CORPORATE
COMMUNICATIONS

Recent Titles from QUORUM BOOKS

CORPORATE COMMUNICATIONS

A Comparison of Japanese and American Practices

WILLIAM V. RUCH

Quorum Books
Westport, Connecticut • London, England

Library of Congress Cataloging in Publication Data

Ruch, William V.
  Corporate communications.

  Bibliography: p.
  Includes index.
  1. Communication in management—Japan. 2. Communi-
cation in management—United States. 3. Corporations—
Japan. 4. Corporations—United States. I. Title.
HD30.3.R82   1984   658.4′5′0952   84-1973
ISBN 0-89930-028-6 (lib. bdg.)

Library of Congress Catalog Card Number: 84-1973
ISBN 0-89930-028-6

First published in 1984 by Quorum Books

Greenwood Press
A division of Congressional Information Service, Inc.
88 Post Road West, Westport, Connecticut 06881

Printed in the United States of America

10 9 8 7 6 5 4 3 2 1

Copyright Acknowledgments

   The following publishers and sources have generously given permission to use extended
quotations from copyrighted works:

From *The After Hours*, by David W. Plath. © 1964 by the University of California Press.
   Reprinted by permission of the publisher.
From *The Anatomy of Dependence*, by Takeo Doi. © 1971 Kodansha International. Reprinted
   by permission of the publisher.
From *Communication in Organizations*, by Everett M. Rogers and Rehka Agarwala-Rogers.
   © 1976 by The Free Press, a Division of Macmillan Publishing Company. Reprinted by
   permission of the publisher.
From *Communication in the Business Organization*, by William Scholz. © 1962 by Prentice-
   Hall, Inc. Reprinted by permission of the publisher.
From *Doing Business in Japan*, edited by Robert J. Ballon. © 1967. Charles E. Tuttle.
   Reprinted by permission of the editor.
From *The Emerging Japanese Superstate*, by Herman Kahn. © 1970 by Hudson Institute.
   Prentice-Hall, Inc. Reprinted by permission of the publisher.
From *For Harmony and Strength: Japanese White-Collar Organizations in Anthropological Per-*

Dunsing, pp. 5–6, *Supervisory Management*, September 1976. © 1976 by AMACOM, a division of American Management Associations, New York. All rights reserved. Excerpted by permission of the publisher.

The following firms and individuals have granted permission to quote from their in-house publications and correspondence:

From *Alcoa News*, courtesy of Aluminum Company of America, p. 10, June 1982 issues.

From *Bendix 81* and *82*. Reprinted by permission of The Bendix Corporation.

From *The Burlington Look* and the *Burlington Employee Handbook*, courtesy of Burlington Industries, Inc.

From *Dresser News* publication, courtesy of Dresser Industries, Inc.

From *Emhart NEWS*, courtesy of Emhart Corporation.

From "Employee Response Strong to RJR World Readership Survey," in *RJR World* (October 1981). Reprinted with permission. © 1981 R.J. Reynolds Industries, Inc.

From *ETHYL INTERCOM*, courtesy of Ethyl Corporation.

From "Face-to-Face Meetings Keep Channels Open," in *The Gifford-Hill Times* (February, 1982). © 1982 Gifford-Hill & Company, Inc., Dallas, Texas. Reprinted by permission of *The Gifford-Hill Times*.

From *Ford World*, courtesy of Ford Motor Company.

From *Formula*. © 1981 Rohm and Haas Company. Reprinted by permission.

From correspondence from Jerry T. Robbins, General Motors Corporation. Reprinted with permission.

From *GM TODAY* and GM policy and guidelines on employee communications, courtesy of General Motors Corporation.

From *Grace Digest* and *Grace News*. Used with permission of Robert Edward Brown and W.R. Grace & Co.

From *Headquarters News*, courtesy of AMAX Inc.

From "How to Succeed in Japan." © 1974 by Japan External Trade Organization. Reprinted by permission.

From *iabc news*, courtesy of International Association of Business Communicators.

From correspondence from James B. O'Connell, Director, Internal Communications, International Business Machines Corporation. Reprinted with permission.

From "Japan's Welfare Load Too Heavy to Carry," by Eiko Fukuda. International Writers Service.

From correspondence with Director, Public Relations and Advertising, Kaiser Steel Corporation. Reprinted with permission.

From *Measure*, courtesy of Hewlett-Packard Company.

From the *Mixer*, courtesy of Hercules Incorporated.

From "Quality Circles Work at Plastics Inc." in *AnchorScope* (Winter 1981–82), courtesy of Anchor Hocking.

From *Sonoco News*, courtesy of Sonoco Products Company.

From correspondence from James H. Mayes, Director of Publications, Standard Oil Company (Indiana). Reprinted with permission.

From correspondence from Texaco Inc. Reprinted with permission.

From correspondence from Emmett Nathan, Manager, Employee Communications, Western Electric. Reprinted with permission.

From *Xerox World* and *Managing at Xerox*, courtesy of Xerox Corporation.

From Public Relations Departments, Nissan and Matsushita, permission to print their company songs.

To
Dorothy and Weston

Contents

Illustrations

Tables

Preface

The subject of this book is corporate communication as it is practiced in Japan and America. But in Japan more so than any other country of the world it is impossible to discuss communicating without first examining the Japanese culture and the history of that culture.

During my two-year teaching assignment in Japan, I was enthralled with what I saw going on around me. Where else would you see ancient festivals stop traffic as they proceeded, sometimes solemnly and sometimes raucously, through crowded streets? Once when I was on a panel at Ehime University, I was asked why American media concentrated on the ancient parts of Japan rather than on the modern aspects. My answer was that that was what Americans were interested in—remnants of the past which influence the present. There's much of that in Japan, some of it discussed here.

For the discussion of American corporate communication, I rely heavily on two sources: publications of American companies themselves and publications of professional business communication organizations. In a survey of Fortune 500 corporations in 1980, I requested copies of company publications for use in my classes at San Diego State University. Many companies complied and continue to mail the materials each month. These publications were useful in this study for three reasons: 1. they are the best source available for the subjects quoted from them; 2. they show the concerns of American managers today, since the publications are considered to speak in behalf of management; and 3. they demonstrate the excellent quality of writing in company publications today. Consequently, long quotes from them are included throughout this book.

Another important source of information for this book was the International Association of Business Communicators. That organization's publications each month are full of useful information of the current state of American business communication. To a lesser but no less important extent, the publications of the American Business Communication Association were used to supplement the text.

Acknowledgments

Not being fluent in Japanese, I am in greatest debt to the Japanese authors who underwent the long and difficult process of learning English and then writing in that foreign language.

Next I am deeply indebted to the American companies who provided publications used extensively in this study. No letter ever sent to a company went unanswered, and in most cases the aid requested was granted. Their materials in the form of illustrations and quotations appear throughout the book.

The same is true for materials used from organizations such as the International Association of Business Communicators, the American Business Communication Association, the National Association of Suggestion Systems, the Quality Circle Institute, and the American Productivity Center. NBC sent transcripts, without question or charge, of two recent programs on Japan. Louis C. Williams, Senior Vice President of Hill and Knowlton, Inc., sent the transcript of a talk he gave about Japan. Myron Emanuel, former Director of Business Communications Programs, Towers, Perrin, Forster and Crosby, sent a copy of an article about Japan he had written. Dr. John Gould of the University of Southern California sent materials he obtained at a meeting in Tokyo of the Japan Business English Association.

From Japan, Mr. Saburo Haneda of Tokyo and Dr. Mikito F. Nakamura of Nishinomiya offered helpful suggestions, ignoring the imposition of my communicating with them in English instead of Japanese.

Finally, I extend my sincere thanks to Quorum Books Editor Lynn Taylor and Production Editor Lynn Sedlak Flint, both of whom provided the professional guidance needed to see this project through to completion.

CORPORATE
COMMUNICATIONS

Introduction

It is the unseen infrastructure of all organizations everywhere. At different times it is formal or informal, direct or indirect, personal or impersonal, oral or written or nonverbal. Its frequency increases geometrically with each human added. So fast is it growing in importance that futurists talk of the coming Information Age; some say that era is not only here but that it started decades ago. "It" is communication—the transfer of thought from one person to another.

The central role of communication in organizational life has been largely overlooked by everyone except organizational theorists. As one writer said in reference to culture, if birds and fish were suddenly endowed with scientific inquiry, they would probably overlook the air and water. So it is with humans and communication, particularly in organizations.

Only in the context of falling productivity has the American manager discovered the value of good communication; he has been forced to in order to compete with foreign companies in which communication is used thoroughly and to great advantage in various techniques. Some of them—such as quality circles from Japan—are being adopted all over the world. As a result, there is interest today in the American organization in all communication techniques.

This book describes those procedures and compares them to similar methods in use in Japan. It is impossible, however, to discuss a corporate communication system without first discussing the overall climate of a corporation. That in turn requires a review of different management philosophies and their origin, and these cannot be adequately presented without some understanding of the culture in which the organization functions and, finally, of culture in general. That is the plan of this book.

After a brief discussion of culture, I describe in Part I for Japan and Part II for the United States the influence of corporate culture and climate on the organization's communication program and the techniques of communication used in each corporation.

In Part III, I attempt a comparison of the countries, corporations, and corporate communication programs and try to draw some conclusions.

Volumes have been written on the subjects of culture, of the form culture takes in Japan and America, of organizations, of management, and of communication. Each topic is too broad to be covered in much detail here. Only those aspects of each that contribute to an understanding of communication in the business organization in the two countries are included here.

Also, it soon becomes clear in a study such as this that we all use terms improperly in reference to the Japanese management system. "Lifetime employment" is not employment for life but for the duration of one's career, which can last in most cases only to age 55. The term was introduced in the Taisho era (1912–1926), when the life expectancy of the Japanese male was 44 years of age, and most died before retirement. Today, "career employment" would be more accurate.

"Bottom up" or "bottoms up" management refers to management communication that is really initiated at the middle levels of the organization. "Middle up" management would be more accurate.

Quality control circles, although once exclusively concerned with quality control, now deal with all aspects of organizational life. So "quality circle" is a more proper term for modern groups.

Finally, references to groups in Japanese companies should be references to teams. The groups of employees who function so successfully in Japanese companies are obviously teams, and it is that quality about the persons involved which assures their success. Referring to them as teams would be more accurate.

Nevertheless, in the interests of quick communication, we retain usage in this book of the more common, less accurate terms.

WHAT IS CULTURE?

Culture is the sum of the learned parts of our environments, "our social legacy, as contrasted with our organic heredity," said Clyde Kluckhohn in *Mirror for Man*.[1] It is what causes an American child to hear a puppy go "bow wow," while the Japanese child hears "wan wan"; it is what makes that puppy a pet in those two countries and a potential meal in Taiwan.

Mary Beres and James Portwood present an anthropologist's definition of culture as a "frame of reference which members of a group have found beneficial for survival in dealing with their particular common environment, and have, therefore, retained and transmitted to successive generations."[2] It is a way of thinking and believing. "Whether a healthy adult feels hungry twice, three times, or four times a day and the hours at which this feeling recurs is a question of culture," observes Kluckhohn.[3]

One acquires both a personality and culture long before he can comprehend either. "To survive," explains Dean Barnlund in a chapter in *Intercultural Encounters with Japan*, "each masters the perceptual orientations, the cognated biases, the communicative habits of his own culture."[4] Kluckhohn suggests that the primary question in anthropology is, "What makes an Italian into an Italian, a Japanese into a Japanese? The process of becoming a representative member of any group involves a molding of raw human nature."[5]

Through communication and socialization is culture transmitted, the raw human nature molded. This is true of societal culture and organizational culture, the latter heavily influenced by the former. Research has shown the sequence of influence to be culture—individual behavior—organizational functioning.[6] Employees learn how to behave in the cultural context and in so behaving shape their organization.

Their language determines a great deal about those employees' perceptions and thinking patterns and thus their behavior. It encourages thinking in certain ways and discourages thinking in other ways.[7] Language is the source of important cultural differences between peoples. But as Barnlund states in *Public and Private Self in Japan and the United States*, "even if all meanings could be expressed in all languages, cultures would still create unique norms for human encounters."[8]

Culture over a period of years demonstrates to an individual which behaviors are opposed and which approved according to what is punished or rewarded. It is a process that occurs on a daily basis. As we will see when we discuss the Japanese culture in Chapter 1, those are not the same behaviors in all societies.

CULTURAL OPPOSITES

As any resident of one country who visits the other can tell you, not only are American and Japanese cultures different, but in many respects one is exactly opposite to the other. Automobiles travel in the left lanes in Japan and the right lanes in America. Light switches, door handles and faucets all are operated in opposite directions in Japan than in America.[9] The Japanese carpenter manipulates saws and planes by pulling, not pushing as do American carpenters. Japanese farmers pull the mattock toward them, while their American counterparts drive the spade away from them. Even the wind and rain storms that we call hurricanes and they call typhoons move in opposite directions, though neither is under human control.

When a Japanese beckons to someone, he does it palm down; Americans motion with palm up. When counting on their fingers, every Japanese starts with the thumb as most Americans do. But instead of beginning with a clenched fist and one-by-one extending the fingers, the Japanese begins with the hand open and, beginning with the thumb, tucks the fingers tightly into a fist with the thumb buried under fingers. Counting continues with six to ten by opening the fingers on the same hand; Americans tend to use the other hand.

Writing is from top to bottom or right to left on a page, instead of left to right, so naturally books printed in Japanese and English start at opposite ends. Names are presented surname first and given name second; there are no middle names in Japan.

"Japanese say 'east-north,' 'west-south,' " says Shozo Yamaguchi in *We Japanese*, "not 'north-east,' 'south-west.' " The Japanese estimate " 'four or three' when Westerners say 'three or four.' "[10] Seven and all numbers containing it are considered bad luck in Japan and good luck in America. Yamaguchi notes that "Japanese say *achi-kochi* (there-here); Westerners say 'here and there.' "[11]

The foreigner in Japan learns that questions beginning with the negative must be answered carefully. "Aren't you going to the faculty meeting today?" If you are, you answer no. If you aren't, say yes.

The average Japanese does not, as an American would, smile broadly on formal photographs because he or she is trying to suppress individuality. The highest compliment you can pay to a Japanese about a photograph is: "You look just like anybody." Americans, of course, like it best when someone tells them their picture looks just like them.

When telling about the death of a parent, wife, child, or other close relative, a Japanese often smiles, his face in no way revealing the grief he feels, in direct contrast to a Westerner's expression under similar circumstances. This custom comes from a desire to suppress all signs of deep emotion and not inflict personal grief on another person.[12]

Finally, not an opposite but certainly different is the Japanese gesture to someone he is not sure is referring to him. The Japanese puts his finger, with a wide swinging motion of his arm, to the tip of his nose while saying "*Boku?*" (Me?). Americans point to the middle of the chest for the same purpose.

Nearly every day of my two-year assignment in the country brought a surprise regarding Japanese customs. For example, I had brought with me a huge, warm, hooded, red parka. I hadn't known when I packed it whether I would ever use it; I also hadn't known that men in Japan at that time just didn't wear red. I was advised to have it dyed before I could comfortably wear it, so it was unstitched and dyed black by a local cleaning establishment.

One occasion that allowed me to wear that parka was a skiing trip to Mt. Zao in northern Japan. I met friends in Hiroshima and Kobe; we joined others in Tokyo, where we caught a train north. After a few minutes on the train, as it moved slowly out of the station, our guide, a student at prestigious Tokyo University, discovered that we were on the wrong train. She notified the conductor, and to our surprise he stopped the train and took us back to the station! Where else in the world would that happen?

It is in the train, by the way, where one of the more unusual Japanese customs occurs. Men remove and carefully fold their trousers to prevent them from wrinkling while seated on the train.[13] Knee-length white underwear, much like American summer pajamas, worn over a pair of white boxer shorts, protects the men's dignity.

The school year began in April and ended in March. Twice each year everyone changed clothes to winter or summer uniforms, regardless of the temperature. That was a custom that amazed Townsend Harris, first U.S. consul to Japan in the mid-eighteenth century. He noted it in his diary:

The Japanese have *fixed days* for their change of clothing. The *law* settles the matter beforehand, and no inclemency of weather can postpone the change. The following are the periods and changes of their dress for our year 1857: On the first day of the fourth month, April 24, they threw off their wadded clothes and put on unwadded ones, but of thick materials. On the fifth day of the fifth month, May 23, they will put on their summer clothing. On the first day of the ninth month, October 18, they will resume the same clothing as that put on on the 24th of April. On the ninth day of the ninth month, October 26, they will put on their winter clothing. This is made of the same material as the previous change, only it is thickly wadded with cotton or silk wadding.[14]

Much of modern Japanese life has ancient origins.

At faculty meetings every Tuesday afternoon, I experienced an aspect of Japanese life that is getting worldwide attention: group decision making. For as long as it took, and that was frequently several hours, a subject was discussed at length by every member of the faculty who wished to speak on it. He or she stood up at his or her place and talked. The others listened intently. When everyone who wanted to had had his or her say, the principal, who had also expressed his opinion, stood up and announced the group's consensus. I was told that often the consensus was contrary to what the principal himself had advocated; but the group's decision was clear, and his job was to announce it. The system is called *matomari*, meaning "adjustment," and it is admittedly a time-consuming system; but its main advantage, as we shall see in Chapter 5, is that, having played a part in making the decision, everyone feels committed to carrying it out.

NOTES

1. Kluckhohn, *Mirror for Man*, p. 26.

2. Beres and Portwood, "Explaining Cultural Differences," in *Organizational Functioning in a Cross-Cultural Perspective*, ed. England, Negandhi, and Wilpert, p. 139.

3. Kluckhohn, *Mirror for Man*, p. 21.

4. Barnlund, "The Public Self and the Private Self in Japan and the United States," in *International Encounters with Japan*, ed. Condon and Saito, p. 38.

5. Kluckhohn, *Mirror for Man*, pp. 198–99.

6. Beres and Portwood, "Explaining Cultural Differences," p. 141.

7. Barnlund, "Public and Private Self in Japan and the United States," p. 23.

8. Ibid., p. 133.

9. Japan Air Lines, printed on envelope of direct mail piece.

10. Yamaguchi, *We Japanese*, p. 41.

11. Ibid., p. 50.

12. Ibid., p. 51.

13. Kawasaki, *Japan Unmasked*, p. 34.

14. Harris, *The Complete Journal of Townsend Harris*, pp. 352–53, as cited in Moloney, *Understanding the Japanese Mind*, p. 10.

PART I

JAPAN AND THE JAPANESE CORPORATION

1

The Culture of Japan

Japan today is unique in several important ways. It is the only non-Western industrialized nation.[1] A great economic power, it is not a great military power.[2] Japan is the only major nation to have renounced war or the use of force as a means of settling international disputes.[3]

The Japanese call their country Nihon or Nippon, which means "the origin of the sun," as it appeared to be from China. Yamaguchi explained the origin of "Japan": "The ancient Chinese called the country Zippon. This pronunciation was expressed by Marco Polo with the spelling of 'Zipangu,' from which 'Japan' " is derived.[4]

Japan has 120 million people living in an area of 142,728 square miles, smaller than California but half again as large as Britain and bigger than East and West Germany combined. It is an archipelago whose numerous islands stretch into a 2,000-mile arc which, if superimposed on the American East Coast, would extend from Maine to Georgia, from 45° longitude to about 25°,[5] with the larger cities of Tokyo, Kyoto, Osaka, and Kobe clustered around North Carolina.[6] Its climate roughly corresponds to those same regions of the United States.

Japan's shoreline is 17,000 miles long—double that of the United States. The island-country, of course, shares no borders with another country. At its closest point, the land is about 125 miles from the Eurasian continent, separated from it by a shallow depression occupied by the Sea of Japan.

About 85 percent of the country's land area is mountainous—one is never out of sight of mountains. Three-quarters of the land surface consists of slopes over fifteen degrees.[7] Only about 15 percent of the land is arable,[8] an area that would fit into the state of West Virginia.[9]

There are 1,000 mineral springs, half of them "hot," and between 150 and 300 volcanoes. Ten percent of all volcanoes that erupted in historic times are located here.[10] In addition to the four main islands of Honshu, Kyushu, Hokkaido, and Shikoku, there are some 3,300 islets and rocks, many unarable and uninhabited.[11]

Present-day Japan is more homogeneous than any other major country in the world.[12] It is comprised of 99.4 percent Japanese and 0.5 percent Koreans.[13] There is also a small group of Chinese and another of Ainu (which in their own language means "man"), who are regarded as the aborigines of Japan. It is believed they came from Siberia.[14] The Ainu were driven steadily northward by Mongol invaders until they settled in northern most Hokkaido. They were of proto-white stock, a group which split off from the white race so early that not all of the characteristics of the Caucasians had developed.[15]

This chapter covers first and very briefly the long history of Japan followed by a discussion of the experience of the average Japanese citizen today.

BEGINNINGS

The country was founded, according to Japanese tradition, in 660 B.C., by the Emperor Jimmu, a descendant of the sun goddess Amaterasu.[16] Archaeologists say the country was first inhabited about 3000 B.C.

The place of origin of the Japanese people is unknown; however, it is believed to have been the northeast Asian mainland via Korea. Harvard professor and former ambassador to Japan Edwin Reischauer provides this information: "During the last ice age, which continued until about 11,000 years ago, Japan was joined by land to the rest of Asia. Since Japan was the geographic end of the line, peoples who wandered into it could not move on but stopped and mixed with those who came later."[17] Later migrants arrived from the south via Formosa (Taiwan) and the Ryukyu Islands, which include Okinawa. Management consultant Mitsuyuki Masatsugu explains further in *The Modern Samurai Society*:

The ancestors of the Japanese people were an exquisite mixture of unneighborly races that arrived from the north, the west, and the south—quite contrasting areas. Thus it is a plausible proposition that the nature-loving character of the Japanese people, manifested in the art of flower arrangement, landscape gardening, and the like, was brought in from the north and that the pugnacious temperament, evidenced in so much warfare, was inherited from the south.[18]

The Japanese today are homogeneous in race, history, language, religion, and culture. Chie Nakane, professor of social anthropology at Tokyo University's Institute of Oriental Culture, explains how that was accomplished:

Archaeological research has shown that during the Jomon period a single culture spread over the whole of Japan: between this time and the beginning of the historical period (fifth century A.D.), continental culture along with wet paddy cultivation may have left a considerable influence, particularly in western Japan, and may have helped the development of the Japanese state formation, but the numbers of continentals actually moving into Japan seems to be very small, and these were quickly and readily absorbed into the native population, so that there is no indication that these new elements formed a separate stratum from the Japanese. There is no evidence of significant movement into the islands of non-Japanese after this period.[19]

In 1949, archaeologists made startling discoveries of stone-chipped tools of the mesolithic, possibly paleolithic, era before 8000 B.C. They believed that this was evidence of an ancient culture that evolved on the islands, contradicting common beliefs of migrations into the area in later periods.[20]

The racial structure of the Japanese is Mongoloid, "like the Chinese, Koreans, Vietnamese, Thais, Burmese and even American Indians," explains William Forbis in *Japan Today*. "The strong Mongoloid strain gives all Japanese straight black hair, brown or black eyes, and the epicanthic fold of skin that extends from the upper eyelid down over the inner corner of the eye."[21]

Diplomat Ichiro Kawasaki in *Japan Unmasked* described his countrymen as perhaps physically the least attractive of all races in the world, with the possible exception of Pygmies and Hottentots. Members of the Mongolian race, like the Japanese, have flat faces, high cheekbones, oblique eyes. Anatomically, they have disproportionately large heads, elongated trunks, and short, bowed legs.[22] But emotionally and mentally the Japanese are very strong. Forbis explains:

At some quiet, still, central place in the Japanese psyche, the people of Japan hold, without concession, to esthetics, ideals, and societal bonds unchanged in twenty centuries. More than any other nation of the East, Japan has adopted, adapted, co-opted, or even stolen the best of the West. But also more than any other nation of the East, Japan has remained itself. The Japanese do not admit the West is best. Japan is ineluctably and intractably alien, not in the sense of hostile but in the sense of different.[23]

The first and most important influence, however, was from the East. Princeton University Professor Marius Jansen states in *Japan and Its World*, "China was the source of Japan's writing system, its cultural values in literature, philosophy, and thought, and its institutional examples in government and law. . . . China was also the channel for the religious values and sectarian development of Buddhism."[24] Jansen presents these reasons for the Chinese influence:

1. Japan was farther away from its sources of influence than was any other major country.
2. China was the only external influence into modern times.
3. The China model endured; for the Japanese it was classical antiquity, a Renaissance Italy, and an eighteenth-century France all in one.
4. China was a special sort of model in that it made no particular effort to sell itself; it didn't have to.
5. The contact was episodic, prompted by Japanese leadership during periods of need.
6. China's definition of Chineseness is cultural rather than geographical or racial, making it possible for Japanese intellectuals to realize membership in the Chinese cultural order.[25]

Buddhist missionaries from China brought their culture along with their religion and Confucianism, from which the Japanese developed their own philosophical tradition. The Confucian tradition stressed order and harmony in society, a fact important in understanding the philosophical foundation of Japanese management, which rejects Western individualism.[26] Forbis explains this internalization process this way:

For something over two thousand years, an emperor or empress belonging to the same family as Hirohito has ruled or reigned over Japan. Beginning in the twelfth century, however, a series of military shoguns (which at first was just another name for "general") seized and exercised real power, in the name of the emperor. The dynasty that left the most definitive print on Japan was the shogunate of the Tokugawa family, who, governing from 1603 to 1867, sealed Japan off from the rest of the world. This was a gesture unique in world history— a gesture of a nation that felt so complete in itself that it wanted no outside advice or advantage, a gesture stemming from a confidence that it knew all it needed to know and from a fear that whatever intruded would upset its order and its peace.[27]

No Japanese was allowed to leave the country, and only a few Dutch and Chinese were allowed to enter for trade purposes, but they were confined to Deshima, an island in Nagasaki harbor. Some 30 million people lived in the closed country—80 percent of them farmers, 7 percent samurai, 3 percent merchants, 2 percent artisans, and 8 percent officials, priests, actors, and outcasts.[28]

It was during the Tokugawa period that Christianity was excluded from Japan. The religion had been admitted in the preceding period of Japanese history because it was part of the cultural package that the country needed. Many Japanese, particularly on the island of Kyushu, accepted the religion and inspired anti-Buddhist sentiment. They destroyed most of the Buddhist statues and temples on that island. The

result was government opposition to the religion in the form of perse-
cution of Christians, forced participation in "stamping on the cross"
ceremonies, and death to many. Some Christians emigrated to Macao
and other places. Christianity was totally eliminated during the Tokugawa period.[29] For two centuries thereafter, a ceremony of "stamping
on the cross" was conducted to prevent the religion's revival.[30]

Everything changed for Japan, however, because of the action of one
American. Commodore Matthew C. Perry opened the doors to Japan
and forced the shogun to accept an American consulate.[31] Perry delivered a note from President Millard Fillmore demanding trade relations
with Japan.

The letter described Perry as an officer of the highest rank in the U.S.
Navy, proposed friendship and "commercial intercourse" between the
two countries, described the wealth of the United States, and explained
that only eighteen days by steamship separated the two countries.[32] Perry
then withdrew to Okinawa for the winter, promising to return early the
following year for a reply.[33] Marion Dilts in *The Pageant of Japanese History*
describes Perry's second arrival:

Perry returned in February 1854, with ten ships instead of four, armed with
two hundred and fifty guns, came ashore with a brass band and a great parade
and made presents to the highest officials of whiskey and champagne, standard
literary works, rifles, revolvers, clocks, perfume, a sewing machine, a telegraph
and a toy locomotive.[34]

The outcome was forced treaties with the United States and Britain in
1854 and with Russia and Holland in 1855.[35]

The Japanese, who had been about equal to other countries when the
doors to the outside were closed, were startled to learn how much ahead
of them the outside world had moved.[36] Japan had dropped far behind
Europe in scientific and industrial achievements.[37] So the country sought
a remedy. Kawasaki explains that Japan became the Occident's eager
pupil. The government sent delegations abroad to learn Western techniques and sciences. Students, chosen carefully, went to England to learn
methods of the navy and merchant marines, to Germany for law and
medicine, to France for silk filature.[38]

In 1868, in addition, the chronological name was changed from Keio
to Meiji, since eras are named for the reigning emperor, and the city of
Edo was renamed Tokyo, to which the capital was moved from Kyoto.[39]
The Meiji era is comparable in Japanese history to the period from the
sixth to the ninth centuries when the Japanese imported Chinese
civilization.[40]

Japan emerged in 1868 from the almost total isolation believing the
emperor to be the father of the national family.[41] That family remains

today. All members of the national family were not equal. Ruth Benedict in *The Chrysanthemum and the Sword* explains, "Until the middle of the nineteenth century only noble families and warrior (samurai) families were allowed to use surnames."[42] Everyone else acquired names in the Tokugawa period; most of them were combinations of words from nature or the environment. One of the worst punishments a samurai could suffer was to have his family name extinguished. To have a mark recorded against one's name today is a serious matter, for it disgraces one's whole family, living and dead.[43]

There are indications the nation of Japan is more of a family than any other. Where else, for example, does the government maintain genealogical records of the entire citizenry? "No one is anonymous," explains Forbis, "and all ancestries and relationships are matters of public record."[44] Masatsugu points out that everyone in the country believes himself to be distantly related to all others: "If we follow any Japanese family far enough back into history, it will be traceable to one of four clans: Minamoto, Taira, Fujiwara, or Tachibana. Since all four of these clans regard the Emperor as their founder, all Japanese are, theoretically speaking, one large family."[45]

Frank Gibney in *Japan: the Fragile Superpower* describes the Japanese national character today:

Japan's *nation society* is unique. A tightly threaded, two-thousand-year-old mesh of human fabric, it has an extraordinarily broadly based culture, a low common denomination of artistic tastes and living standards, and a talent for narrowing the national energies to well-defined tasks or objectives.... Their unities came naturally from long incubation in their own island society. Thus, when they borrowed the arts or inventions of other nations, they generally did so confidently and purposefully. It takes an extraordinarily self-confident culture to assimilate so many outside influences without losing its own identity.[46]

Only a quarter of a century after emerging in 1868 from its total isolation, Japan defeated Russia in battle and was recognized as a great nation by the rest of the world.[47] It took a while longer for events to convince the Japanese themselves of their standing as a leader among the world's nations: in 1964 the country hosted the Olympic Games; and in 1979 the leaders of the industrialized countries met in Tokyo for the first time.

THE JAPANESE EXPERIENCE

Richard Halloran describes the experience of the Japanese nation from the point of view of an individual in *Japan: Images and Realities*:

You may think I am presumptuous to say that I am typical of all Japanese because there are an infinite variety of people in Japan, just like any country. But we Japanese are a very unified people and we live in a closely knit society in our small island country. We Japanese have the same basic beliefs and traits and language whether we live in the city or the countryside, or in northern Honshu or southern Kyushu. It can be said, in my opinion, that we Japanese have a definite national character. Conformity is important to us, and we Japanese soon hammer down the nail that sticks up.[48]

The life experience of the average Japanese is today very different from that of the average person in other countries. The result is an individual who reacts in a particular way to his company and his country.

As a newborn, the Japanese is coddled and fondled and loved by everyone. As he grows, he is with his mother all of the time, carried on her back in the daytime and sleeping by her side at night. He is seldom disciplined, even for throwing something through the paper partitions between rooms in the small Japanese house. Halloran's description continues:

When I was a little child, I had a great deal of freedom. My parents allowed me to do almost anything I wanted, especially since I was the eldest son. I suppose this explains why we Japanese are so self-centered. Child psychologists say that a person's basic personality is formed during the first four years of life, and that is when we Japanese are the most permissive with our children. I can remember, just before I reached school age, that my parents began telling me for the first time that I couldn't do certain things. They didn't tell me that it was right or wrong, but that I mustn't do it because of what other people would think. All through my childhood after that, my parents would remind me that I must conduct myself so that other people would think well of me and of our family. My father, who was very strict, taught that I must respect his authority immediately and without question. I think this is why we Japanese have such deep respect for older people and for authority. We have a saying: "There are four things in life to be feared—earthquake, thunder, fire, and the wrath of an angry father."[49]

When the Japanese child enters school, the real world takes hold of his life. To be assured of a secure job in one of the country's finest large corporations, the candidate must be a graduate of one of the country's ten or so top universities. To accomplish that, he must first be accepted by one of a select group of excellent high schools which prepare students to pass the entrance examinations to these universities. It is interesting that once admitted to a university, a student has little motivation to work hard. It's admission that counts to potential employers.[50]

The same holds true for middle schools which prepare their students for entrance to the best high schools and for elementary schools which prepare their students for the middle schools. Believe it or not, it also holds true for kindergarten and nursery schools. Students take examinations for entrance to the best ones, for which their parents have had to send the children to an expensive preparatory course. So if a person is to have a chance to be employed by one of the best corporations in the country, his parents must begin to plan for him when he is three or four years old.

While under pressure that an American would certainly find extreme for so early an age, the Japanese child's life changes in another way. Suddenly with school as important as it is in his life, a regimentation enters his life at home and in school. Parent and teacher clamp down on him. Feelings formerly expressed to the amusement of everyone now have to be suppressed.

From my second-story apartment in Matsuyama, I could look into the small wooden homes that surrounded our building. More than once, in one particular house, I saw the father of a young student who was having difficulty concentrating grab the child by the neck and shoulders and shake him into a studious wakefulness.

The Japanese girl undergoes the same type of training; in some respects it is even more harsh. Before the war, she was taught to sleep with her legs together. In marriage, she is expected to do the best to please fastidious in-laws. There is a correct way to do everything, and she is expected to know what it is and to do it under the watchful eye of her mother-in-law.

So burdensome are these mental constraints that when in a position that releases them of such pressures, the Japanese behave as though different people. An example is the record of atrocities in China and Southeast Asia during World War II. Another example is their attitude at home. Kawasaki observes, "If a street is littered or a public park is in a disgraceful state, the average Japanese does not give a hoot. The degree of selfishness, rudeness, and inconsideration shown in public conveyances in Japan also cannot be surpassed."[51]

Forbis explains these traits this way:

Although society in peacetime Japan provides a "web" relationship of behavior that holds down violence, when the constraint is off in battle on some foreign shore—when the soldier gets into a situation for which there is no specific ethic—the animalistic barbarity that resides in every man can come out. The Japanese also fight all the harder because of the shame that cowardice or surrender causes in the eyes of society. They were cruel to prisoners of war partly because they were contemptuous of them for *being* prisoners.[52]

As a result, 27 percent of prisoners in Japanese camps died during World War II, compared to 4 percent of POWs in German camps.[53]

On the other hand, because they had not been told how to behave in the event of capture during the war on the theory they would fight to the death for the emperor,[54] Japanese prisoners of war were exceedingly helpful in supplying information about their army to their captors.

So intense had been their indoctrination to be fighters for the emperor that soldier holdouts were found to be living in the jungles of Asia long after the war's end. Michael Gibson in *The Rise of Japan* describes one of them: "Shoichi Yokoi, an Army sergeant, evaded capture in 1944 and hid in the jungles of Guam for twenty-eight years. He was discovered by fishermen on 24th January, 1972. On returning to Japan, he insisted, 'I have brought my rifle back with me. I will return it to the Emperor.' "[55]

It is easy to understand how release from such pressures could cause atrocities such as the "rape of Nanking." The chaplain of Jonan told me that his uncle had participated in a gang rape of a young Chinese woman during the war; afterward they buried her upside down in the ground and, holding her legs apart, sliced her in half with a sword.

Though under normal conditions the Japanese considers that behavior extreme, Walt Sheldon in *Enjoy Japan* explains that the Japanese, polite at home and in their own groups, are far different elsewhere. They may there express feelings that had to be curbed most of the time. The Japanese say of this fact, *Tabi no haji wa kakisute,* "Throw away your shame in whatever place you visit." It's all right, away from home, to get drunk, stagger through the streets, and shout obscenities at the top of your lungs.[56]

Part of the pressure on the average Japanese is protecting his sense of honor, imposed on him from the ancient code of Bushido. In a course at Syracuse University in psychoanalytic theories of personality, my professor suggested that it was this code that caused the Japanese to attack Pearl Harbor, in retribution for Admiral Perry's "intrusion" of Tokyo Bay. (Is it just coincidence that when U.S. Consul Harris pressured the Japanese for a meeting with the shogun, the meeting took place on December 7, 1857?[57]) My professor said that, know it or not, the Japanese are duty-bound to repay America eventually for the atomic bombing of Hiroshima and Nagasaki. Some might say that they are doing that now in the marketplace.

Kawasaki finds another reason for Pearl Harbor. When Japanese began to emigrate to the United States in large numbers, Congress enacted in 1924 the Exclusion Act, placing Japanese immigrants on a quota and virtually outlawing their entrance. This, Kawasaki speculates, could have placed the Japanese on the warpath that culminated in the attack on Pearl Harbor.[58]

Another part of the pressure on a Japanese is the obligation he is taught to feel to others. *On* is the word that describes personal obligations that must be repaid; those who fail to do so are held in contempt. Herman Kahn quotes a definition of *on* by John Whitney Hall and Richard Beardsley in *The Emerging Japanese Superstate*:

On is a beneficence handed down from one's superior. It institutes an obligation (*ongaeshi*) to the superior on the part of the person who receives it or enjoys its benefits. By its very nature, *on* always connotes a hierarchical relation between two specific actors; the obligations that arise from *on* therefore are not part of an abstract code or principle but have at least shades of difference, inasmuch as the specific participants in one relation differ from another.[59]

This duty, of course, intrudes into the business organization. Managers in organizations have to cope with a complex set of reciprocal obligations. The manager who once granted a favor to a colleague in another department knows that someday his colleague must reciprocate.[60]

Giri describes the sense of loyalty one feels to all groups of which one is a member. This explains the success of group activity in the Japanese corporation and the low level of turnover in Japanese companies. Kahn again quotes Hall and Beardsley:

Giri is an all-pervading force in the behavior of all classes of people and in all walks of life.... Although the complexities and ambivalences of *giri* must be taken into account, it operates because of the universal need for respecting and expressing "human feelings" (*ninjo*) in social life that exists in closely knit communications.... The sanctions of *giri* are to be found in society in the mores, customs, and folkways, and not in the laws.[61]

Giri thus influences everything in society. More than once, for example, while walking down a street, I saw a motorist whose car had stalled trying to push it by himself out of the way of traffic. And more than once, I helped push. I learned that the Japanese sense of obligation prevented the other Japanese from helping to save the poor motorist a lifelong obligation of returning the favor. They were doing him a favor by not helping!

These qualities of Japanese life give only a partial picture. Foreigners are surely puzzled by the all-inclusive "sincerity clause" which appears at the end of Japanese contracts: "When a dispute arises concerning this contract, the two parties will talk it over with sincerity." Even in billion-yen deals, Japanese do not set detailed provisions, but rely on the "sincerity clause" to protect all interests.[62] Kawasaki explains that other character traits contribute to the success of the Japanese: discipline, the ability to relax and enjoy life, business acumen, community spirit, love for education, unity and competitiveness, and a driving sense of guilt and obligation.[63]

The Japanese individual, it is said, marries a wife and respects the emperor according to Shintoism, even though that religion was banished by the constitution and became powerless in 1945.[64] He dies a Buddhist. Throughout his life, he observes other customs of both religions—such as visiting a Shinto shrine on holidays—and mixes these with observances of Confucianism (which is really a philosophy of life) and Christianity. Masatsugu points out that although less than 1 percent of all Japanese are Christian, some 1.4 million Bibles are sold in Japan annually, as are about 9 million copies of partial editions of the Gospels of Mark and Luke. One in ten people in Japan buys a Bible every year![65]

When asked to describe themselves in national character surveys, the Japanese selected one word constantly: "diligent." The total choosing that word has increased from 55 percent in 1953 to 66 percent in 1973. Those who select that word are generally higher in age, education, and occupational status.[66]

Changes are occurring. An article in the *Japan Times* reports that "quality of family life in Japan deteriorated during 1982 because of such negative factors as growing juvenile delinquency problems and a higher divorce rate."[67]

The one area in the world where, like no other, the Japanese can be compared to other ethnic groups is Hawaii. Japanese achievements compare well with those of the other twelve ethnic groups in the islands. The Japanese comprise only 27 percent of the population. Yet the government is largely Japanese with a Japanese governor and senator and 75 percent of the state legislature being Japanese. Also 90 percent of all schoolteachers and 60 percent of all plant managers are Japanese. They are at the bottom among the ethnic groups in the divorce rate, in juvenile delinquency, and in families on welfare.[68]

Maurice Bairy, in "Motivational Forces in Japanese Life," a chapter in Robert Ballon's *The Japanese Employee*, compares Japanese work habits with those of other nations:

Always active, most Japanese get up very early to go to work or school and, doing so, complain very little. Granted the fact that they work easily, they nevertheless work, generally speaking, only moderately; as a matter of fact, their best— their work done *isshokenmei* ("with all strength")—is commonly equivalent to merely an average performance in the West. More remarkable than any flamboyance of temporary performance is their constancy; faithfully, day after day, hour after hour, they accomplish their assigned tasks with patience and perseverance. The pressures of society and their training of former years have taught them to regard work, almost unconsciously, as such a favored and valued component of life that their participation in it has become a completely natural and spontaneous action. Meanwhile, satisfaction in performance has a different meaning in Japan from the one it has in the West, where it equates mainly with a promotion of personality and an affirmation of independence. In Japan, however, satisfaction in performance is pleasure in having accomplished whatever was expected by the group and by Japan as a whole, and it results in relaxation and a sense of harmony.[69]

Kiyoshi Seike described very succinctly the character of the Japanese when he said: "He does what he is expected to do, he says what he is expected to say, he abides by an intricate code of etiquette."[70]

NOTES

1. Vogel, *Japan as Number 1*, p. 5.
2. Cleaver, *Japanese and Americans*, p. 236.
3. Agee, "Bendix in Japan," p. 16.
4. Yamaguchi, *We Japanese*, p. 377.
5. Cleaver, *Japanese and Americans*, p. 59.
6. Reischauer, *Japan: The Story of a Nation*, p. 4.
7. Pezeu-Massabuau, *The Japanese Islands*, p. 36.
8. Cohen, "International Aspects of Japan's Economic Situation," in Council on Foreign Relations, *Japan Between East and West*, p. 109.
9. Cleaver, *Japanese and Americans*, p. 59.
10. Langer, *Japan, Yesterday and Today*, pp. 9–11.
11. Burks, *Japan*, p. 6.
12. Masao, "The Japanese Language and Intercultural Communication," in Japan Center for International Exchange, *The Silent Power*, p. 57.
13. *The World Almanac and Book of Facts, 1982*, p. 552.
14. Yamaguchi, *We Japanese*, p. 130.
15. Reischauer, *Japan: Past and Present*, pp. 9–11.
16. Gibson, *The Rise of Japan*, p. 9.
17. Reischauer, *Japan: The Story of a Nation*, p. 9.
18. Masatsugu, *The Modern Samurai Society*, p. 2.
19. Nakane, *Japanese Society*, p. 141.
20. Burks, *Japan*, p. 32.
21. Forbis, *Japan Today*, pp. 62–63.
22. Kawasaki, *Japan Unmasked*, p. 26.
23. Forbis, *Japan Today*, p. 4.
24. Jansen, *Japan and Its World*, p. 9.
25. Ibid., pp. 10–13.
26. Sours, "Influence of Japanese Culture on Japanese Management Systems."
27. Forbis, *Japan Today*, p. 9.
28. Dilts, *The Pageant of Japanese History*, pp. 258–61.
29. Masatsugu, *The Modern Samurai Society*, pp. 22–23.
30. Dilts, *The Pageant of Japanese History*, p. 278.
31. Forbis, *Japan Today*, pp. 10–11.
32. Allen, *Japan*, p. 5.
33. Reischauer, *Japan: The Story of a Nation*, p. 109.
34. Dilts, *The Pageant of Japanese History*, p. 276.
35. Adams and Kobayashi, *The World of Japanese Business*, p. 29.
36. Reischauer, *Japan: The Story of a Nation*, p. 110.

37. Masatsugu, *The Modern Samurai Society*, p. 7.

38. Kawasaki, *Japan Unmasked*, p. 174.

39. Ibid., pp. 173–74.

40. Ibid., p. 175.

41. Aoki and Dardess, *As the Japanese See It*, p. 261.

42. Benedict, *The Chrysanthemum and the Sword*, p. 50.

43. Embree, *The Japanese Nation*, p. 153.

44. Forbis, *Japan Today*, p. 82.

45. Masatsugu, *The Modern Samurai Society*, p. 19.

46. Gibney, *Japan*, p. 39.

47. Cleaver, *Japanese and Americans*, p. 18.

48. Halloran, *Japan*, p. 215.

49. Ibid., p. 224.

50. Cleaver, *Japanese and Americans*, p. 220.

51. Kawasaki, *Japan Unmasked*, pp. 85–86.

52. Forbis, *Japan Today*, p. 19.

53. Gibson, *The Rise of Japan*, p. 91.

54. Benedict, *The Chrysanthemum and the Sword*, pp. 30–31.

55. Gibson, *The Rise of Japan*, p. 108.

56. Sheldon, *Enjoy Japan*, p. 190.

57. Moloney, *Understanding the Japanese Mind*, p. xvii.

58. Kawasaki, *Japan Unmasked*, p. 29.

59. Hall and Beardsley, *Twelve Doors to Japan*, as cited in Kahn, *The Emerging Japanese Superstate*, p. 50.

60. Bettignies, "Japanese Organizational Behavior: A Psychological Approach," in *Management Research*, ed. Graves, p. 87.

61. Hall and Beardsley, *Twelve Doors to Japan*, p. 49.

62. Awaya, "Japan's 'Unwritten' Law," p. 12.

63. Kawasaki, *Japan Unmasked*, p. 229.

64. Delassus, *The Japanese*, p. 113.

65. Masatsugu, *The Modern Samurai Society*, p. 22.

66. Cole, *Work, Mobility and Participation*, p. 230.

67. "Family Life in Japan Deteriorated in '82: Government," p. 2.

68. Kelley, "Japanese Management and Cultural Determinism."

69. Bairy, "Motivational Forces in Japanese Life," in *The Japanese Employee*, ed. Ballon, p. 57.

70. Seike and Terry, *Contemporary Japanese Houses*, as cited in *Public and Private Self in Japan and the United States*, ed. Barnlund, p. 60.

2

The Japanese Corporation: Background and Structure

The Japanese corporation, while not too different from the American corporation, offers an interesting contrast in certain respects. This chapter examines the origin and growth of the Japanese corporation, its structure, the group activities that are so prevalent in it, and some aspects of Japanese management's emphasis on human relations.

The fact that the basic structure of the Japanese corporation is very similar to that of the American corporation is not a matter of chance. "We learned most of our production and management methods from you in America," an executive of Toshiba has said. "And most of our manufacturing equipment also came from America. All we did was modify them to fit our special circumstances."[1]

In the postwar period, a time referred to as the Hungry Cage by modern Japanese, specific changes were mandated for the Japanese industrial system by the Occupation forces. Hideaki Okamoto explains:

First, the commerce law was amended so that boards of directors were legally required in place of "control by stockholders" which had already been only nominal. Thus, "control by trustees" was instituted. Second, auditing by certified public accountants was introduced to replace ritualized inspection of the books by internal auditors. Third, top management, in order to be accountable to trustees, assumed responsibility for detailed company operations and reported to the board of directors. Fourth, a controller system was gradually adopted. Fifth, management by committee was introduced, so that general managers' committees, directly in line with the board of directors, were formed. Finally, top management training programs, patterned on American models, were introduced.[2]

So it is not surprising that Japanese and American corporations are structurally the same. However, as Takeo Fujisawa, cofounder of Honda Motors Company, once observed: "Japanese and American management is 95 percent the same and differs in all important respects."[3]

HISTORY

Rodney Clark notes in *The Japanese Company* that, unlike Britain and the United States, where the company arose as a means of organizing business after much industrial development, in Japan "the company arrived almost at the moment when the country can be considered to have entered the modern world, and it was adopted immediately in order to make the growth of industry easier."[4]

During the Tokugawa period, Japan was ruled by hereditary regents, or shoguns, of the Tokugawa family. It is interesting that a form of elitism has developed in Japan today among persons who have this kind of historic name. Acquaintances of mine often told me whether their names were common ones—Yamamoto, Nishimura—or historic and exclusive ones—Fujiwara. Clark describes early Japanese society:

The country was divided into domains, each ruled over by a lord who owed allegiance to the shogun. There were four main social orders. The highest of these (except for a small number of court nobles attendant on the importent emperor) was that of the warriors or samurai. Their function was to administer the state. The second and largest order was that of the peasants, whose honourable task was to provide the wealth of the nation and the means to support the samurai. Below these stood the artisans. The last of the four orders was that of the merchants, condemned to inferiority in Confucian theory because they merely distributed goods that others produced.[5]

The feeling today that a Japanese corporation is a family has very definite historic origins. During the Tokugawa period the family was a group called a house, or *ie*, a word that referred to both the physical dwelling and the group of persons living in it. The house was a legal entity in the same sense that a corporation is today. Members were subservient to the househead, who managed the household for the benefit of everyone who lived there.

By the middle of the nineteenth century, after three centuries of rule by the Tokugawa shoguns, the feudal order disintegrated. In 1868, the last Tokugawa shogun lost power in favor of the Emperor Meiji, who began to Westernize the country and made industrialization a high priority.

The social order that existed then also contributed to today's Japanese system. Feudal Japan was a composite of isolated village communities, each centered around its work and each self-sufficient. "People rarely left the village in which they were born and under the Tokugawa administration passes were needed to leave one's district," states Michael Isherwood.[6]

Village households were arranged by seniority of residence in the community. "The Meiji reformation simply transferred these principles and practices from the country into factory and office," according to Isherwood.[7] People were accustomed to spending all of their time—on and off the job—with the same people. As we'll see, this is an important quality of present-day Japanese business life.

The Japanese trace the origin of their business community to the samurai, who dominated Japanese life for more than seven centuries and "who became industrialists, bankers, and traders after the Meiji Restoration," according to Halloran.[8]

At first samurai were both landowners and fighters. But as castle towns grew, fighting became too technical and each feudal lord needed retainers to pursue the art of war. So the samurai were cut off from the land.

In time of peace—like the Tokugawa period—samurai were parasitic. As lords lost their economic power, some samurai broke away. Seeking ways to improve themselves and their country, they went to the cities and made liaisons with merchants. They studied foreign languages, sciences, and religion and gave the country a ready supply of administrators when they were needed.[9]

First among fifteen points to which George Copeman attributes "The 30-year Japanese Miracle" is that "the feudal samurai tradition comes right into modern industry and gives a special code of behavior to the managerial and supervisory grades."[10] Others share this view despite the fact, stated well by Arthur Koestler in a *Life* magazine article, that the Meiji Restoration in a single generation "metamorphosed Japan from a feudal society into one of the leading industrial and military powers of the world—a feat unparalleled in human history."[11] The business community, much supported by government during this period, gradually developed its own power and soon worked as an equal partner with government in constructing Japan's industrial economy.[12]

The result is that "Japan is now first in shipbuilding and the production of cameras and motorcycles, second in automobile manufacturing, and third in steel, paper production, and petroleum refining," says M. Y. Yoshino in *Japan's Managerial System*.[13] Japanese companies have become dominant in cameras, radios, television sets, and hi-fi equipment, all the result of a national consensus by business organizations two decades ago to target consumer electronics.[14] Their attention has turned to computers and robots, and they have gained the lead in the latter and are closing in on world-leader America in the former.

In the late 1970s, Japan had 40,000 robots in operation, about five times more than the United States and European Economic Community combined.[15] According to the NBC White Paper, "If Japan Can, Why Can't We?" by 1980 there were 45,000 robots in operation in Japan to America's 5,000.[16] It was reported on that program that some Japanese plants are so automated that the third shift each day is run entirely by computer-assisted machines. There are no people.[17]

All of this is the outcome of Japan's effort to cope with labor shortages and to reduce the costs of production. Japan's second-largest steel company, NKK, opened a plant in Ogishima in 1976 that is so highly automated that it can produce more steel than the plant it replaced with fewer than half the workers. Although it cost $3 billion and took ten years to build, the plant has tripled the average productivity per worker.

The NBC program also reported that Mazda made 740,000 cars in 1974, when it had 37,000 workers. By 1979, it had only 27,000 workers, but it turned out a million cars. The feeling in Japan is that this kind of efficiency can be achieved in all areas of production in all industries and that this is only the beginning.

The remarkable aspect of all of this is that Japan has achieved it in only the fourth decade after its near total destruction of industrial capacity. The Japanese corporation through which the country is achieving its successes deserves worldwide study.

STRUCTURE

Japanese business today includes some 5 million enterprises, of which over 600,000 are in manufacturing, but only about 700 of them account for most of the country's production. The 25 percent of these manufacturing companies which are incorporated employ some 65 percent of the work force.[18]

The close cooperation between business and government in Japan has earned it the name "Japan, Inc." worldwide, to the distress of many Japanese. The organizations most responsible for planning and controlling government–business interrelationships is the Ministry of International Trade and Industry (MITI), roughly equivalent to but much more powerful than the U.S. Department of Commerce.

Among MITI's duties are steering industry toward advantageous activities, creating mergers among companies in declining industries, persuading companies in depressed sectors to reduce capacity, and forming consortia to exploit foreign sources of raw materials and markets.[19] Because MITI has no statutory authority, it tries to accomplish all of this through persuasion. Industry does not have to comply. MITI has drastically reshaped Japanese business by abolishing some industries and establishing others, deciding what companies should build plants in what locations and ordering docks where needed and removing others. There is no doubt that MITI has been responsible to a large measure for turning Japan into an advanced industrial nation.[20]

The interests of Japanese businesses are protected by several organizations. The Federation of Economic Organizations has a membership of 100 major trade or industrial associations and some 750 major firms. This is the most influential group.

The Japan Committee for Economic Development has 1,500 individual members. Its function is to coordinate members' business interests.

The Japan Federation of Employers' Associations includes about 30,000 employers. It represents members in labor–management matters.[21]

The Japanese Chamber of Commerce represents medium and small businesses. It also has some influence in government.[22]

A part of the Japanese business world not duplicated in America is the *zaibatsu*, a huge combination of interconnected and interdependent companies, usually several smaller ones to a single big company, in an individual industry. Richard Caves and Masu Uekusa describe the *zaibatsu* as a collection of "manufacturing, trading and financial corporations, with a group generally including oligopolistic firms from a number of industries but few rivals in individual product markets."[23]

Before the war, the four most powerful *zaibatsu* (Mitsui, Mitsubishi, Sumitomo, and Yasuda) controlled 70 percent of all bank deposits. Three of them controlled over 50 percent of all coal output and more than 50 percent of merchant shipping. Two dominated two political parties and were able to manipulate government fiscal policies to gain large subsidies and ultimately to influence the entire economy.[24]

Mitsui was preeminent among the four. According to John Roberts in his comprehensive historical account, *Mitsui, Three Centuries of Japanese Business*, its "sprawling empire embraced every significant sector of industry, finance, and commerce, and employed as many as three million people domestically and overseas.... Controlling as it did one of the major prewar political parties in Japan, Mitsui could influence legislation, arrange the appointment of friendly cabinets, and make its imprint on foreign policy."[25] Roberts said that, independently or in collaboration with other *zaibatsu*, Mitsui could thwart power-hungry bureaucrats and militarists, promote necessary reforms, and topple governments.[26]

Although outlawed during the Occupation, the *zaibatsu* gradually regained power. A difference, though, is that ownership today is dispersed among shareholders instead of a single family owning the entire operation as it did before the war. The four largest today are the same four that were strongest before the war. Supportive services and ties between companies in a *zaibatsu* include interlocking directorates, preferential credit, coordinating committees, sharing of raw materials and products, and mutual ownership.[27]

Today Mitsubishi is the largest *zaibatsu*, described in *Business Week* as

"Japan's biggest industrial, trading, and banking conglomerate. Sales of the 28-member group totaled $123 billion in the fiscal year ended March 31 (1981), and banking assets were $103 billion."[28]

Although American stockholders consider themselves owners of the company and do not hesitate to attend annual meetings to question officers and members of the board of directors, the Japanese shareholder views his holdings in quite a different way. Since companies pay fixed dividends, the shareholder views his investment as a savings account or even a postal savings account. He is not likely to question the management of either of those. Why should he question his return on investment in a company?[29]

The fact that the debt–equity ratio of a typical Japanese firm is 20:80 (meaning that only 20 percent of its funding is shareholder equity and 80 percent is bank financing) causes management to be more attentive to bankers than shareholders.[30]

An unusual aspect of Japanese corporate annual meetings is the presence of *sokaiya*, paid professional shills whose job it is to move the meeting along with minimum interference from shareholders. Herbert Glazer reports on this phenomenon in "The Japanese Executive," a chapter in *The Japanese Employee*, stating that the *sokaiya* "fill the room where the meeting is held with shouts of 'Approve!' 'No Objection!' and 'Move on with the meeting!' Since other stockholders are too timid to object to such harassment, *sokaiya* are able to insure that no questions arise during the meeting."[31]

Composition of the board of directors of Japanese companies also differs from that of American boards. In Japan, most members are also employees—usually top managers; in America, the reverse is true—most are outsiders. Also, the board of directors in Japan generally includes former union officials. "Nikkeiren, the Japanese Federation of Employers' Associations, recently surveyed 534 large companies and discovered that 992 out of 6,121 executives, or 16.2 percent, had been influential union leaders," reports Masatsugu.[32]

Since most Japanese board members are also officers of the company, their duties as directors are not much different from their regular duties. Being a director is, of course, a prestigious achievement for an employee; however, it is largely a symbolic rank. The board of a Japanese corporation is a ceremonial body charged with matters of form only.[33] The directors act chiefly, when they do, as mediators in disputes.

Like American directors, Japanese board members are elected by shareholders at the annual meetings. The size of Japanese boards is usually slightly larger than the size of American boards; a survey of 1,112 leading Japanese corporations by the Toyo Keizai Publishing Company revealed that the average number of directors is 14. They range in size from 5 to 37, with more than half of the firms having 14 to 20 members on the board.[34]

Top management officers of the large Japanese corporation include the chairman of the board, president, managing directors, department heads, section heads, and branch managers.[35] There are usually about ten vertically arranged divisions of responsibility in the Japanese business organization.

The president is ultimately responsible for decision making in the Japanese firm. The unique *ringi* system of decision making, to be discussed in Chapter 5, means that most of the president's decision-making authority is indirect.

Managing directors correspond roughly to the vice-presidential level of American businesses. They seem to have the greatest influence in the decision-making process.

Department heads are usually aged 45 to 52. Several of these report to one managing director. Some companies also have deputy or assistant department heads.

Section heads are aged 35 to 45. About three report to one department head. Some companies also have assistant section heads, usually aged 32 to 38.

Finally, three or four branch managers report to one section head.[36]

The most senior and respected managing director is in charge of the personnel department,[37] which is certainly not the case in American corporations. But in Japan, "the Personnel Department is all-important," according to Gibney.[38] This is due, of course, to the great emphasis in the Japanese corporation on human relations.

A useful department in this company is the *somu-bu*, "general affairs department," which handles duties not covered by any other department. Its responsibilities include public relations, company mail, interdepartmental relations, and maintaining files.[39]

The hiring process in the average Japanese company also differs considerably from its American equal. Candidates must pass a company aptitude test as part of the applications process.[40] Also, when the Japanese hiree enters his company, he is not being hired for a single job. He is merely hired into the company to serve in whatever capacity he is needed. If he is a white collar worker, he assumes the honored title of *salariiman*, a Japanization of "salaryman." About one-fifth of the labor force calls itself by that term.[41]

Japanese companies have adopted a ranking system in which employees are assigned a rank based on their academic background, length of service, and ability. The number of ranks per company varies. Toyo Rayon, for example, has 30 ranks, with the new employee being assigned to one of the lowest 3. Promotion depends on performance; however, there is a set number of years an employee remains in a rank. The one with the worst performance remains in rank for the maximum period.[42]

The supply of labor available to the Japanese firm is about to undergo change, according to the *Economic Survey of Japan (1979–80)* published by the *Japan Times* of Tokyo. The labor force is getting older and more educated and includes more women, the survey states. The rate at which the average age of the population is rising is four times faster than in Western countries. The number of university graduates is rapidly rising, from 120,000 in 1960 to 370,000 in 1979.[43]

Until recently, the Japanese corporation has been almost totally racist and sexist due to the homogeneous social system it maintains, which can tolerate little cultural diversity. "To the extent that women or ethnic minorities," William Ouchi notes in *Theory Z*, "are culturally different, they cannot succeed in Japan."[44] Their careers will be limited to lower levels of management, Ouchi explains. However, the survey states that at least for women that is changing for several specific reasons, among them (1) the shortening of the total child-rearing period by the reduction in the number of offspring; (2) the spread of labor-saving electrical home appliances and the replacement of housework by external services; and (3) the deepening devotion to work which accompanies the trend toward higher educational achievements.[45]

Another aspect of the Japanese business that differs from the Western system is a dependence on subcontractors. In a pyramid-style system, subcontractors work with sub-subcontractors and those with sub-sub-subcontractors and so on for four or five levels. Six major car manu-facturers, for example, subcontract about 70 percent of their material cost, compared to 30 to 40 percent in Europe and the United States (except Volvo, which matches Japan).[46]

This subcontracting system allows Japanese companies to compete successfully through rapid technological change. Wage levels at subcon-tracting companies are lower and benefits provided employees fewer.

Businesspersons in Japan operate in a military metaphor. In the 1960s, rejecting American methods, they looked to their own history for con-cepts to strengthen their own unique system. They studied primarily these books: the eighteen-volume biography of Ieyasu Tokugawa, foun-der of Japan's last great military dynasty; *Sun Tzu*, the Chinese classic on military strategy; and the 1938 edition of the *Operations Manual of the Imperial Japanese Army*. They learned from these to equate business management with the tactics of war.[47] That thinking permeates business life today in Japan, beginning with a new employee's orientation.

New employees fresh out of high school or the university undergo a military-style orientation at an industrial company described by Thomas Rohlen. The one-month program includes a 5:30 wake-up, calisthenics, inspections, lectures, sports activities, and other team activities. All of this is in specific uniforms. The lectures are on the "expectations that all will demonstrate a 'fighting spirit.' " Others are on:

the subject of "love" . . . [how] to make a success of their future marriages through a cooperative attitude and teamwork between husband and wife.... The last day of training is the occasion for a series of ceremonies which mark the return of the participants to society and seal the bonds formed among the trainees and between them and the company.... Dressed in their business suits for the first time in a month, the men stand at attention while the president addresses them on the now familiar themes of cooperation, company loyalty, comradeship and fighting spirit.[48]

Some companies go a step further and actually send their new employees to train with the Self-Defense Force—Japan's army—to instill in them a military discipline.[49]

It's interesting that industrial spying is rampant with spies using the same techniques of the best Cold War sleuths. A *Newsweek* article, "Japan's High-Tech Challenge," in the August 9, 1982, issue, states that "over the past 30 years Japanese firms have spent more than $10 billion in fees and royalties for foreign technology that American and European companies were only too willing to sell."[50] With Japan's successes in world markets, their competitors are reluctant to share technology, so Japan, it appears, is resorting to new methods. When Hitachi and Mitsubishi Electric employees were caught in an FBI sting operation trying to purchase IBM software secrets, a Japanese spokesman said that the FBI was trying to damage America's chief industrial rival.[51] It is obvious, however, that, perhaps because they are operating in their military metaphor, the Japanese are beginning to accomplish that very well all by themselves.

NOTES

1. Emanuel, "Productivity Improvement—Japanese Style," p. 1.
2. Okamoto, "Management and Their Organizations," in *Workers and Employers in Japan*, ed. Okochi, Karsh, and Levine, p. 179.
3. Interview with Taizo Ueda, Senior Economist, Honda Motor Company, Ltd., Tokyo, July 1, 1980, as reported in Pascale and Athos, *The Art of Japanese Management*, p. 85.
4. Clark, *The Japanese Company*, p. 13.
5. Ibid.
6. Isherwood, "Check Your Own Check-List," in *Business in Japan*, ed. Norbury and Bownas, p. 184.
7. Ibid., p. 185.
8. Halloran, *Japan*, p. 74.
9. Best, *Christian Faith and Cultural Crisis*, pp. 5, 6.
10. Copeman, "The 30-year Japanese Miracle: Lessons for the West," in *Why the Japanese Have Been So Successful in Business*, ed. Furstenberg, p. 86.

11. Koestler, "Her Course Is Set," p. 68.

12. Halloran, *Japan*, p. 74.

13. Yoshino, *Japan's Managerial System*, p. 273.

14. Ramsey and Gibney, "Japan's High-Tech Challenge," p. 50.

15. Pempel, *Policy and Politics in Japan*, pp. 60–61.

16. "If Japan Can, Why Can't We?" transcript, part 2, p. 17.

17. Ibid., part 2, p. 16.

18. De Mente, *How to Do Business in Japan*, p. 38.

19. Sinha, *Japan's Options for the 1980s*, p. 19.

20. Forbis, *Japan Today*, p. 6.

21. Pempel, *Policy and Politics in Japan*, pp. 29–30.

22. Masatsugu, *The Modern Samurai Society*, p. 40.

23. Caves and Uekusa, "Industrial Organization," in *Asia's New Giant*, ed. Patrick and Rosovsky, p. 495.

24. Warshaw and Bromwell, *Japan Emerges*, p. 10.

25. Roberts, *Mitsui*, p. 5.

26. Ibid.

27. Forbis, *Japan Today*, p. 374.

28. "Mitsubishi: A Japanese Giant's Plans for Growth in the U.S.," p. 128.

29. Glazer, "The Japanese Executive," in *The Japanese Employee*, ed. Ballon, p. 79.

30. Imai, *16 Ways to Avoid Saying No*, p. 133.

31. Glazer, "The Japanese Executive," p. 80.

32. Masatsugu, *The Modern Samurai Society*, p. 155.

33. Glazer, "The Japanese Executive," p. 81.

34. Yoshino, *Japan's Managerial System*, pp. 197–98.

35. *The Japan Business Guide*, p. 32.

36. Ibid., p. 33.

37. Ouchi, *Theory Z*, p. 24.

38. Gibney, *Japan*, p. 183.

39. De Mente, *How to Do Business in Japan*, p. 48.

40. Emanuel, "Productivity Improvement—Japanese Style," p. 1.

41. Plath, *The After Hours*, p. 36.

42. Financial Times, *Japan*, pp. 44–45.

43. Japan, Economic Planning Agency, *Economic Survey of Japan*, pp. 210–13.

44. Ouchi, *Theory Z*, p. 92.

45. Japan, Economic Planning Agency, *Economic Survey of Japan*, p. 215.

46. Watanabe, "Technological Linkages Between Formal and Informal Sectors of Manufacturing Industries," as cited in Sinha, *Japan's Options for the 1980s*, p. 12.

47. De Mente, *How to Do Business in Japan*, p. viii.

48. Rohlen, "Sponsorship of Cultural Continuity in Japan: A Company Training Program," in *Japanese Culture and Behavior*, ed. Lebra and Lebra, pp. 334–35.

49. Masatsugu, *The Modern Samurai Society*, p. 161.

50. Ramsey and Gibney, "Japan's High-Tech Challenge," p. 49.

51. "Japscam for Computer Spies," p. 7.

3

The Japanese Corporation: Employees

Japan's only natural resource in any abundance is its people so the country goes to great lengths to protect its people. In the past, as we've seen, the Tokugawa shoguns sealed off the country from outside influences. More recently, the government decided to record its history selectively by deleting from history books references to its "acts of aggression" in China and Southeast Asia during World War II.[1]

It is doubtful, however, that the government can prevent stories such as those of the atrocities from being passed on, and, as they are, they are distorted, without government interference. When I lived in Japan, schoolchildren who had been born after World War II were asked what about the past they would like to experience if they could. A surprisingly large number said they would like to see the beauties of the fire bombing of the cities during the war. Their elders had told them how enjoyable it had been to stand on a hill or a mountain and watch the fires burning below them! Most of the children had heard the glorified descriptions in their own family groups, which in Japan are very important.

More important than the family group for the Japanese employee, though, is his or her work group. Each individual work group is also very important to a corporation. To be sure a group and all of its members perform well, the Japanese company invests much time and money on good employee relations. In this chapter, we examine group life in the Japanese company and a company's emphasis on employee (human) relations.

GROUPS

From the Tokugawa days of isolated villages whose residents depended on one another for survival, the Japanese have learned to adapt to group living and working. Favoring group to individual activity, once a matter of survival, has become a matter of preference. "From primary school to the university, the student is encouraged to act and think of himself primarily as a member of a group, rather than as an individual," say Robert Marsh and Hiroshi Mannari in *Modernization and the Japanese Factory*. "Thus, before a person ever enters a company, he has normally developed a collectivity orientation, and upon entering the company, he transfers this to the new group setting."[2] Richard Pascale and Anthony Athos in *The Art of Japanese Management* call the work group "the basic building block of Japanese organizations."[3]

Japanese are motivated to achieve through the group both group goals and corporate objectives. One's membership in a group is conditioned on working according to its direction, showing deference to other members of the group who are superior in age and service if not ability, and not seeking recognition for his contributions to group work.[4]

The fact that an employee may stay in the same group for the duration of a career means that maintaining group harmony and cohesiveness benefits everyone. Halloran expresses the Japanese view:

We Japanese don't like individuality, and even the word *kojin*, which means "individual" in our language, has a rather bad meaning. If we Japanese say a man is *kojin-teki*, or individualistic, we mean that he is egotistic and wants to do things his own way rather than getting along with his group. My foreign friends sometimes tease me, "Why don't you stand up for your rights?" They don't understand that we Japanese don't think much about rights.[5]

Because the semiannual bonuses depend on group achievement, cooperation in and support of group activity become important for very practical reasons. Friedrich Furstenberg in *Why the Japanese Have Been So Successful in Business* describes the value of groups to the organization:

One must therefore agree with W. H. Brown, the American observer, who states: "It is precisely this group orientation of the managers, their team work and the existence of harmonious personal relations, which give to Japanese organisations their strength and efficiency. This type of organisation does not suppress the special capabilities of an individual. It allows him the broadest possible scope. The faults of a person, likewise, are obscured, since they are counter-balanced by the strengths of his colleagues. Finally, a feeling of group satisfaction is engendered because each one contributes to the vital activity of the undertaking and shares in it.[6]

Plath, however, states why harmony is not an end in itself:

Group harmony is important to the extent that it contributes to group achievement, but harmony per se is not an "ultimate" goal.... A happy family is desirable, but family members' performance is not conditional upon happiness. In Lord Avebury's terms, the Japanese ideal stressed the Happiness of Duty much more than the Duty of Happiness.

It is the group's goals that matter most, and what matters about them is that they are the group's goals, regardless of their "content." They usually will be expressed as the wishes or decisions of the head, but it is taken for granted that the head will not announce selfish wishes but only those which have group consensus.[7]

The Japanese have a slogan for it: "Extinguish the self and serve the group."[8] Morinosuke Kajima, head of the Kajima Construction Company, expressed it this way: "There is no more perfect feeling than the knowledge of duty well discharged."[9]

"The stability of the working group," say Norbury and Bownas, "takes precedence over everything. The rule is to avoid any unnecessary embarrassment or offense to others, particularly within one's own group."[10] "Strength of character," Benedict explains, "they think, is shown in conforming not in rebelling."[11]

Insights on group activities in the Japanese corporation of a few Americans who work in them were included in a *Fortune* magazine article. A Fujitsu employee stated:

Half my time is spent working with other groups, and if I get them angry I can never get them to push and pull with me. So I have to be polite outside my section, but with my own people I don't have to be polite.... It's always "we" and "they." There are very many opposing groups and conflicts. There is no harmoniousness. If there were, meetings would be shorter, ten to fifteen minutes instead of half a day, and they wouldn't go to seven at night. But it is a rule in Japanese society to strive to attain harmoniousness. That's why, if possible, you want 100 percent concurrence in any decision.[12]

A Japan Air Lines employee explained the power of groups in relation to a president's decision-making authority: "If the president went ahead without the approval of the groups concerned, he'd be removed in some face-saving way, whether by elevation to chairman or being made the president of a subsidiary."[13]

Advantages of group work were accentuated by the oil shortage of 1973. That international event was especially harmful to this country, which imports 90 percent of all of its energy resources.[14] A mobilization of Japan's real resource—its people—was required to respond to and overcome the impact of drastically increased prices. It was during this period that from 35 to 40 percent of Japanese companies began emphasizing groups and group activities.[15] However, while dependence on the group in business organizations is of relatively recent origin, as is the corporation itself, in Japanese history, the dependence on social groupings in the Japanese culture is not so recent. Robert Cole in *Japanese Blue Collar: The Changing Tradition* provides its background:

We can clearly identify this group spirit as a characteristic of Japanese social structure at least as far back as the sixteenth century, which saw the full flowering of feudalism in Japan. At that time, the politically decentralized government allowed the absolute rule of local magnates over their subjects. The followers of these local rulers were closely clustered around them in compact territorial units. The *daimyo* wielded absolute power over his vassals and in turn guaranteed them their fiefs. But Japanese group consciousness goes back to the even more distant past. Strong clan-like social organization seems to have been a persistent feature throughout Japan's history.[16]

In the modern Japanese corporation, membership in the right group is more important than any other aspect of an employee's life. It controls everything. According to Nakane, "There is almost no social life outside the particular group on which an individual's major economic life depends."[17] So getting into the right group is an important goal for a Japanese employee, even more important, the Japanese say only half-facetiously, than that of choosing a wife.

The benefits to the employee of belonging to a group begin on the first day of work. Although he is still required to find his place within his group, the employee receives special advantage from membership in his group. Other members extend to him their support both on and off the job—in finding a residence, for example. "The new employee," Nakane states, "is in just about the same position and is, in fact, received by the company in much the same spirit as if he were a newly born family member, a newly adopted son-in-law or a bride come into the husband's household."[18] By Japanese custom, in a family of daughters, a husband of one of them is often adopted into the family to assume its name and the rights and responsibilities of a son.

Socialization into the organization is also facilitated by group membership. Anyone who has ever worked his way into a job in an American company knows it takes months, even years, to understand what is truly happening around you. Think of the advantage of having someone explain the company and the personalities in it to you in the beginning!

Recalcitrant behavior of an employee can be controlled through the group also. Little such behavior usually occurs beyond occasional willfulness; whatever nonconforming behavior does occur is handled with understanding and sensitivity. Extreme cases, such as shutting oneself off from the rest of the group, receive a response in kind, ostracism, an intolerable situation for the average Japanese. It is not likely that an employee would expose himself to that possibility.

The frustrations of the organization are improved by the groups. Responsibilities are shared by group members. There is not the American-style clear delineation of individual responsibilities set forth in job descriptions. To define individual duties by job description, the Japanese feel, means that when that worker is absent from the job his duties stop. Group members in Japan, on the other hand, help one another and cover for one another. Marsh and Mannari explain, "Norms of mutual help among employees are strong enough so that even in an assembly line setting, work is not totally individualistic."[19]

The quality that organizations try to inculcate most of all in groups and, for that matter, throughout the organization is *wa*, or harmony. Striving for harmony in daily life is as old as the country itself. The original name of the country was *Yamato*, meaning "great harmony."[20] The first part of the first article of the constitution of Prince Shotoku in 604 said "*Wa* is a virtue, and make it a rule not to dispute."

Wa can be traced to the Confucian idea of natural law, which was supposed to be the basis of society—between ruler and ruled. It should also be the basis of relationships between individuals who should strive for harmony. Rohlen describes it as "the cooperation, trust, sharing, warmth, morale, and hard work of efficient, pleasant, and purposeful fellowship."[21]

A quality of Japanese group life that must be unique is a social interdependence, called *amae* by psychiatrist L. Takeo Doi and defined by James Bartholomew as "a desire to presume on the good will or emotional support of another."[22] This desire exists between all members of a group, but it is especially strong in two special and unusual relationships: *sempai–kohai* and *oyabun–kobun*.

In *sempai–kohai* relationships, the young Japanese employee has the security of being apprenticed informally to a senior member of the management staff. Sometimes the relationships are assigned, with the junior employee receiving the name of his *sempai* on the first day of work. Takie Sugiyama Lebra in *Japanese Patterns of Behavior* explains that, in this relationship, "a *sempai* employee plays the role of an elder brother toward a *kohai* employee."[23] The senior member looks after and advises the junior member, who reciprocates with hard work and a great deal of respect. Albert Craig explains that a superior addresses his subordinates in familiar terms that express his acceptance of and affection for them. "This suggests a paternalistic warmth, and kindly concern for the future of the junior, his training and his welfare in general. The junior accepts this, is respectful and works hard."[24] Bairy observes that the communication between such individuals and between those in similar relationships in Japan serves a broader purpose than transmitting ideas between the individuals; it provides an "emotional message."[25] Such a relationship does develop on occasion in American companies, but it is neither as common nor as planned as is the Japanese style of the interaction.

The *sempai–kohai* relationship steadies the new employee as he learns to interact within the company; it helps his socialization. If an employee is having difficulties, it is attributed to his lack of a *sempai*. If an employee is successful, his *sempai* takes much of the credit. Peter Drucker refers to the *sempai* as a "godfather."[26]

The person selected as *sempai*, Rohlen states in *For Harmony and Strength*, must "be the same sex as the newcomer, a little older (one source said ten years is about right), gregarious, and knowledgeable. Most importantly, they should be models of good work habits and proper attitudes."[27]

Sometimes *sempai* intercede in the authority structure of the company. An office chief may pass instructions to the employee through his *sempai*, who is able to explain the assignment and the reasons for it. A *sempai* might also intervene to explain an employee's errors.

A *sempai* may have several employees apprenticed to him. The more influential he is, the more young employees he will guide. Ernest van Helvoort in *The Japanese Working Man: What Choice? What Reward?* explains the pervasiveness of the relationship:

Sempai groups may coincide with units of the formal organization, but frequently they will not and their influence may extend into every corner of the enterprise. The formal organization, therefore, is covered with a barely visible web of personal interrelationships, which has a direct impact on the workings of the whole structure.[28]

Similar to a *sempai–kohai* relationship but different in that the feelings between the individuals are deeper is the *oyabun–kobun* arrangement. *Oya* means "parent," and *ko* means "child." It is a parent–child relationship between adults; the *sempai–kohai* relationship in comparison would be teacher–student, for example. Although the words *oyabun* and *kobun* have lost some of their appeal because they have been adopted and used extensively by the underworld in Japan, the relationship is much in evidence in business.

The *oyabun–kobun* arrangement can also exist between whole organizations. Sinha reports, "It is not unusual to find a large business or an industrial firm to act as the *oyabun* to a number of affiliated and subordinate companies and to treat each as 'child-company.' "[29]

Naturally there are some disadvantages to the group system. James Abegglen mentions the most important one in *The Japanese Factory*: "Widely disparate groups of employees who are homogeneous within each group in experience and outlook but ill-equipped to communicate with each other"[30] interfere with the corporation's total communication effort.

There is also the possibility, as Jon Woronoff explains in *Japan: The Coming Social Crisis*, that demands of various groups on an individual may be conflicting. One's obligations to the company may overwhelm his duties to family, for example. Woronoff also speculates that the dominance of groups in a person's life prevents him from realizing and developing his own personality.[31]

Personnel procedures may create problems for a group. For example, Rohlen explains that "transfers may be initiated by problems in office or factory groups, but no group leader has much power over who will be assigned to his unit."[32] Group stability is frequently interrupted by transfers of members or turnover of employees who retire or quit.

Rohlen points out also, "The size of office and factory groups is not determined by considerations of group dynamics, but by the work load and other external factors. In consequence, many groups are too big to be organized on a small-group model."[33]

With increasing company size, group members are experiencing a sense of alienation from the company, Rohlen reports. Group orientation also tends to segregate employees by age, providing little chance for interaction between working groups of different ages. Expanding corporate activities are also removing the group leader from participating in group activities—the leisure-time ones, for example—because of the demand of his work.[34]

So important are groups to the functioning of the Japanese economy, both in business and in society in general, that Vogel explains that the greatest threat to Japanese-style democracy comes from neither the left nor the right. Instead, the real threat, says Vogel, "is the dissipation of group cohesiveness. ... with unorganized groups there is no way to reach an understanding." [35]

HUMAN RELATIONS

Japan has always had to depend on its human resources to make up for its severe lack of other natural resources. Japanese managers take human relations very seriously.

In addition to the training the new employee undergoes, he receives continuous training throughout his career. Yoshi Tsurumi, professor of international business at City College of New York, asks Japanese managers what they regard as their most important management functions. "If it's not first on the Japanese manager's list, training subordinates is always mentioned at least second or third."[36] When he asked American managers the same question, none has ever mentioned training as an important managerial function. Rohlen reports that Westinghouse made a study of employee development in Japan and in its own company in the United States. The company found that Japanese companies spend much more time and money developing people.[37]

The Japanese manager above all else, says Boye De Mente, must be "expert in human relations."[38] What does that entail? Here is how Konosuke Matsushita, head of Matsushita Electric Industrial Company, Ltd., answered that question: "First we must really know what a human being is. If one wants to raise sheep, one must first learn the nature of sheep. So with the human heart."[39]

Japanese businesspersons have been found in surveys to prefer a boss who is "exacting in business conduct but warm-hearted on the personal level."[40] He must also feel that his boss trusts him implicitly; without that sense of trust, he will find it difficult to commit himself totally to the company, as is expected of him.

Toshiroh Sakata of Sharp Corporation attends employee weddings and makes hospital visits as part of his human relations work on the job. "Weddings, hospital visits—these are some secrets of good human relations," says Sakata, who takes pride in his close relationship to each of the 100 people who work for him. "Out of 100, I know the hobby, sports interest, and health condition of each of them—and that makes for good relationships."[41]

Toward creating a spirit of unity among workers, Japanese companies are known to have company songs, company uniforms worn by everyone in the organization, and exercise sessions for employees either before the day begins or during the work day. Kawasaki explains the practice:

Japanese workers gather on factory grounds and engage in calisthenics before starting the day's work. They are cheerful and humor is always present. For instance, when someone gets confused and starts bending in the wrong direction, laughter and smiles flit throughout the factory and pervade in the workshop for the rest of the day. Factories in Japan thus cater to the Japanese taste for some kind of regimentation and formal order, thereby fulfilling the Japanese yearning to "belong." In many factories such as the giant Matsushita Electrical Works, the president himself addresses the entire crew every morning in order to exhort them to greater efforts.[42]

Some of these techniques are being used with American workers by Japanese plants operating in the United States. An item in the *San Diego Union* referred to one such company: "Promptly at seven each morning, workers at Kyocera International line up on rows, each standing on a dot in the parking lot beside Balboa Avenue. The color of their uniforms is their designation of rank. Then come the calisthenics, and finally a pep talk from CEO Arthur Jonishi or one of his aides."[43]

During these exercise sessions, workers often sing the company song, which combines, usually, patriotism with paternalism. Matsushita was the first company to have a song. In its present form, this is it:

A bright heart overflowing
With lives linked together,

Matsushita Denki.
Time goes by but as it moves along
Each day brings a new spring.
Let us bind together
A world of blooming flowers
And a verdant land
In love, light and a dream.

We trust our strength together in harmony.
Finding happiness,
Matsushita Denki.
Animating joy everywhere,
A world of dedication,
Let us fulfill our hopes,
Shining hopes,
Of a radiant dawning
With love, light and a dream.[44]

And here is the company song of Nissan:

Looking at Mt. Fuji surrounded with white clouds in the morning, we gather with a great hope toward the future. We are the cream of technology. We will devote all our labours, a result of sweat and hard work, to achieve prosperity and happiness in this world. This is a pride we at Nissan take. Nissan, the leader of the country's industry.[45]

The emphasis on human relations in the Japanese company may be in response to what the employee considers his rights. "First, he must not be embarrassed in any way. Second, he should not be asked to do any work outside of his duties as he sees them. Third, he should not be criticized for expressing individualism. And fourth, he should not be forced to do anything against his wishes—unless for a 'group' cause," all according to De Mente.[46]

Probably the first of those is the most important one to a Japanese. It's the well-known Oriental desire to save face. I experienced it firsthand.

When I worked with a youth group in a local church in Matsuyama, I did everything I would have done with a similar group in America. Most of our activities were well attended because young people wanted the opportunity to practice English.

One year we had a Halloween party. The group bobbed for apples, even though the young Japanese considered it unhygienic. Then we began to play games. In one game, we turned off the lights and had three candles in the middle of the floor on which the group was seated in a circle. It was a follow-the-leader game, and it gave them a chance to be uncharacteristically and joyously silly. I reached over and pinched the cheek of the person next to me, and they all did the same to the persons beside them. I turned to the person on the other side of me and ran my finger all around the face. They did the same.

After a few minutes of laughter and mimicry, I told them the game was over and we turned on the lights. Of course, the faces of the two individuals next to me were covered with bright red marks from the coloring I had smeared all over my fingers after the lights went off. I had played the game with American youngsters, and they thought it was a good joke on the persons whose faces were colored red. But this group was so completely embarrassed for the two victims that they wouldn't look at them. Without a word, the two washed their faces and returned to the group to join other activities. No one said a word about it the rest of the evening.

Assured of these basic rights, including not being embarrassed in any way, the Japanese worker responds by committing himself totally to his work. For example, he doesn't take a prolonged vacation; entitled to fifteen to twenty days a year, the Japanese employee takes only an average of five days.[47] "Few, if any, dare to take this officially stipulated leave in full," reports Kawasaki, "for fear their colleagues may think ill of them as being selfish or frivolous. At most they will take only a few days off and then work for the rest of the year without grumbling."[48] Twelve national holidays, listed on Table 1, make up somewhat for missed vacation time.

Absenteeism is low. A study by an American firm determined that absenteeism in Japan runs only 4 to 5 percent annually.[49]

However, all of this does not mean that every day is sheer bliss for the Japanese worker. Drucker observes, "What they experience in their daily lives are tensions, pressures, conflict, and not unity. They see intense, if not cutthroat, competition both among the major banks and among the major industrial groups. And the Japanese are themselves involved every day in the bitter factional infighting that characterizes their institutions."[50]

Nakane explains, "The Japanese system naturally produces much more frustration in the members of lower status in the hierarchy; and allows the head to abuse the group or an individual member."[51]

Woronoff reports that the Japanese employee does not feel obligated to give fair value in work for wages received. The attitude of many office employees is that physical presence is all it takes to fulfill any such obligations.[52] Although they work long hours, the density of that work is poor.[53]

American employees of Japanese companies (in Japan) had much to say about attitudes of workers in a *Fortune* magazine article. Discussing disharmony in his work environment, a Toyota Motors employee said:

There's a myth about all the politeness. At the lower levels people under 30 are always shouting at each other, but when they get older and reach the *kakaricho*

Table 1
Japanese National Holidays

Date	Holiday
January 1	New Year's Day.
January 15	Adult's Day—to honor young people who have reached 20 years of age, voting age.
February 11	National Foundation Day—to celebrate the accession to the throne of Jimmu, the first emperor.
March 21	Vernal Equinox Day—to celebrate the coming of spring. People visit ancestral graves.
April 29	Emperor's Birthday.
May 3	Constitution Day.
May 5	Children's Day.
September 15	Respect for the Aged Day.
September 23	Autumnal Equinox Day—to celebrate the first day of autumn.
October 10	Health-Sports Day—to encourage young people to enjoy sports.
November 3	Culture Day.
November 23	Labor Thanksgiving Day—to celebrate a good harvest in the countryside.

(chief clerk) and *kacho* (section chief) classes, they become more subtle.... When there is something really wrong between two people they just don't talk to each other.[54]

A Fujitsu employee said:

If you're narrowly brilliant—say, a very good circuit designer—but with no ability at manipulating people, you are going to be very frustrated. In a Japanese company, most of the work is manipulating people or getting support for your ideas. In Japan the more you can get people to do what you want, the more brilliant you are seen to be.[55]

A survey conducted by the Ministry of Labor in Japan showed that there are many emotional and mental disturbances among Japanese workers. Among workers' complaints, as reported by De Mente, were "having to work too fast, incapable supervisors, unappreciative man- agement, crowded working and living conditions, traffic and pollution problems, and having to maintain the delicate human relations that are the basis for the Japanese business system."[56]

However, these feelings don't always work against the corporation. Cole explains why:

It is quite possible that workers may have low morale and work satisfaction and still manifest high work motivation and commitment to work. For example, comparative data for Japan and the United States show that Japanese blue-collar workers generally register more dissatisfaction (controlling for industry) on such measures as "work pace too fast," "bored with job," and "job provides opportunity to display ability." This may be because they have good reason to hold higher expectations on these matters. In any case, although these differences serve as measures of morale and work satisfaction, they do not necessarily tell us that Japanese workers have lower work motivation or commitment to work. On a crucial measure of desire to change jobs, which taps the probability of individuals trying to take action to relieve dissatisfaction, Fujita reports that the Japanese respondents were markedly less likely to want to change jobs.[57]

How much of that attitude is due to the difficulty a Japanese employee has in changing jobs, though, is not clear.

The safety valve in Japanese corporations is the fact that group members spend a great deal of leisure time together. Whether it's participating in recreational activities on the company premises or visiting a bar together, the group that works together also plays together. "Typically," report Pascale and Athos, "for every twenty-five hours spent at work, a Japanese spends one socializing after hours with his group."[58]

At the earliest possible time, four members of my school's faculty invited me to join them for a trip to Omogo, a tourist resort on the island of Shikoku. We drove for five hours over steep mountains to reach it—a huge, beautiful canyon with large boulders on which people sat eating a picnic lunch. After a leisurely afternoon walk around the area, we bathed in the hottest water I had ever tried to enter and spent another five hours driving home. Needless to say, we knew one another a great deal better at the end of the day than we had before, which of course is the point of such excursions.

Although an informal gathering, the custom of group members visiting a local bar together after leaving work—which Jonan faculty members did not do—is so important to performance on the job that the employee who fails to participate risks serious sanction.[59] Nakane reports that some employees remain in the bars drinking until well after the last train has left.[60]

This aspect of group life is important to the maintenance of cohesiveness. Conversations during these sessions are about work. Behavior not tolerated at other times—infantility, rudeness, vulgarity, boisterousness—is accepted here.[61] Status does not accompany the group into these activities. Thoughts that could never be expressed by either leader or member in the office are suddenly acceptably articulated over the sake glasses. A Japanese tradition says that anything said over drinks is excusable and should be forgotten.[62] Pressures are released. The welfare of the group is enhanced. Productivity continues to improve, and so do the company's profits. Here is one man's experience at one of these informal after-work sessions:

One time I was out drinking with some men in my section from the office and the section chief was there. Nobody really likes him because he is cold to us. He knows he will not go any higher in the company but that many of us will, and he is jealous. Anyway, we were all rather drunk and I laughed at the section chief for pinching the fanny of one of the office girls when he thought no one was looking. I told him he was a lecherous old fool. The next day he greeted me as usual and had forgotten all about it. Of course, he was drunk too and maybe he didn't remember.[63]

It is certainly not true, however, that every *salariiman* attends these sessions. A survey by Yasuda Trust and Banking Company found that more than 40 percent of salarymen never go to bars, cabarets, or clubs. Of employees in leading positions, a large percentage go once a month, though, and some more frequently.[64]

Employees also share dinners and even weekend excursions together—never taking their spouses along. That's just the way it is done in Japan; it is not a sign of marital trouble. However, a survey of Hitachi Company employees found that 70 percent of the respondents said their job is the most important single thing in life—more important even than their wives.[65]

The next chapter reviews some qualities that the Japanese worker considers the outstanding features of his work.

NOTES

1. "War Atrocities, Revisited," p. 29.
2. Marsh and Mannari, *Modernization and the Japanese Factory*, p. 179.
3. Pascale and Athos, *The Art of Japanese Management*, p. 125.
4. Yoshino, *Japan's Multinational Enterprises*, p. 164.
5. Halloran, *Japan*, p. 225.
6. Furstenberg, *Why the Japanese Have Been So Successful in Business*, p. 12.
7. Plath, *The After Hours*, pp. 76–77.
8. Ibid., p. 78.
9. Hewins, *The Japanese Miracle Men*, pp. 238–39.
10. Norbury and Bownas, *Business in Japan*, p. 185.
11. Benedict, *The Chrysanthemum and the Sword*, p. 207.
12. "Outsiders Inside Japanese Companies," p. 116.

13. Ibid.

14. Reischauer, *Japan: The Story of a Nation*, p. 3.

15. Hanada, comments, Japan-America Business Conference.

16. Cole, *Japanese Blue Collar*, p. 14.

17. Nakane, *Japanese Society*, p. 10.

18. Ibid., p. 14.

19. Marsh and Mannari, *Modernization and the Japanese Factory*, p. 180.

20. Masatsugu, *The Modern Samurai Society*, p. 64.

21. Rohlen, *For Harmony and Strength*, p. 47.

22. Bartholomew, "Cultural Values in Japan," in *Business and Society in Japan*, ed. Richardson and Ueda, p. 244.

23. Lebra, *Japanese Patterns of Behavior*, p. 87.

24. Craig, "Functional and Dysfunctional Aspects of Government Bureaucracy," in *Modern Japanese Organization and Decision-Making*, ed. Vogel, p. 12.

25. Bairy, "Motivational Forces in Japanese Life," in *The Japanese Employee*, ed. Ballon, p. 54.

26. De Mente, *How to Do Business in Japan*, p. 16.

27. Rohlen, *For Harmony and Strength*, p. 130.

28. van Helvoort, *The Japanese Working Man*, p. 116.

29. Sinha, *Japan's Options for the 1980s*, p. 15.

30. Abegglen, *The Japanese Factory*, p. 44.

31. Woronoff, *Japan: The Coming Social Crisis*, pp. 40–41.

32. Rohlen, "The Company Work Group," in *Modern Japanese Organization and Decision-Making*, ed. Vogel, p. 200.

33. Ibid., p. 201.

34. Ibid.

35. Vogel, *Japan as Number 1*, p. 128.

36. "Made in Japan," p. 9.

37. "Japanese Management: Can It Work Here?" p. 17.

38. De Mente, *How to Do Business in Japan*, p. 16.

39. Hewins, *The Japanese Miracle Men*, p. 342.

40. Imai, *16 Ways to Avoid Saying No*, p. 21.

41. Stephens, "Visions: The Rising Sun of Productivity," p. 7.

42. Kawasaki, *Japan Unmasked*, p. 42.

43. Morgan, column, p. B-1.

44. Provided by Matsushita's Public Relations Department.

45. Provided by Nissan's Public Relations Department.

46. De Mente, *How to Do Business in Japan*, p. 25.

47. Cunningham, "A Return to Balance," p. 21.

48. Kawasaki, *Japan Unmasked*, pp. 40–41.

49. Cunningham, "A Return to Balance," p. 21.

50. Drucker, "Behind Japan's Success," p. 83.

51. Nakane, *Japanese Society*, p. 13.

52. Woronoff, *Japan: The Coming Economic Crisis*, p. 36.

53. Woronoff, *Japan: The Coming Social Crisis*, p. 182.

54. "Outsiders Inside Japanese Companies," pp. 115–16.

55. Ibid., pp. 116, 120.

56. De Mente, *How to Do Business in Japan*, p. 55.

57. Cole, "Changing Labor Force Characteristics and Their Impact on Japanese Industrial Relations," in *Japan: The Paradox of Progress*, ed. Austin, pp. 206–7.

58. Pascale and Athos, *The Art of Japanese Management*, p. 127.

59. Plath, *The After Hours*, p. 39.

60. Nakane, *Japanese Society*, p. 124.

61. Lebra, *Japanese Patterns of Behavior*, pp. 116–17.

62. Nakane, *Japanese Society*, p. 125.

63. Halloran, *Japan*, pp. 238–39.

64. Adams and Kobayashi, *The World of Japanese Business*, p. 98.

65. Delassus, *The Japanese*, p. 145.

4

The Japanese Corporation: Three Outstanding Characteristics

In describing their corporation, most businesspersons in Japan list three qualities in this order: lifetime employment, the seniority-wage system, and enterprise unions. These important characteristics are discussed in this chapter.

LIFETIME EMPLOYMENT

The aspect of Japanese business life which has attracted widest attention is lifetime or career employment. It is a development of Japan's industrial system since World War II, primarily, that served a definite need in the economy at that time. Most believe that it was a reaction to a competitive labor force after the war and was achieved by union efforts.

Others trace the origin of lifetime employment to the Meiji Restoration. Until about 1918, Japanese workers were very mobile. Skilled workers moved frequently to earn higher wages and attain higher rank. Wages were determined by rank of job or type of skill rather than by age or years of service in the same company. Employers found the most skilled workers the least controllable. The system at the time resembled in many respects the present methods of employment in the West.

Lifetime employment was introduced after World War I, when measures were taken to overcome a recession. As noted previously, the average life expectancy in the country at that time was only 44 years, so the term "lifetime employment" was accurate. Today the idea would be better expressed by "career employment."

During this period in Japan's industrial history, new production techniques were used and new equipment installed. Skilled workers were less essential to new assembly-line procedures; instead, companies needed workers trained to do their own special work. So corporations concentrated on training their own labor force and began taking measures to retain those employees.

Hirees needed a certain amount of education to begin with, so recruitment focused each year on new graduates. New employees were trained, and the best were retained as permanent employees. "A disciplined labor force makes lifetime employment practical," states a *Fortune* magazine article. "Japanese workers come in the door properly trained by the family, by the school system, by the entire society."[1]

To illustrate how the no-layoff policy works, the NBC White Paper "If Japan Can, Why Can't We?" described what employees at Mitsubishi experienced when changes had to be made:

Five years ago, Mitsubishi's Hiroshima shipyard used 11,000 tons of steel a month. Now it uses 2,000. The government decided that as a matter of national policy, Japan should reduce its shipbuilding capacity and turn that to something else, such as building drilling rigs for oil exploration.

Mitsubishi's Hiroshima yard cut its work force by 1,700, but no one was fired or laid off. This oil rig off New Jersey's coast was built by some of the shipyard workers. Others were transferred to other Mitsubishi operations or loaned to other industries.[2]

So entrenched in Japanese management philosophy now is the no-layoff policy that dismissal of an employee is limited to only a few reasons. Here are some listed by Imai:

1. Failure to satisfactorily perform his duties due to incurable mental or physical illness.

2. Such poor performance and attendance that he is deemed unfit for the performance of his duties.

3. A scaling-down of the business operation for some unavoidable reason.

Nowhere is it stated that an employee may be dismissed for a mediocre performance. Since there is no job description, there are no criteria against which to judge performance. ... Japan's collective decision-making makes it difficult to pin the responsibility on a single individual.[3]

The employee who decides on his own to change jobs, according to Imai, will do so for one of three reasons:

The first reason concerns the job itself, such as lack of recognition and limited advancement, and inability to utilize one's own ability. The second concerns human relations—self-centered reasons including dissatisfaction with management, unsatisfactory personal contacts, and uncongenial company atmosphere.

Table 2
Job Changes per Worker in Selected Countries

Country	Job Changes					
	None	**One**	**Two**	**Three**	**Four**	**N.A.**
Japan	71.5	14.8	5.4	2.2	1.3	4.9
United States	23.0	17.9	18.2	13.3	27.0	0.7
United Kingdom	41.4	23.8	14.6	7.7	12.2	0.3
West Germany	56.1	24.9	12.5	3.6	1.8	1.1
France	52.4	22.6	10.2	5.3	9.0	0.4
Sweden	47.1	24.2	13.7	5.4	8.7	0.8

Source: Japan Prime Minister's Office, "White Paper of the Youth," 1978, p. 52.

The third concerns environmental reasons, such as low salaries, dissatisfaction with working conditions, and the insecurity of the company's future.[4]

Imai explains that it is also very difficult to resign a position in a Japanese factory; in fact, it is often more difficult than getting the job:

When one wishes to resign, he must submit a notice of resignation. Often the management turns down such a request. He can, of course, resign in spite of the management's opposition but it takes strong nerve to do so, since harmony is one of the greatest virtues in Japan. Besides, an unamicable departure often means an unfavorable settlement of separation allowances.[5]

Lifetime employment policies often mean that a Japanese employee over 30 cannot change jobs. Table 2 compares Japanese "job hopping" to that in selected Western countries. The difference is so great because the Japanese job changer could only be given beginner's work, but he would have to be paid according to his age. His salary and his work would not correspond.[6]

Also, mental and emotional barriers exist between newcomers and workers who started their career together in an organization. They are regarded as having deficiencies in their personalities because they did not fit themselves into the social structure of their previous organization. They are seen too as disloyal to their first employer. They are believed to lack the harmonious personalities needed to get along in the orga-nization. So the employee who changes jobs faces rejection in the new company, regardless of how competent his effort.

Nakane reports of one employee who left his original employer after ten years to work for another company. "Although he served his new company for twenty years and rose to be the manager of its London office, he was never fully accepted."[7]

Beginning in 1970, some companies started hiring employees who were in mid-career for their technical expertise. These employees have never been treated like regular employees. Their pay has been a step or two below those of their own age group because it would have been unfair, employers felt, to employees who had been with the company all of their working lives to do otherwise.[8] These employees experience discrimination in other ways also. Nakane presents this testimony of a job-changer:

You know, it is not something to be explained logically. There were all sorts of disagreeable statements about me; it was not done in the context of formal business procedure but rather in the informal circumstances and networks in which I was unable to participate. It was, in fact, just like an old mother-in-law in a traditional Japanese household getting at her young daughter-in-law over the salting of the pickled vegetables. She can never get it right, in the mother-in-law's eyes; either there's too much, so she's wasting salt, or there's too little so she has no idea how things should taste. So whatever I did invited criticism and complaint. There was never anything factual or any tangible reason. Rather it all came from spite—from their feeling that there was a new man who hadn't worked in the company from the start as they had done. In a situation like this, a man can achieve his potential only when his boss is powerful enough to protect him against his colleagues. And when his boss retires, or if he should happen to leave, he would find himself in a quite intolerable situation.[9]

Only about a third of the Japanese work force, most of them employees of the 1,000 largest companies, is covered by career employment policies; however, it is also practiced by some medium and small firms.

Not all employees of companies which do follow the practice are covered. Only workers for whom employment will probably be continuous are included. These workers also receive semiannual bonuses of three or four months' wages.

It should be noted that in smaller companies without lifetime employment policies the relationship between workers and the company is geared for the long term. It is not a transitory arrangement.[10]

Here is what a young American employed in Japan by Isuzu Motors had to say about lifetime employment in a *Fortune* magazine article:

Even workers who are secure in terms of employment are not so secure in terms of job content. If you don't do your job well, you're going to do the job nobody wants—you're going to get old in that chair, and it's nerve-racking.... If I were working for GM in Detroit, more than likely the job would be very defined and narrow. Here you'll be in marketing awhile, and then you'll be sent to corporate planning, and then to working on products. That would be pretty tough to do in an American company.[11]

Other benefits granted by the average Japanese company to employees, as listed by De Mente, are these: free wedding ceremonies and receptions, free honeymoons, free baths, and meals for which they pay only a nominal sum.[12] One employer went so far as to advertise for brides for his workers.[13]

An article in *Ford World* included these additional benefits given employees in Japan: "subsidized dormitory living, subsidized apartments and housing, low interest loans, extensive company-provided medical services, recreational facilities, a library, beauty and barber shops, and a scholarship fund for orphaned children."[14] All benefits are also extended to the employee's family. They may shop at the company store for "food and hard goods at attractive prices."[15]

One company is reported to provide, an addition, free funerals for the employee's entire family.[16] An item in *Industrial Relations News* referred to this benefit: "A Kyoto, Japan, company is offering the ultimate employee benefit. It has acquired a tomb capable of holding the remains of several thousand people to enable its workers to be together in death as they were in life."[17]

Temporary and part-time workers are excluded from all of these benefits, as are those employees who join the company in mid-career.

Retirement age for most employees in Japan is still 55; however, the trend toward extending it to age 60 is gaining momentum. Opposition is waged by employees worried about promotion opportunities. As of January 1980, 40 percent of all firms still held age 55 as their retirement age.[18] However, about 95 percent of Japanese companies today reemploy retired workers or extend the employment period for their workers who reach retirement age, so that about half of those who retire at 55 are still working at 60. The *Economic Survey of Japan* describes the trend:

The move to extend the retirement age has been mounting gradually, since the days of the labor shortage during the early 1970s. The move intensified as an increasing number of workers began reaching the retirement age amid slackening demand for labor following the first oil crisis. By 1978, extending the retirement age became a major issue, and in 1979, an agreement was reached between management and labor in the steel and private railway industries—both leaders in the management labor field—to extend the retirement age to 60.... According to Economic Planning Agency's survey of corporations (1,547 listed firms, January 1980) the number of firms that have extended, will extend, or are contemplating the extension of retirement age, has surpassed the 60 percent mark.[19]

At retirement, the Japanese employee receives no pension. Instead, he is given a lump sum equal to several years' salary; afterward, he must live on a small government stipend. Extending the retirement age will take some of the pressure off providing for himself and his spouse in those last years. There are far too few homes to care for old persons in Japan to help the retiree who runs out of funds. The system of older persons living with their children is changing too. In the past 75 percent of all older people lived with their children.[20] Many wives today, however, work and don't have time to care for their own families and parents too. More and more young people are moving to big cities and living in apartments where facilities are too scarce to allow older members of the family to live there as well. So changing social conditions in Japan may force corporations to make lifetime employment truly "lifetime" by helping retirees care for themselves the rest of their lives through adequate pension plans.

Almost all corporate recruiting efforts for white collar workers are directed to university students, who, when hired, are expected to stay with the company until retirement. Myron Emanuel notes that in the 1980s graduates are choosing to go to electronics firms. Only a few years ago, their choice was with automobile manufacturers, and before that it was steel companies.[21] (Blue collar workers are recruited from junior and senior high schools; clerical employees come from senior high schools.) This annual recruitment drive assures a spread in the ages of workers.

After about a year's probation, the employee is given tenure status. We listed above the grounds for dismissal. Ouchi feels that such a step is a very serious matter for any worker:

An employee will not be terminated for anything less than a major criminal offense, and termination is a harsh punishment, since the one who has been fired has no hope of finding employment in a comparable firm and instead must turn either to a minor firm that pays comparatively low wages and offers little security, or else must return to his hometown.[22]

In his early years, the employee receives training in corporate operations, moving from department to department to acquire an understanding that will serve him and the company well later. Woronoff, however, presents a different point of view on the system:

There [in management], the personnel is shifted about incessantly to get more experience and a feel for the company. This upsets even what little incipient professionalism there is. Generalists may have been all right in the older companies, and where personal relations are all that count, but Japan now has too many companies in highly specialized fields and carrying out work in markets requiring in-depth knowledge. Its personnel is often a bit amateurish here. Similarly, the training which places stress on discipline, loyalty, ability to follow orders, and so on naturally does not enhance a person's capacity for imagination or drive. It is also a bit stifling for innovation. Even at the level of R&D, the Japanese have shown considerable talent at picking up other people's ideas, taking them a step further, and turning out products that are truly innovative. But basic research and creativity are often lacking.[23]

Career employment, however, does not mean that employees' capabilities are ignored. More able employees receive the choice assignments, higher bonuses, and promotions that come a year or two before their peers. Everyone knows who the most promising employees are during these early years. Yet, says Yoshino, "there is a minimum acceptable age for every position, and even the most competent are not promoted before they reach the prescribed minimum age level."[24] Also, those who are selected to move ahead of their peers, explains Vogel, "can be promoted only if they enjoy the respect and approval of their associates; this prevents the growing distinctions from being overly disruptive."[25]

Of 100 employees who enter a company together, 10 will be advanced to department head; a few of them will make it to director, and only 1 might make it to president.[26] The result is a very competitive situation where "every co-worker is a rival."[27]

As stated previously, recruitment is limited to graduates with those hired at the same time, forming a peer group that may last for the rest of their careers. For the following five or ten years, the *salariiman* will rotate jobs in various sections of the company. During this period great demands are made on the employee's initiative, contributing to his on-the-job development. At the end of this period, the employee will have reached his first threshold: the position of *kacho* (section chief). He may go no further, but his years of experience will be valued by the company. "Experience is seen as something that cannot be taught," Ballon points out. "It is a function of age, and is manifested in what could be generally called human relations. In this context, the manager is expected to develop into a generalist rather than a specialist."[28]

After twenty years or so another hurdle is reached: *bucho* (department head). Again some will remain in this position, usually until retirement at age 55 or 60. Then they will be transferred to a related firm to continue working at reduced wages. Those that are promoted to directorships while serving as *bucho* are not asked to retire at the usual age.[29] Retirees receive three and a half to four years' salary granted in one lump sum. At the age of 60, they also qualify for a state pension.

Outsiders are puzzled about how the fluctuations of a business can accommodate the lifetime employment system. Flexibility is achieved in adjustments made to total temporary or part-time workers, consultants, subcontractors, and overtime of employees. Companies are also careful not to exceed their work force beyond what they would need in a recession economy.

Kawasaki Motors Corporation recently demonstrated how it responds to the need to reduce its work force. It had to cut 50 out of 591 employees, according to the *NAB* (National Alliance of Business) *Clearinghouse Showcase*, a monthly employment and training digest.

To avoid laying off workers, the company gave cash incentives to 5 employees who retired early, assigned 35 employees to projects outside of their job duties in the plant, and sent the remaining 10—welders, painters, motorcycle assemblers—to work for the city until business picked up. The 10 renovated City Hall and painted fire stations and other municipal buildings while receiving their full pay and benefits from Kawasaki.[30]

The main advantage to the company of the lifetime system of employment is the retention of trained workers. Kawasaki, for example, has a ready trained source of skilled employees when business improves. Employers are more willing to invest in training workers they know will remain to use it for the company's benefit.

Another advantage of the policy is the motivation it provides workers. They identify more fully with the company and seek the highest productivity to benefit the company. Automating plants with robots is accepted by workers not threatened with job loss. Robert Hayes who visited six Japanese factories in preparation for a *Harvard Business Review* article found, "Japanese workers in the companies I visited willingly worked up to 60 hours of overtime per month (3 hours per day) when demand was high," recognizing that a no-layoff policy requires a work force level that lags behind sales demand.[31]

A curious fact about lifetime employment is that it does not apply to women. Although a large percentage of women work, they do so only until they marry. Thereafter, they may continue to work but not as regular employees of large firms. "Only one percent of management jobs are held by women. Japanese business is a man's world," noted one television documentary.[32] Although women comprised 33.8 percent of the Japanese work force in 1980, only 19.8 percent of working women have permanent jobs. The rest could be laid off from jobs considered supplementary.[33]

SENIORITY-WAGE SYSTEM

Closely allied to career employment and the aspect of Japanese business that makes it possible is the seniority-wage system. This was granted gradually to white collar workers after 1940, prior to its being given to blue collar workers. Management based wages on age and length of service to give workers security. The nature of the work done was not a consideration.

Seniority is rigidly observed. Promotion to lower-level management positions can often be determined on the employee's first day of work. "Every Japanese who joins a company upon graduation knows that in 15 years he will be promoted to managerial level, even if his first assignment may be clipping newspaper articles," states Imai.[34] The system corresponds well to the Japanese respect for age.

However, the cost of an aging work force could be prohibitive in a recession. Older workers are reluctant to leave a job after attaining a certain wage level for fear they could not command the same pay in another company. Some employees also would prefer a wage system that somehow takes performance into consideration. At present it rewards outstanding work only minimally. Emanuel explains that, although an entering engineer will start at roughly the same pay as a high school graduate and will stay even with him for the first year or so, he will gradually pull ahead. The engineer will quadruple his starting salary by retirement; the high school graduate will only triple his. In addition, the engineer will receive a higher bonus twice a year than the high school graduate.[35]

Until recently, the system has emphasized demerits over merits. "The protruding nail will get hammered down," is a well-known Japanese saying. Changes have already begun, however. About a fourth of firms surveyed by the Economic Planning Agency have revised their wage systems since 1975. Half of the companies studied are moving toward revising their wage systems, and a large number of firms are establishing wage systems which give special consideration to ability or to the assignment. The trend is toward recognizing the contributions that specialists can make to the business.[36]

ENTERPRISE UNIONS

To counter the advance of unionism after World War I, many large firms created joint labor–management conference systems, called factory committees or councils.[37] The move kept unions out. Labor disturbances, when they occurred, were protests of unfair labor practices.

When career employment was introduced, the trained labor force stabilized. Both the horizontal job market and the horizontal labor union disappeared. After World War II, enterprise unions—representing employees in single companies—arose, accounting eventually for 90 percent of labor union membership.[38] By 1949, some 6 million workers belonged to 30,000 unions.[39] The primary impetus to unionism in Japan was the support given it by the Occupation forces.[40]

In the turmoil of postwar Japan, every worker faced problems in making a living. To protect themselves against uncooperative employers, the workers organized unions which demanded large wage increases, participative management, and an end to the status system among employees. They used group pressure to attain their goals.[41]

There are 70,000 enterprise unions in Japan today.[42] The union accepts as members only regular employees—white and blue collar—of a single company; the union is thus independent of outside influences. Only about a third of the labor force is unionized. Regular employees up to the department manager level are automatically members.[43] It is easy to understand why the typical union member is more sensitive to the welfare of the company than is his American counterpart.

Typical of many Japanese labor unions, the Toyo Kogyo's Workers' Union was organized immediately after the Second World War. Its first decade was characterized by conflict, as was true of many unions in Japan. Its second and third decades saw a gradual improvement in working conditions as Japan's economic growth forced Toyo Kogyo's management to meet or even anticipate union demands.

The energy crisis, however, came just as Toyo Kogyo was introducing the rotary engine, and thus hit the company hard. Since then the union has sought to cooperate with the company. "The union is willing to sacrifice anything to maintain job security," says union Vice President Daisaku Nishida. The last strike was in 1976.[44]

Japanese workers forego the full-time labor representatives and outside support during strikes and other crises for the right of permanent employment. Each enterprise union has complete freedom to collect dues, form and revise a constitution, call strikes, and elect officers.[45] Most enterprise unions are also loosely affiliated with one of the four national trade union centers or federations.[46] The only issue likely to arouse the union is unfair discharge of one of its members. Nakane states, "The single most important union success was the gaining of the right of appeal against summary dismissal or layoff."[47]

Twice a year—in May and November—employees of large and medium-size companies engage in "offensives." These are the times when the sizes of the bonuses which usually equal about 4.4 months' salary or more are decided. Activities include slogans, speeches, and leaflets. Strikes are possible but always short; they are intended to demonstrate that disharmony has erupted.[48] If there is a strike, employees wear armbands and headbands, wave flags, and sing songs that sound very militaristic.[49]

A visiting group of Ford executives and officials of the UAW learned about the Japanese union, as described in Ford World:

The Japanese call their management style the "work together" method. Mamoru Tanabe, an executive vice president of Nippondenso—Japan's largest automotive parts supplier—told the Ford–UAW study group that the Japanese cannot understand the continual confrontation between managements and unions in the West. According to Tanabe, Japanese managements believe managements and unions must proceed together to the same destination—prosperity for the company and happiness for the union members. If there is no company, there is no union.

The union in Japan is generally notified of actions and decisions before they are enacted. Monthly meetings are held between management and union representatives to discuss many items, including production schedules, productivity and work improvement matters. The meetings are held at the department, plant and company headquarters level. These extensive union and employee consultations—and the high degree of mutual trust—are considered key factors to a company's success and to the good relationship managements have with unions.

Union officials generally show great interest in promoting productivity and growth. Because of their concern for the success of the enterprise, they avoid actions that would damage the total effort. Both managements and unions are willing to subordinate special interests for the long-run performance of the business.

The Japanese labor–management relationship is based on a history of cooperation and recognition of mutual interests rather than on a record of past adversity. An important key to this relationship is the Japanese sense of family and the unwritten commitment on the part of management to providing lifetime employment for most employees.[50]

Although variations of the lifetime employment system and the seniority-wage policy exist in the United States, the enterprise labor union is uniquely Japanese. It could never work in America.

NOTES

1. Bruce-Briggs, "The Dangerous Folly Called Theory Z," p. 44.
2. "If Japan Can, Why Can't We?" transcript, part 2, p. 10.
3. Imai, *16 Ways to Avoid Saying No*, p. 31.
4. Imai, *Never Take Yes for an Answer*, p. 32.
5. Ibid., p. 36.
6. Drucker, "Japan Tries for a Second Miracle," p. 7.
7. Nakane, *Japanese Society*, p. 106.
8. De Mente, *Japanese Manners and Ethics in Business*, pp. 35–36.
9. Nakane, *Japanese Society*, p. 106.
10. Kim and Lunde, "Quality Circles: Why They Work in Japan and How We Can Make Them Work in the United States."
11. "Outsiders Inside Japanese Companies," pp. 115, 122.
12. De Mente, *How to Do Business in Japan*, p. 35.
13. Hsu, *Iemoto*, p. 205.
14. "They Cost Less Than in the United States," p. 9.
15. "Japan Diary," p. 12.
16. Nakane, *Japanese Society*, p. 10.
17. "Until Death Do Us Part?" *Gifford-Hill Times*, March 1982, p. 3.
18. Japan, Economic Planning Agency, *Economic Survey of Japan*, p. 215.
19. Ibid., p. 216.
20. Forbis, *Japan Today*, p. 41.
21. Emanuel, "Productivity Improvement—Japanese Style," p. 1.
22. Ouchi, *Theory Z*, p. 17.
23. Woronoff, *Japan: the Coming Economic Crisis*, p. 40.
24. Yoshino, *Japan's Managerial System*, p. 237.
25. Vogel, *Japan as Number 1*, p. 141.

26. Masatsugu, *The Modern Samurai Society*, p. 208.

27. Ibid., p. 87.

28. Ballon, "Management Style," in *Business in Japan*, ed. Norbury and Bownas, p. 128.

29. Ibid., p. 129.

30. "Elsewhere," *iabc news*, March 1982, p. 10.

31. Hayes, "Why Japanese Factories Work," p. 64.

32. "Japan, Inc.: Lessons for North America."

33. Trater, *Letters from Sachiko*, p. 186.

34. Imai, "Taking Care of Your Japanese Staff," in Japan External Trade Organization, *How to Succeed in Japan*, p. 173.

35. Emanuel, "Productivity Improvement—Japanese Style," p. 2.

36. Japan, Economic Planning Agency, *Economic Survey of Japan*, pp. 220–22.

37. Okochi, Karsh, and Levine, *Workers and Employers in Japan*, p. 493.

38. Ibid.

39. Ibid., p. 495.

40. Ibid.

41. Sumiya, "Contemporary Arrangements," in Okochi, Karsh, and Levine, *Workers and Employers in Japan*, p. 56.

42. Emanuel, "Productivity Improvement—Japanese Style," p. 2.

43. De Mente, *How to Do Business in Japan*, p. 131.

44. Gray, "Japan, Corporate Strategies for the 1980s," p. 40.

45. Cole, "Enterprise Unions," in *Business and Society in Japan*, ed. Richardson and Ueda, p. 38.

46. De Mente, *How to Do Business in Japan*, p. 133.

47. Nakane, *Japanese Society*, p. 18.

48. Hsu, *Iemoto*, pp. 208–9.

49. De Mente, *How to Do Business in Japan*, p. 132.

50. "Common Ground, Mutual Goals," p. 8.

5

Organizational and Cultural Influences on Japanese Corporate Communication

Communication in the Japanese firm is integrated totally into all corporate operations. There is nobody with sole responsibility for communication—a manager, corporate communication. The responsibility for communicating is charged to every single employee. As we shall see, it is at the lower levels of the organization where communication is the most intensive. From there it travels in an upward direction.

Certain aspects of Japanese corporate life influence considerably the communication that takes place in a firm. Some of them have already been discussed: group activity and lifetime employment. Others will be discussed in this chapter: decision making and quality circles.

In addition, qualities of the Japanese culture have an inevitable effect on Japanese corporate communication. These include the complex nature of the Japanese language and a cultural awareness of and dependence on nonverbal communication. We begin this chapter by discussing these.

LANGUAGE

The Japanese language is one of the most unusual in the world. Yale historian John W. Hall has said, "Japan is the only true world power that does not have a 'world language.' . . . In many ways Japan remains the most culturally distinct and intellectually inaccessible of the great powers and this fact impedes greatly the exchange of ideas and sentiments with the rest of the world."[1]

Only Korean is strikingly related to the Japanese language. Japanese is kin also to the Ural-Altaic (Mongolian, Manchu, Turkic) and the Polynesian lingual families.[2] It was a spoken language until about A.D. 400, when Chinese books began to arrive and the Japanese began to fit the Chinese ideographs to their own language, a process achieved mainly in the ninth and tenth centuries.[3] The result is the same as various nationalities using the same Arabic numerals for a counting system to which they apply their own words. Chinese and Japanese can look at the same symbols and apply their own language.

There are a total of 49,000 *kanji* (Chinese characters), the most complex requiring 48 strokes.[4] In 1946, the American Occupation pressured the Ministry of Education to select the most common ones for everyday use. Of the 1,850 selected, children learn 881 in elementary school and the rest later.[5]

The Japanese eventually developed two syllabaries: *hiragana*, used for all those Japanese words for which there is no Chinese character; and *katakana*, used for all foreign words, including those adopted from Dutch, German, Portuguese, and English, among other languages. Both syllabaries have 48 characters. In addition, the language may be written in Roman letters through *romaji*.

One result of this incredibly complex system of language is a very cumbersome typewriter, described by Forbis:

The standard typewriter—*taipuraita* in Japanese—is large, heavy, cumbersome, and slow. It consists of a type case, bigger than a chessboard, that contains more than two thousand characters, and a cylindrical carriage, holding the paper, that can be moved anywhere—backward and forward, and from side to side—over the case. Having positioned the carriage over the chosen character, the operator presses the machine's single key, whereupon a mechanical finger reaches down, plucks out the desired type, impresses it on the paper through the inked ribbon, and replaces it. The type case is so hard to memorize and the process so inefficient that large business enterprises keep only a few machines, together with the skilled women who run them for formal communications. Most letters are written by hand.[6]

This situation changed in the late 1970s with the invention of a Japanese-language word processor, an accomplishment until then considered impossible. The key innovation, according to Dr. Shigenori Matsushita, associate chief engineer of computer and OA systems at Toshiba's Information Systems Business Group, was the linkage of *kanji* characters with phonetics.

The Japanese-language word processor has brought enormous savings to business operations; each one added is like an extra employee. Use of the word processor increased productivity 8.6 percent between 1978 and 1981 in Toshiba's Engineering Department. Takuma Yamamoto, president of Fujitsu, attributes to the word processor the fact that there has been no increase in his company's indirect costs despite corporate growth of from 15 to 20 percent. At Toyo Kogyo, preparation of the Japanese Department of Transportation certification forms for the seven variations on the 929 model of the Mazda, a procedure that used to take 55 hours, took only 10 hours.[7] Office automation has begun to change clerical work in the Japanese corporation even in the difficult Japanese language.

Probably nowhere else in the world is the connection between language and culture so evident as in Japan. "Human culture without language," Kluckhohn states, "is unthinkable."[8]

De Mente describes language in Japan as the "primary repository and transmitter of Japanese culture."[9] Reischauer says language defines the Japanese "more distinctly than any other feature in their culture."[10]

In this vertically structured society, the language includes different levels of speech—low, common, and high—representing the status of the speakers, and different language is used by men and women. One speaks to all superiors with respect, to all subordinates with low-level words, and with equals with common, familiar terms.

It is these rules of social etiquette which make Japanese a complex language. It should be a simple one. No other major language uses so few sounds.[11] There is no singular and plural, no genders, no articles, no declensions, no conjugations; grammar is simple; the vocabulary is rudimentary.[12]

So although a foreigner might learn the language very well, the rules of society make an attempt to use the language, especially in business, very risky. Stanley Holt, who directs the *Reader's Digest* operation in Japan, has said, "Sensitivity to cultural patterns is far more important for you to communicate more effectively. Even if you learn the language, you are not going to think like a Japanese."[13] A failure to use the precisely proper terms of respect would do more damage than the appreciation engendered by the attempt to learn and use the language. The problem becomes one of culture rather than language in communication.

NONVERBAL COMMUNICATION

In Japan, an important part of the message is transmitted without words. "To the Japanese," explains Kunihiro Masao, "language is *a* means of communication, whereas to the people of many other cultures it is *the* means."[14] If given a choice, the Japanese would prefer not to use words. A proverb says, "Not to say is better than to say."[15] To the Japanese, nonverbal communication is often more important than verbal communication.[16] For them, the verbal message accompanies the nonverbal cues instead of the other way around, as in other cultures.[17] The Japanese, Bairy explains, keep a "constant alertness to the ambient milieu through a steady communication and exchange."[18] Kawabata Yasunari,

Japan's Nobel Prize-winning novelist, has said that the Japanese communicate through unspoken understanding, a type of telepathy, because for them truth is in the implicit rather than in the stated. They call it *ishin-denshin*, "communication by the heart."[19]

In Japanese corporations, as in Japanese life generally, nonverbal communication between two or more people is constant. Many important aspects of Japanese life are rarely, if ever, verbalized, reports Helmut Morsbach. "Even if verbalising something, there is often a large element of understatement, and silence is valued for its powers of communication."[20] Words are often considered unnecessary to Japanese when Americans feel the need for lengthy explanations. Inazo Nitobe said in *Bushido, the Soul of Japan*, "To give in so many articulate words one's innermost thoughts and feelings is taken as an unmistakable sign that they are neither profound nor very sincere."[21]

The Japanese "have a positive mistrust of verbal skills," Reischauer reports, "thinking that these tend to show superficiality, in contrast to inner, less articulate feelings that are communicated by innuendo or by nonverbal means."[22] A proverb expresses the Japanese view: "The mouth is the entrance of calamity."[23] Rather than rely on verbal communication, the Japanese prefer to have others infer what they want to say from what they did not say and from their mannerisms.[24] "Words are paltry against the significance of reading subtle signs and signals and the intuitive grasp of each other's feelings," explains Lebra.[25]

Often the Japanese use vague language and rely on nonverbal communication to avoid confrontation. "To the Japanese, vagueness is a virtue," according to Jack Seward. "To be exact is to be impertinent and arrogant, in that it assumes superior knowledge. To be vague is to be courteous and humble."[26] Instead the Japanese, as Imai states so well, prefer "subtle, implicit, open-ended, obscure understatement."[27] If they feel what they have to say will be disagreeable to the listener, the Japanese soften the tone of the message or they give a positive answer and then forget the whole thing. Imai lists these ways a Japanese says no by indicating yes:

The first, and perhaps most typical, way to imply no is to say yes and then to follow this with an explanation which may last half an hour and which, in effect, means no.... The second way to imply no is to be so vague, ambiguous, and evasive in reply that the other side loses track of what the issue was.... The third way is simply not to answer the question and to leave the matter unattended.... Other ways include abruptly changing the subject, criticizing the other party, or suddenly assuming a highly apologetic tone.[28]

Japanese conduct dialogues in circles, say Pascale and Athos, "widening and narrowing them to correspond to the other's sensitivity to the feedback."[29] They have a word for the routine: *haragei*, "the art of the belly."[30] One member of our faculty at Jonan used to call it simply "reading stomachs." Here is one Japanese employee's experience in this regard:

One day in the office, a man who works near me went to the desk of the section chief and talked to him for a long time. I could not hear what they were saying, but I noticed that the section chief looked in my direction several times. After they finished talking, the man went back to his desk without saying anything to me. But the next day, when we met in the washroom (I think he deliberately followed me there) we discussed our work and he made a slight reference to one of my accounts, saying he hoped it was as accurate as the last time the auditors looked at it. Right away, I was sure he had seen something wrong, and I was not surprised when the section chief called me over. He discussed something else but mentioned briefly that particular account and said he knew the auditors would find it in order whenever they checked it. That night I stayed late in the office to go over the account and found a bad mistake, which I corrected. Nothing else was ever said about it.[31]

The main reason for all of the circumlocution is the long-term working relationships of the Japanese employment system. Knowing that they will spend a long time working together and be dependent on one another to varying degrees, Japanese employees are eager to keep peaceful relations with one another.

Nonverbal communication is a means of both discovering the status of others, through name cards, and of showing respect when appropriate through the bow.

One of the first things a newcomer to the country notices about the Japanese society in general but about Japanese business in particular is that everyone uses name cards. There is a very good reason for it.

Until two Japanese businesspersons know the position of each other, for example, they find it difficult to communicate. The name cards inform the receiver of the status of the presenter and the degree of formality required in dealing with him. Without the cards, a person has no clue of relative rank and can't speak, eat, or sit. "When speaking, he is expected always to be ready with differentiated, delicate degrees of honorific expressions appropriate to the rank order between himself and the person he addresses," explains Nakane. "Behavior and language are intimately interwoven in Japan."[32]

When confrontation is unavoidable and one's own superior issues a reprimand, the Japanese response is with another nonverbal sign: a smile. Another person is not supposed to be burdened with one's problems in life, so in times of pain and suffering, every sad feeling hides under a smile.[33]

Besides respectful language, the bow enables the Japanese to show respect for one another. The person of lower status bows lower, longer, and more frequently. It is easy for a person watching to discern the relative status of the persons bowing.

A bow that is proper for one person might be an insult to another who stands in a different relationship to the one bowing. Benedict explains that bows range from a mere inclination of the head and shoulders to "kneeling with forehead lowered to the hands placed flat upon the floor."[34]

There are differences, too, in men's and women's bows. Forbis explains that "men bow with hands at sides and arms rigid; women place their palms on their thighs."[35]

Another method of showing respect, by the way, is sucking in the breath between clenched teeth.[36] The same noise, however, may also serve as "a prologue, embarrassed and yet eloquent, to refusing to do some requested favor," according to Forbis.[37]

Clothing in Japan, as everywhere, communicates. Uniforms in all areas of Japanese life communicate status and make conversations with the proper honorifics possible, even among strangers.

Mrs. Takashi Fujioka, an American who just recently moved to Japan with her husband, finds the uniform important in her daily life:

Everyone's status is identified by his "uniform!".... Dark suits, worn summer and winter, identify you as a respectable businessman. Many Japanese won't do business with you if you're wearing a light suit. When I go to the local market-place, I wear an apron. Don't laugh—it's my "uniform"—it identifies me as a neighbor and housewife. It's very important that people can identify your status by your uniform so they know how to react to you and they know what you expect from them. If they don't know your status, they feel very uncomfortable around you.[38]

Intonation or voice tones can communicate a great deal in Japan. Certain words can be expressions of mild reproach or the worst possible insult, depending on the tone with which the words are uttered or shouted.

Finally, the physical layout of a Japanese office communicates. The desks of supervisors and managers are often in the same large room as those of their employees. Only the conference rooms and toilets are separate. In one such room, lines of desks face one end of the large room where facing them is the desk of the vice-president.[39] In some rooms, section heads sit with their sections, the desks arranged together.[40]

Other methods of nonverbal communication in Japan are seating arrangements, silence, and eye contact. In seating, the person farthest from the door has the highest status. There is a great deal more silence in Japanese conversations than one notices in other countries, but there is much less eye contact. Subordinates avoid looking superiors in the eye.

Also, from samurai days, the expressionless face in Japan has been considered important to hide one's feelings from adversaries.

It is easy to agree with Imai when he says, "In the typical Japanese communication, one has to be able to hear between the lines."[41]

CORPORATE STRUCTURE

Certain aspects of the structure of the Japanese company influence communication. One of them is the group; communication in groups is mainly horizontal. A good relationship among group members is nurtured, and communication among group members is encouraged.

"The Japanese philosophy" says De Mente, "is that the company with good human relations will succeed, while the company with bad human relations will fail."[42] It is to everyone's best interests to establish open communications among group members, particularly when those employees will be working together for the rest of their working lives and much of their decision making will be through consensus. Section leaders are called upon to improve communication within their sections.[43] If there is a negative side to this system, it is that the success of interpersonal relationship within groups sometimes makes communication between groups difficult.[44]

The essence of the specialized group activity called quality control circles, or, more properly today, quality circles, discussed later in this chapter, is communication. The members spend a great deal of time in horizontal communication, choosing problems to be solved, analyzing them, and then proposing solutions. Then an oral presentation gives the members an excellent opportunity, perhaps their first, to communicate with top management.

The informal grouping of individuals into groups called *habatsu* provides opportunities for communication outside formal channels.

Finally, the junior–senior relationship between group members, referred to in Chapter 3 as *sempai–kohai*, affects communication between those individuals and, indirectly, the entire group. "Viewed in qualitative terms," says Craig, "what is most striking about the personal tie is the easiness of the relationship between junior and senior. This easiness sustains an unimpeded two-way flow of communication."[45] In addressing the superior, a subordinate uses high-level language with its more honorific expressions. Information is transmitted between different levels of the hierarchy much more easily than it is in the American corporation.

Such a relationship between junior and seniors in different groups or even different offices enhances the business conducted between groups or offices. "*Sempai–kohai* working in separate offices," reports Rohlen, "constitute important informal channels of communication and influence that operate behind the scenes."[46]

The *ringi* system of decision making, discussed later in this chapter, is not only a form of corporate communication; many believe it is the most important form of corporate communication in the Japanese organization. Yoshino explains:

The system does, to a degree, fulfill the functions of both coordination and communication. As we noted earlier, it is not uncommon for the group sponsoring a particular proposal to consult with others prior to the preparation of the *ringisho*. Thus, a proposal may, to a degree, reflect the views and opinions of a number of managers concerned with the particular decision, and a certain amount of coordination is thus undertaken at the lower levels before a proposal is officially prepared. The circulation of the proposal also serves, up to a point, as a means for communication and coordination.[47]

Ouchi reports that because of the Japanese firm's qualities such as lifetime employment, an organizational culture develops which facilitates communication among employees.[48] The more common experiences among employees, the easier it is for them to communicate. "This commonality," says Ouchi, "provides them with a shorthand form of communication."[49] Americans lose that atmosphere of familiarity through constant changing of jobs, usually between companies. Japanese also acquire a broader knowledge of the company in being moved from job to job, thus increasing communication success. Bairy elaborates:

The hierarchy of each Japanese industrial unit usually includes a number of layers of members of the same age, often graduates of the same university, who maintain firm solidarity within their own age-groups. Shifted all through their careers from one part of Japan to another so that they might become acquainted with all branches of a firm and all other employees and officials of it wherever located, they quite understandably develop a natural spontaneity and unity of views and purposes in harmony with the entire group. The achievement of such familiarization is a strong enhancement of any firm's effective communication among its own members and with its outside associates.[50]

DECISION MAKING: THE RINGI SYSTEM

Among the top concerns of managers everywhere, Drucker has said, is making effective decisions.[51] Certainly one of the most unusual methods is Japanese consensual decision making. Known as *ringi seido*, "written proposal system," it is a system of middle-up management, of consultation to reach consensus, of subsequent writing of the proposal, the *ringisho*, of circulation of the proposal for approval by those whose opinion helped to shape it, and finally, of approval or rejection by top management.

The *ringi* system is believed to have been used in the civil bureaucracy in the early Meiji era and to have been adopted subsequently by private corporations.[52]

Craig reports, "In *On Serving One's Lord* (*Jikun teiko*) written in the 1730s, Kani Yosai, discussing the division of labor between lower and upper officials, argued that 'rough drafts (*aragoshirae*) should be made by lower officials and then polished by higher officials.' "[53]

Abegglen in *The Japanese Factory* refers to the Japanese process of reaching decisions as strikingly different from the American method of decision making and the clearest distinction between American and Japanese business organizations.[54]

Yoshino defines *rin* as "submitting a proposal to one's superior and receiving his approval" and *gi* as "deliberations and decisions."[55] The *ringi* system includes all of these. Yoshino calls it "much more than just a procedure; it represents a basic philosophy of management deeply rooted in Japanese tradition."[56] More than 90 percent of large Japanese firms and numerous smaller ones use this decision-making technique.[57] Yoshino explains the rationale for the system:

A system of decision making had to be devised to allow for some degree of de facto decentralization of task performance to the lower levels without decentralization of *formal authority* in decision making. Simultaneously, the system had to allow for decision making by group participation and consensus. To meet these criteria, the *ringi* system was devised.... Given Japan's sociocultural background, it was her answer to the problem of administering an organization that is too large to be managed through informal person-to-person contact of managerial personnel.[58]

An employee, usually one on a lower echelon of the management hierarchy, is assigned the task of preparing the *ringisho*. He is not likely to know all there is to know about the subject, and so he is forced to consult with others on his own management level and on levels higher than his to be sure he prepares a complete and acceptable proposal. Through informal discussion and formal meetings, an agreement is reached, and only then is the *ringisho* prepared for circulation among the executives, sometimes several dozen, for their approval. Those who do approve apply their seal (*han*) to it and pass the document along. Executives who have disagreements apply their seal, too, but add their comments as well. Disagreements between lower-level employees are settled by higher-level managers. De Mente reports, "Anyone who disapproves passes the document on without stamping it—or puts his seal on sideways or upside down to indicate conditional approval."[59]

The process of broad consultation before a decision is reached is called by the Japanese *nemawashii*, meaning "binding the roots of a plant before pulling it out," according to Vogel.[60] Even when the *ringi* system is not used for decision making, issues receive almost continuous consultation between those concerned with the subject of the decision. "The reverse side has its reverse side," says a Japanese proverb.[61] "The consultation," says Vogel,

varies from mundane detail to broad general issues, and usually it takes place in a climate of great mutual confidence and support.... Usually the executives in an organization are reluctant to move until a consensus is reached, but if the issues are sharply drawn and the executives must make a choice, they try to gain widespread support before making these decisions.[62]

The system focuses on the problem, not on the answer. Not all possible solutions are given to avoid forcing people to take sides. Vogel explains:

Nowhere in the process is there a fully organized presentation of several options to higher officials, and nowhere is there a neat package of conclusions flowing from higher levels. Good decisions emerge not from brilliant presentations of alternatives but from section people discussing all aspects of the questions over and over with all the most knowledgeable people.[63]

The *ringi* system is used only for those issues which are complex and medium- to long-term and require a high degree of coordination. Personnel matters are not so handled. General strategy questions are discussed in meetings and *ringisho* drafted only when necessary.[64] For unimportant matters, the system serves to circulate information about decisions already made.[65]

The president is ultimately responsible for either approving or not approving the *ringisho*. In most cases, he approves it without modification because of the long process of approval that created it. His role is to legitimize decisions made by group consensus.

"Whether or not a *ringi* proposal is approved by the president is primarily determined by who has approved it by the time it gets to him. If all or most of the more important managers concerned have stamped the *ringisho*," De Mente explains, "chances are the president will also approve it."[66] Once approved, the project is implemented by the person who proposed it.

A part of the *ringi* system, as it is of Japanese management in general, is the manipulation of others. Imai observes, "In Japan a good manager is one who knows how to manage his superiors."[67]

Two young Americans who work in Japanese companies indicated in a *Fortune* magazine article that the reverse is also true. An employee of Fujitsu states:

I have noticed that when our president wants to have a decision made his way, he'll arrange what seems like a random-chance meeting with one or a few section chiefs and he'll just casually drop a suggestion: wouldn't it be good if something is done in this area? Then he goes back and waits while they go through all the motions, prepare the budget, make the analysis, circulate the plan, and get everyone's agreement. Then they'll come back to him. He'll say, "Okay, good idea." They will get all the praise. It was their idea.[68]

An American employee of Nissho Iwai explains that some people who are considered good leaders in Japan don't make decisions at all but find out instead what the decisions are.[69]

Drawbacks to the *ringi* system do exist. For one thing, some middle managers may be reluctant to allow the drafting of the *ringisho* to proceed unless they have approved it. Some employees who should be involved in the procedure may inadvertently be omitted, causing resentment or worse. Other problems are summarized by Susumu Takamiya:

1. It is apt to degenerate into mere red tape, the curse of bureaucracy. Emphasis tends to be placed on the techniques of documentation in order to obtain the top man's approval. The document further tends to be passed around to too many offices, accumulating a large number of seals. In the case of a certain large company, as many as 30 seals had to be obtained for one single *ringisho*; it often took one month before it reached the president.

2. The system permits evasion of responsibility. Usually it is far from clear what all these seals really mean, and to what extent or in what respect the people affixing them assume responsibility.

3. The procedure tends to dilute the top leadership concerning overall policy making, since *ringi* decisions by the president regard individual operations. The criticism is often heard that Japanese top management does not exercise leadership as it should.

4. The president's approval by the *ringi* system is tantamount to prior supervision of the subordinate's work, which tends to give the false impression that supervision is completed and that the follow-up is not needed anymore. For the same reason, subordinates will neglect the necessary reporting to their superiors.[70]

Other weaknesses of the *ringi* system, according to Yoshino, involve changes to organizations and culture in Japan and the indifference of busy employees. Growing corporate organizations have slowed down still more the already time-consuming process at a time when rapid managerial responses and decisions are required. That combined with a trend toward impersonalization of the employer–employee relationships and the erosion of traditional values have reduced the loyalty and commitment to some degree on the part of Japanese managerial personnel.

Also, because responsibility under the *ringi* system is dispersed, attitudes of employees become apathetic and complacent to the entire process. In some firms, managers examine *ringisho* only casually; placement of their seal of approval does not actually represent careful consideration and judgment. Cross-sectional and interdepartmental rivalries tend to limit the effectiveness of the *ringi* system even more.[71]

The problem that receives most discussion is the unclear responsibility of a *ringi* project. Caves and Uekasa agree with Yoshino that it presents a problem: "Staff support for the planning function can be quite weak because the substantive proposal comes from nonspecialized personnel, and there is no way for alternatives to be systematically explored. The system can be slow and precludes fixing definite responsibility for action taken."[72]

Furstenberg disagrees: "It may be thought that this method of decision making amounts to complete abrogation of responsibility. But such an interpretation is fallacious. Decisions are planned and carried out by middle management who are allowed a great deal of discretion and hence of responsibility."[73]

The technique, though time-consuming and a little cumbersome, includes many benefits. Shared information improves the *ringisho* to a level of perfection that would otherwise be impossible. The system plays an important part in downward communication.[74] Involvement of executives on various levels ensures fast implementation of the subject of the *ringisho*. Vogel reports, "Occasionally top Japanese bureaucrats talk enviously of their Western counterparts who can simply give out orders or directives of plans, but when pushed they acknowledge that the Japanese system works better in the long run."[75] To that I would add that the Japanese system works better in the long run *for the Japanese*.

Benefits of the *ringi* system, De Mente explains, vary by company.

In some it is little more than a formality, and there is pressure from the top to eliminate the system altogether. In other companies the system reigns supreme, and there is strong opposition toward any talk of eliminating it. The system is so deeply entrenched in both the traditional management philosophy of the Japanese and in the aspirations and ambitions of younger managers that it will no doubt be around for a long time.[76]

In the midst of changes that success is bringing to the Japanese corporation, many executives are calling for changes to the decision-making system. "As one executive put it," says Yoshino, " 'Japanese management must transform itself from management by seals to management by objectives.' "[77]

Some companies have already taken steps to improve the *ringi* system, if not replace it, including standardizing and simplifying formats of *ringi* documents, clarifying routes for their circulation, reducing the number of employees who examine a proposal, allowing those examining the proposal to express their opinions as they examine it, submitting the proposal directly to top management in urgent cases, clarifying the responsibilities for each level of management within the framework of the *ringi* system, and taking up *ringi* proposals at executive committee meetings.[78]

One method of replacing the *ringi* system being used by some companies is long-range planning. By scheduling company affairs in longer time frames, management eliminates the possibility of reacting to *ringi* proposals individually.

QUALITY CIRCLES

That part of Japanese management which is actually being adopted throughout the world is the quality circle, a participative method whereby a group of employees, usually a work team that performs similar duties and reports to a single supervisor, meets one hour a week to discuss problems of their work. They pinpoint the problem, analyze it, and suggest solutions to management, which retains decision-making authority to accept or reject the solutions. The objectives of the quality circle system are to improve communication, particularly between line employees and management, and to identify and solve problems.

A specific framework that requires participation of the company's top management is essential to success of the procedure. "In most cases," says Ouchi, "a circle undertakes a study project that can be solved within about three months, and which should take no longer than six months."[79]

Participants include from as few as 3 to as many as 25 members; ideal size is from 7 to 10. Their supervisor serves as leader, and an outside facilitator participates. A steering committee oversees the group's work. Assumptions of the quality circle system include these:

1. Individual workers are recognized as human beings with the intellectual desire to participate in solving work-related problems.
2. Individual workers have the capacity to grow and develop to be better than they already are.
3. Individual workers are the experts on the job who know best how to make the job easier and more effective.
4. Individual workers want to contribute their minds and ideas as well as their hands and backs to the job.[80]

Yoshi Tsurumi explains the rationale of the procedure: "Once you accept the notion that rank-and-file workers have just as much at stake in the future of the company as management, it becomes obvious they are also the ones who have the best knowledge of production problems and quality control."[81]

Four distinct steps occur in the operation of a quality circle:

1. Group members identify problems on the job that they feel need solving. Suggested problems may come from top management or from any other source in the organization. The more problems a circle has to work with, the more likely it is to select a satisfyingly challenging one to solve.

2. Members analyze the problem, using any analysis technique required, and they consult with outside experts, as needed. Prior to beginning the circle's work, members are given training in statistical techniques that they will use in this stage.

3. Members suggest a solution to managers in what is called a management presentation. The leader and facilitator invite those members of top management in whose area the subject of the problem falls. Members explain the problem they have been working on, the suggested solution, and the projected cost saving to the company of the change. Acceptance or rejection of the idea remains with management; there is no change in decision-making authority. If it is a relatively minor change which can be approved on the spot, it usually is. If there is a large dollar investment, the decision is passed to higher management for the final decision. An answer is returned in a specified time, usually about five working days.

4. Implementation of the change is ordered or the idea is rejected. On occasion, the problem is sent back to the quality circle for elaboration on an idea or other changes.[82]

Each step in this procedure must be carried out conscientiously for complete success. Throughout industry about 80 percent of quality circle recommendations are accepted by management. David C. McCrary, corporate director of product reliability at Sheller-Globe, says, "Most of these recommendations lead to dramatic cost savings, improved quality, efficiency and productivity. For the people involved in circles, there is a sense of deep personal satisfaction and job enrichment."[83]

U.S. occupational forces introduced modern quality control techniques in 1946 to help the country in reconstruction. From then until 1962, the notion fermented in scientific circles. To overcome the country's reputation throughout the world for poor-quality merchandise, the quality circle was created by the Japanese Union of Scientists and Engineers (JUSE) and Dr. Kaoru Ishikawa, a professor of engineering at Tokyo University, who is considered the father of the quality circle movement.

The Japanese acknowledge that concern for quality control was encouraged by two Americans: Dr. W. Edwards Deming, a former Stanford University professor and an expert on quality control who lectured in Japan on statistical methodology beginning in 1950, and Dr. Joseph M. Juran, a quality control expert who taught courses in management aspects of quality control beginning in 1954. Prior to that, Japan had had only limited experience with modern statistical quality control methods. Dr. Juran, presently head of New York's Juran Institute, Inc., taught that quality control should be "an integral part of the management function and practiced throughout the firm."[84] Dr. Deming assured them that use of statistical methods would eliminate their quality problems in five years.[85] Deming's suggested statistical methods and philosophy include:

1. Innovate with a long-range outlook for the company.
2. Don't accept defective material, workmanship, or products or machines out of order.
3. Eliminate dependence on mass inspection.
4. Reduce the number of suppliers that you have for the same product and demand that they use statistical techniques for quality control.
5. Identify two sources of waste by way of statistical methods and try to reduce them.
6. Use statistical methods for better on-the-job training.
7. Use statistical methods along with supervision to help people do their job better.
8. Eliminate fear throughout the organization to help people to do a better job.
9. Put together a team of people to work on design, research, sales, and production.
10. No longer use slogans or goals aimed at the work force to attempt to increase productivity.
11. Look closely at work standards.
12. Introduce elementary statistics to all employees.
13. Retrain people in new skills to keep them up in new advances.

14. Maximize the use of statistical knowledge in your company.[86]

Emanuel describes the first efforts to apply these techniques:

The first formalized, systematic approach was the Zero Defects (ZD) Program. Workers were organized in small groups and asked for their ideas. The results were astounding. Many Japanese products—almost overnight—established quality standards for the rest of the world.

"The ZD Program was fine for what it did," reported one Labor Relations Director, "but it was a 'top-down' movement and didn't conform to our philosophy of 'bottom up' management, and it didn't unlock our workers' creativity and motivation." Thus, the evolution of ZD Programs to QC Circles.[87]

It was the leadership of JUSE and Japanese industrialists which ultimately created the quality circle. In the Japanese adaptation of the Deming–Juran teachings, each person in the organization, from top management to the rank and file, receives instruction in statistical quality control techniques. More important, they organized study groups to upgrade quality control practices, the predecessor to today's approach.

To publicize the method, in 1962 JUSE started a journal, *Quality Control for the Foreman*. Every communication medium in the country was then used to introduce the method to the nation. In 1964, regional quality control chapters were started, and in 1970, *Fundamentals of Quality Control Circles* was published. In 1968, the first quality control team visited the United States with uncertain success.

In 1971, the first of frequent conferences was held; by the end of 1975, the five hundredth quality conference was held. By that year there were 70,000 quality control circles in operation in Japan. Today it is estimated that there are a million quality control circles being operated in Japan by 10 million workers, one in eight. Although the emphasis in the beginning was on quality control, the focus has broadened to cover all of corporate life. So the term commonly used today is quality circle, instead of quality control circle. Some industrialists refer to the modern approach as total quality control (TQC).

Ouchi reports, "The explanation for the circles' popularity lies in their unique function. What they do is share with management the responsibility for locating and solving problems of coordination and productivity. The circles, in other words, notice all the little things that go wrong in an organization—and then put up the flag."[88]

Ouchi also quotes Joji Arai, director of the Washington, D.C., office of the Japan Productivity Center, as saying, "The average Q-C Circle in Japan produces each year fifty to sixty implemented suggestions per worker. The current record is held by one company that averaged ninety-nine implemented suggestions per worker for a single year."[89]

More than this, however, management has found reductions in absenteeism, tardiness, and work disruption.[90] The result is that between 1948 and 1973 the Japanese gross national product grew two and a half times faster than the world average.[91]

Much of this success must be attributed to the work of the Japan Productivity Center. The center was established in 1955 with the goal of improving the country's productivity by sending study missions abroad, sponsoring management development services, and conducting research for private companies. Financed by the government, by general contributions, by membership fees from private businesses, and by fees for services rendered, the center has invested nearly $250 million in Japan's productivity.[92]

The 1 million quality circles in Japan each solve an average of three problems per year.[93] Certain companies report specific successes with the circles. Nippon Steel Corporation has 8,400 quality circles involving 70 percent of its 52,000 blue collar workers. In one year, the circles completed 15,935 projects, saving the company about $5 per ton of steel products.[94]

There are currently 2,147 quality circles at Toyo Kogyo, makers of the Mazda, with more than 16,000 people participating.[95] As Figure 1 shows, productivity at Toyo Kogyo nearly doubled in only five years. At Nissan Motor Company, 4,161 circles worked on over 30,000 projects in one year, saving about $2.4 million. Nippon Electric Company's Fuchu plant doubled productivity in three years; management attributes about 25 percent of that to worker input through the circles. Sharp Corporation's Tenri plant has experienced a 30 percent jump in productivity every six months for three years, much of it due to quality circles. At Nippon Kokan K.K., some 8,000 workers in 1,480 circles accounted for cost savings of over $86 million in one year.[96]

Toyota Motor Company's customer complaints have nearly totally been turned over to quality circles for solution, saving the company $3 million a year.[97] Toshiba Corporation's Fukuwa Works has had quality circles for a long time. Its 160 circles meet five minutes both before and after work and often during lunch as well. Several ideas of the circles have been incorporated into the plant's machine designs.[98]

At Sontory's Katsura Brewery outside of Kyoto, quality circles have been meeting since the plant opened in 1969. They meet for one or two hours per week—often when the production line is shut down. "Each group has its own theme such as how to be more efficient, how to decrease mistakes, how to decrease the number of unwashed bottles, and how to decrease unsuitable labeling," according to an article in Atlantic-Richfield's *mgr* magazine.[99]

Estimates are that the 10 million Japanese workers who participate in quality circles have achieved savings of about $25 billion for their com-

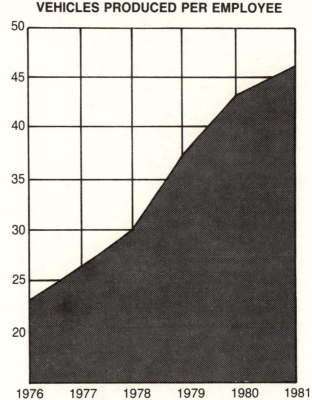

VEHICLES PRODUCED PER EMPLOYEE

Figure 1. Productivity at Toyo Kogyo, makers of the Mazda, has increased 97.8 percent in five years. (Source: "Mazda RX-7," *Business Week*, July 19, 1982, p. 29.)

panies.[100] Donald C. Bauder, financial editor of the *San Diego Union*, reported that Japan's productivity gains from 1970 to 1981 were 110 percent, highest among eleven industrialized countries studied. The United States, with a 34 percent gain, was second to last.[101]

NOTES

1. Gibney, *Japan*, p. 145.
2. Seward, *The Japanese*, p. 163.
3. Reischauer, *Japan: The Story of a Nation*, p. 31.
4. Forbis, *Japan Today*, p. 130.
5. Ibid.

6. Ibid.

7. Gray, "Japan, Corporate Strategies for the 1980s," p. 45.

8. Kluckhohn, *Mirror for Man*, p. 24.

9. De Mente, *Japanese Manners and Ethics in Business*, p. 105.

10. Reischauer, *The Japanese*, p. 380.

11. Forbis, *Japan Today*, p. 127.

12. Delassus, *The Japanese*, p. 68.

13. Japan External Trade Organization, *How to Succeed in Japan*, p. 203.

14. Masao, "The Japanese Language and Intercultural Communication," in Japan Center for International Exchange, *The Silent Power*, p. 56.

15. Yamaguchi, *We Japanese*, p. 176.

16. De Mente, *How to Do Business in Japan*, p. 82.

17. Doi, "Some Psychological Themes in Japanese Human Relationships," in *Intercultural Encounters with Japan*, ed. Condon and Saito, p. 20.

18. Bairy, "Japanese Ways," in *Doing Business in Japan*, ed. Ballon, p. 4.

19. Burks, *Japan*, p. 203.

20. Morsbach, "Reflections on Relationships," in *Business in Japan*, ed. Norbury and Bownas, p. 194.

21. Nitobe, *Bushido, The Soul of Japan*, as cited in Barnlund, *Public and Private Self in Japan and the United States*, p. 133.

22. Reischauer, *The Japanese*, p. 136.

23. Yamaguchi, *We Japanese*, p. 178.

24. Imai, *16 Ways to Avoid Saying No*, p. 101.

25. Lebra, *Japanese Patterns of Behavior*, p. 115.

26. Seward, *The Japanese*, p. 170.

27. Imai, *16 Ways to Avoid Saying No*, p. 124.

28. Ibid., pp. 7–8.

29. Pascale and Athos, *The Art of Japanese Management*, p. 97.

30. Reischauer, *The Japanese*, p. 136.

31. Halloran, *Japan*, p. 218.

32. Nakane, *Japanese Society*, p. 30.

33. Embree, *The Japanese Nation*, p. 230.

34. Benedict, *The Chrysanthemum and the Sword*, p. 48.

35. Forbis, *Japan Today*, p. 20.

36. Yamaguchi, *We Japanese*, p. 49.

37. Forbis, *Japan Today*, p. 21.

38. "Mandarin Oranges and Origami," p. 10.

39. Bruce-Briggs, "The Dangerous Folly Called Theory Z," p. 44.

40. De Mente, *How to Do Business in Japan*, p. 48.

41. Imai, *16 Ways to Avoid Saying No*, p. 10.

42. De Mente, *Japanese Manners and Ethics in Business*, p. 69.

43. Furstenberg, *Why the Japanese Have Been So Successful in Business*, p. 32.

44. Abegglen, *Management and Worker*, p. 92.

45. Craig, "Functional and Dysfunctional Aspects of Government Bureaucracy," in *Modern Japanese Organization and Decision-Making*, ed. Vogel, p. 12.

46. Rohlen, *For Harmony and Strength*, p. 132.

47. Yoshino, *Japan's Managerial System*, p. 259.

48. Ouchi, *Theory Z*, pp. 41–42.

49. Ibid., p. 42.

50. Bairy, "Motivational Forces in Japanese Life," in *The Japanese Employee*, ed. Ballon, p. 53.

51. Drucker, "What We Can Learn from the Japanese," p. 110.

52. Yoshino, *Japan's Managerial System*, p. 256.

53. Craig, "Functional and Dysfunctional Aspects of Government Bureaucracy," in *Modern Japanese Organization and Decision-Making*, ed. Vogel, p. 24.

54. Abegglen, *The Japanese Factory*, p. 83.

55. Yoshino, *Japan's Managerial System*, p. 254.

56. Ibid.

57. Masatsugu, *The Modern Samurai Society*, p. 171.

58. Yoshino, *Japan's Managerial System*, p. 256.

59. De Mente, *Japanese Manners and Ethics in Business*, p. 87.

60. Vogel, *Modern Japanese Organization and Decision-Making*, p. xxii.

61. Yamaguchi, *We Japanese*, p. 182.

62. Vogel, *Modern Japanese Organization and Decision-Making*, pp. xxii–xxiii.

63. Vogel, *Japan as Number 1*, p. 144.

64. Vogel, *Modern Japanese Organization and Decision-Making*, p. xviii.

65. Craig, "Functional and Dysfunctional Aspects of Government Bureaucracy," in *Modern Japanese Organization and Decision-Making*, ed. Vogel, p. 24.

66. De Mente, *Japanese Manners and Ethics in Business*, p. 88.

67. Imai, *Never Take Yes for an Answer*, p. 5.

68. "Outsiders Inside Japanese Companies," p. 116.

69. Ibid.

70. Takamiya, "Reorganization in Japanese Enterprises," in *Doing Business in Japan*, ed. Ballon, p. 172.

71. Yoshino, *Japan's Managerial System*, pp. 260–61.

72. Caves and Uekusa, *Industrial Organization in Japan*, p. 14.

73. Furstenberg, *Why the Japanese Have Been So Successful in Business*, p. 12.

74. Ibid., p. 71.

75. Vogel, *Japan as Number 1*, p. 95.

76. De Mente, *Japanese Manners and Ethics in Business*, p. 87.

77. Yoshino, *Japan's Managerial System*, p. 262.

78. Ibid., pp. 262–63.

79. Ouchi, *Theory Z*, p. 262.

80. Callahan, "Quality Circles: A Program for Productivity Improvement Through Human Resources Development."

81. "Made in Japan," p. 9.

82. Callahan, "Quality Circles: A Program for Productivity Improvement Through Human Resources Development."

83. "Graybill's GREAT Program Gets People Involved," p. 3.

84. Cole, *Work Mobility and Participation*, p. 136.

85. Ringle, "The American Who Remade 'Made in Japan,' " p. 68.

86. Deming, "What Top Management Must Do," pp. 20–21.

87. Emanuel, "Productivity Improvement—Japanese Style," p. 4.

88. Ouchi, *Theory Z*, p. 261.

89. Ibid., p. 262.

90. Zemke, "Quality Circles: Using Pooled Effort to Promote Excellence," p. 31.

91. Kahn and Pepper, *The Japanese Challenge*, p. 1.

92. "The Japan Productivity Center," pp. 1–2.

93. Gryna, *Quality Circles*, p. 12.

94. Imai, *16 Ways to Avoid Saying No*, p. 138.

95. Gray, "Corporate Strategies for the 1980s," p. 29.

96. "Quality Control Circles Pay off Big," pp. 17–18.

97. "Japanese Attribute Much of Success to Quality Circles," p. 34.

98. Stephens, "Visions: The Rising Sun of Productivity," p. 7.

99. Ibid., p. 11.

100. "Japanese Attribute Much of Success to Quality Circles," p. 33.

101. Bauder, "U.S. Productivity West's Lowest," p. H-18.

6

Communication in the Japanese Corporation

Since earliest times, the Japanese have used various means of communicating. Most people don't know that the smoke signal, whistle, horn, and drum helped the rural residents of early Japan communicate. Drums, for example, called the samurai to the castle. None of these, however, could communicate over long distances. For that they used the letter.

The Persian king in the sixth century B.C. began the exchange of letters on a systematic basis. His letters helped him rule the Persian empire, a practice continued under the Roman empire.[1] There was an exchange of letters between the rulers of Japan and China as early as the third century B.C. It was from Queen Himiko of the ancient Japanese state of Yamatai to the ruler of China.[2]

Another method of communicating in early Japan was the use of way stations. Beginning in the seventeenth century, they were placed every 16 kilometers on all the trunk highways. There men and horses were posted to relay messages, just like the American pony express.

Official post offices were established in 1872, patterned after Britain's. A little earlier telegraphic communication was introduced. When Commodore Perry came in 1853, he presented to the Shogun Tokugawa a Morse telegraph inscribed, "For the Emperor of Japan."[3] Because it was expensive, however, few Japanese could afford to use it at the time. Also, some Japanese considered telegraphy a form of Christian magic and made it a point to sever the cables and cause other disruptions.

In 1908, communication with the United States was begun with the laying of a submarine cable between the countries.[4] "Now," says Minoru Hirota, "the stage of communication has expanded to space. Various kinds of information are delivered via man-made satellites instead of by foot or by horses as compared to a century ago."[5]

Communication has been as important to Japanese society in general as it has been in the Japanese corporation. This chapter examines this role by first reviewing both the formal and informal systems of communication in the Japanese business organization.

COMMUNICATION IN THE CORPORATION

As noted previously, communication is central to Japanese corporate life. Everyone does it constantly, from the chairman of the board to the rank and file. Emanuel states that "in Japan, effective employee communication is viewed in exactly the same manner, and with the same order of priority, as product quality; indeed, the two concepts are inseparable. As one Japanese businessman said, 'We could never achieve our high standards of quality or reach our current levels of productivity without good employee communication.' "[6]

The Japanese corporation collects and processes information more thoroughly than do companies in other countries.[7] However, never is information gathering an end in itself. Vogel refers to it as "a group-centered process closely linked to long-range organizational purposes, permitting an impressive range of information to be concentrated where and when the organization can best use it."[8] This access to information is undoubtedly one of the reasons Japan has become a great industrial power.

At the same time that the Japanese absorb information from the outside, they are virtually unable to transmit messages about themselves to foster understanding of their lives and customs. In a sort of "communication shyness," or passivity, they are unstinting in their efforts to understand others, yet they have little incentive to disseminate information about themselves to the rest of the world.[9]

Communication, both formal and informal, moves in every conceivable direction in the Japanese company. The employee has a special need to know because of the collective form of decision making, according to Clark:

Perhaps the best indication of a general awareness that decisions are made collectively is the very thorough dissemination of information that takes place in many Japanese companies. Dozens of documents seem to be in continuous circulation, so that company members know a great deal of what is going on, even if it scarcely concerns them. There are, of course, the *ringi*, the suggestions and proposals mentioned earlier, which usually start in one department and are passed to collateral departments to be seen by relatively junior managers before being shown to the directors. There are rules and directives in the name of the president, managing directors, or department heads. There are daily or weekly pep talks or discussion sessions, at which salesmen will be told of the operating ratios on the shop floor as well as the sales figures, and production line workers will be given details of the efforts being made to get new recruits. The effects of this generous flow of information are great and good. The knowledge that he is worth informing at all improves a man's morale, particularly if his prospects are limited and his self-esteem depends upon his giving the impression that he is always in the know. Understanding what is happening elsewhere in a company helps people to take a greater interest in their own work, which they can come to see as part of an estimable whole. And, of course, by distributing information so liberally, upper managements ensure that no one who really needs to know something is overlooked.[10]

Of pivotal importance in this system are middle managers, who, while considered the weak link in the communications of an American corporation, are largely responsible for the successful communication process within the Japanese company. "The manager often acts as a symbol of unification within his organization and assumes the role of coordinator as well as communicator," says Imai. "He has to be guided by his subordinates as well as direct them."[11] Managers in Japan, reports an article in *mgr*, publication of Atlantic Richfield, "become mainly communicators whose jobs are to make sure employees understand the 'vision' that comes down from the top, and to carry up the word from below."[12]

For most of his day, the Japanese manager acts as communicator between people in different departments or between his own people and outsiders. Sheldon describes the typical day of a Japanese businessman, showing him beginning the morning by reading cables that arrived during the night from overseas, digesting and answering correspondence, and then joining a conference with his group.[13] Communication in the Japanese corporation, as with all others, starts with the first duties of the day.

Japanese management through the personnel department makes it a chief goal to encourage the continual flow of information and communication between management and employees and among employees.[14] "The Japanese view of the benefits of industrial communication," Bairy explains, "are like those of a fine harvest that follows upon patient, monotonous, and sometimes anonymous cooperation with the laws of nature."[15]

Bairy further explains that in addition to transmitting information from one employee to another, corporate communication is intended to give the receiver of the message "an emotional message." Managers take an interest in each of their employees, and no message exchange takes place between them without some proof of that concern—an inquiry about family, health, hobbies, and so on.

In a book designed to help foreign businesspersons succeed in Japan, the Japan External Trade Organization (JETRO) explains that communication in Japan is more than mere words:

Communication is the most important and it's not a matter of a language barrier. You must establish understanding with the people you are dealing with, whether partners, staff or customers. For business to be done successfully in Japan, you must know the social structure and hierarchical structure of the companies with whom you are dealing.[16]

The emphasis in Japanese corporations is on personal, oral communication as opposed to written forms of communication. The Japanese "hate paper as a means of communication," explains Gibney.

Although some final matters must necessarily be put down in memo form, the exchange of ideas is something they prefer to do face-to-face. Indeed, the oral commitment often counts far more than the written contract. ("I don't care what you write in those memos," one of our Japanese executives cautioned me before one labor negotiation meeting. "But please be careful what you say to them.")[17]

Another reason for Japanese displeasure with written communications in the past has been the typewriter they were forced to use before the invention of the Japanese-language word processor. Gibney reports that mastering the typewriter, still, of course, in use in most Japanese companies, took six months. "Typing the simplest memo can be a major production. The language itself, however, is so vague that clever explanations and attempted niceties of expression may cause more communication problems than they solve. Most Japanese company typewriters, when available, are reserved for unambiguous declarations like financial reports and price lists.[18]

FORMAL SYSTEM

The formal communication system in the Japanese firm, diagrammed in Figure 2, is very similar to that in American corporations. "For general internal information," Furstenberg says, "the methods and aids used in major Japanese companies are similar to those used in Europe."[19] The same applies to America.

Publications

Emanuel, who leads Americans on study tours of Japanese corporations, says this of their written corporate communication:

There are the usual corporate publications that go to all employees, and the best—such as "Nissan News," put out by the company that makes Datsun au-

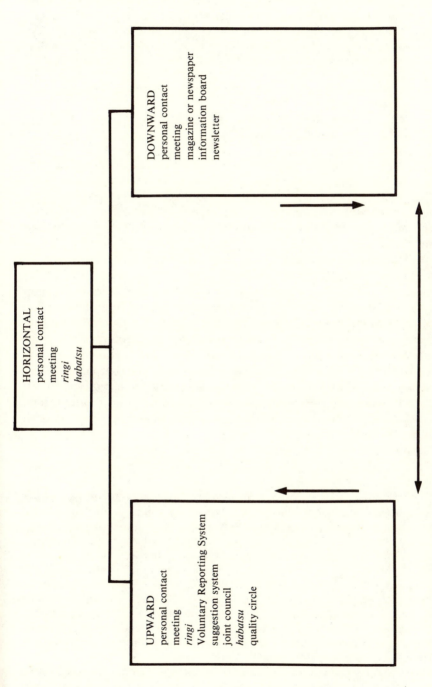

Figure 2. The formal system of communication in the Japanese corporation resembles that in the American company.

tomobiles—are on a level with the best in North America. Most larger firms also sponsor plant publications, excellent bulletin board programs, and regular employee meetings. Considerable use is made of plant-wide loudspeaker messages.

There are generally more nonbusiness features in employee publications than are found in North America because in the Japanese culture, the worker's whole family identifies with his firm.... So almost all company publications consider the family a key audience for articles and stories.... There are no "professional" employee communicators in Japanese industry ... and the positions of "editor," "employee communications manager," etc. are filled by employees as part of their normal rotation and transfer through the organization.[20]

Literally dozens of documents are in continuous circulation to let employees know what is going on. For downward communication, there are print media: company magazines, newspapers and newsletters. There are also bulletin boards, called information boards in Japan, where they are used to communicate with employees much more extensively than they are in the United States.

Morinosuke Kajima, head of Kajima Construction Company, tells of converting his company's monthly magazine from a "sort of literary or entertainment magazine" into a monthly report that stated his opinion on the front page, "stressing the importance of pursuing our business on a permanent basis, instead of seeking temporary profit." A collection of the statements was later distributed among the employees.[21]

At Nissan Motors, the *Nissan News*, mentioned by Emanuel, is distributed to all employees, as is a monthly publication by the company's labor–management council. There are also "local plant publications and each plant has video equipment that shows weekly items from headquarters. In addition, an in-house loudspeaker system links headquarters with Nissan plants."[22]

Rohlen describes the methods of communication used in a Japanese bank:

The company's major instrument of inspiration is its monthly magazine, the Uedagin *News*. Printed on fine paper, filled with pictures, and often sporting several pages of color photographs, the *News* is a sophisticated publication that covers a broad range of subject matter. In addition to editorials, we find articles stating bank policy and messages from leaders, many heavy with ideological rhetoric. Other regular features include such diverse things as round-table discussions, reports of Uedagin events, news from the branches, a monthly child care, health, and home economics section, accounts of foreign travel, discussions of the economy, and announcements of marriages, births, retirements and deaths. A typical issue runs about 70 pages, and, as would be expected of a company magazine, it presents a picture of happy people. Human interest stories and personalized material are two notable emphases of the news staff.

The participation of average members is encouraged through monthly "relay" articles and round-table discussions. In the latter, eight to twelve average members gathered by the magazine staff discuss a common problem or experience in the bank. This form of public discussion encourages a serious outlook, and the participants find themselves voluntarily indicating a strong interest in solving the bank's problems. Their printed comments, then, become testimonials of their commitment to Uedagin. For readers the result is an impression of wide involvement in bank affairs on the part of persons of all ranks. New policies are also discussed in this way, and the *zadankai* (round-table discussion) thus serves to maintain an impression of broad popular consideration and support for decisions handed down by management.

Also serving to publicize the ideology are such documentary enterprises as the periodic writing of the history of the bank and the display of important historical materials. On the bank's twentieth anniversary, a beautifully bound and illustrated volume of over 600 pages was published, and an even larger history is planned to commemorate its twenty-fifth. This publication appears to be intended to serve several purposes. It is written to intensify the awareness of and pride in the history of the institution, and its interminable lists and photographs of past personnel serve as an album of memories for older members.[23]

At Honda, every man keeps a diary of "his work, ideas, thoughts, joys and sorrows"—"an honest record" from which the company claims "to get to know its employees."[24]

Meetings

Much more important to the Japanese corporation is upward communication. Meetings of all kinds are used to communicate information upward in the management chain. "Japan is today the land of meetings," Nakane observed, "and it is far from difficult to find a man who spends more time at meetings than at his desk.... Not only vital issues but those less pertinent are brought under consideration by a meeting."[25]

Meetings in Japan are longer and more frequent than in other countries because of the process of consensual decision making. They allow coordination of work by those on the same managerial level and communication between those on varying levels of the organization. "In the last analysis, they are the best known mechanism for efficient information sharing," state Pascale and Athos.[26]

The style of conducting meetings in the two countries differs, too. Americans invite open and honest confrontation at meetings. Japanese, as they are culturally trained to do, avoid open confrontation. Any subject likely to cause disagreement is discussed in advance of the meeting, and agreement is reached on a solution. During the meeting, then, everyone understands how the issue will be settled, and no one disagrees or loses. In fact, the meeting can provide a formal approval of a decision reached during informal consultation.[27]

When there is a problem to be settled at a meeting or alternative solutions to a problem, decisions are made through consensus. Each person at the meeting expresses his views for whatever length of time he wants. Afterward, the leader of the group makes a decision based on the group's wishes, even when that is contrary to his own preference.

A requirement of the system is the sort of active listening that most Japanese can do and most Americans can't. Pascale and Athos say that Americans listen in an evaluative way, accepting or rejecting ideas presented, which leads to fatigue and listening shortcuts so that they actually absorb only about 30 percent of the message. The Japanese, the authors explain, practice "less-ego listening." "They hold 'principle' in abeyance, regard themselves as one among others in the situation, and thus achieve easy accommodation with the circumstances of the meeting.... This situational ethic enables the Japanese to air different views without falling into a duel of personalities."[28] This contrasts to the American push for a decision, which, as Pascale and Athos observe, "often prompts managers to choose prematurely, based on conceptual analysis and substantive merit, but without due regard for implementational feasibility."[29]

The functions that occur in the meeting in the United States are in Japan performed through the broad, informal system of consultation just described, the formal meeting, and to some extent the *ringi* system.[30] The skillful manager has a network of informal communication channels to call upon when needed within the company and outside, too.

Voluntary Reporting System

Another form of upward communication is a frequent survey of employee attitudes, usually administered by the personnel department and called by some the voluntary reporting system.[31] Annually and often more frequently, questionnaires are distributed to employees asking for their opinion on almost everything in their corporate lives, including satisfaction, office leadership, and personnel problems on the job,[32] as well as much about their personal lives such as rent paid, size of living quarters, hobbies, and desire for a transfer.[33] The results are the basis for changes in the corporation and provide a profile of the morale of each office.[34] It has been said that the system is needed because of the social distance between managers and employees.

Suggestion System

The suggestion system is used for upward communication in Japan, as it is elsewhere; however, its use by the Japanese is more intensive. In one company studied by Marsh and Mannari,

Each worker is encouraged by his foreman to think of a suggestion each month.

A theme is often stressed in a given month, e.g., how can we reduce costs of production? Forms available for writing one's suggestion ask for the person's name, a name for the suggestion, a description of the present method, and a description of [the] idea for a new, better method.[35]

Committees of employees and managers evaluate suggestions submitted by individuals or groups. Some companies exhibit on information boards accepted suggestions, which may also be reported in the corporation's print media.[36]

Pascale and Athos report a Matsushita belief: "A great many people, paying attention each day to how to improve their jobs, can accomplish more than a whole headquarters full of production engineers and planners."[37] In 1979, his company received over 25 suggestions per employee, with some divisions averaging more than 60 per employee. Monetary rewards are given for accepted suggestions, and the best of them receive companywide attention.[38]

At Toyo Kyogo, makers of the Mazda, 1.7 million suggestions were received in 1981 alone, and more than half of these were adopted. Figure 3 shows the huge increase of suggestions made and adopted that year over previous years. Most of them increased the efficiency of a specific work place and helped eliminate wasted time, motion, and money in almost every area of the company.[39]

Joint Councils

A system that is used in both Japan and America is one of consultation between employees and managers mainly for the purpose of upward communication. Furstenberg reported that a 1968 study by the Japanese Productivity Center showed that the most widely mentioned objectives of joint councils were the improvement of understanding and the harmonious running of the business.[40] A similar study of American councils would undoubtedly draw a different response.

Electronic Methods

Facsimile-transmitting machines have been popular in Japan, partly because handwritten messages are so common. Teleconferencing also has been adopted extensively because it meets the basic Japanese office style. Takuma Yamamoto, president of Fujitsu, notes that with teleconferencing one of three monthly senior staff meetings takes place by telephone.[41] All of these methods are covered in great detail in Chapter 9.

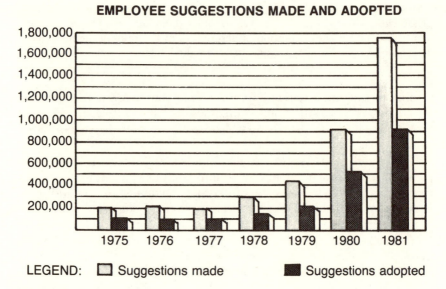

Figure 3. Employee suggestions at Toyo Kogyo have increased nearly ninefold, as have suggestions accepted by the company. (Source: "Mazda RX-7," *Business Week*, July 19, 1982, p. 29.)

Letters

The formal system of communication also includes letters, communications outside the company. As explained previously, letter and memo writing and paperwork in general do not fit well into Japanese methods of corporate communication. Most business transactions take place through personal contact or over the telephone. International business is conducted by telex mainly. "Only the data in inquiries, estimates, offers, etc., are confirmed in writing, often in forms or form letters," state Saburo Haneda and Hirosuke Shima in an article in *The Journal of Business Communication.*[42]

Letter writing in Japan is distinctive in its obligatory polite opening. Gibney explains:

A reminder to pay a bill or an announcement that a new man has joined a bank's board of directors are equal occasions for the obligatory opening remarks about the rude necessity of imposing on one's time or the change of seasons. "Now that spring promises to come," the letter begins, "the first buds of the cherry blossoms can be descried climbing the far-off mountain. Although we hesitate to break in on your very busy schedule, troubled as you are with many worthy pursuits, it is time that necessity compels us to remind you that your firm's indebtedness...[43]

Atsuko Tanaka, professor of business education at Baika Women's College, Kyoto, provides these openings for each month of the year:

January:	In this new season, we are happy ...
February:	In this coldness still prevailing ...
March:	In this early spring season ...
April:	In this mild season of spring ...
May:	In the season of young leaves ...
June:	In this early summer season ...
July:	In the scorching summer heat ...
August:	In this summer heat still with us ...
September:	In this first part of fall ...
October:	With the fresh coolness setting in ...
November:	In this season of late autumn ...
December:	In this busy year-end season ...[44]

Some small companies employ one person to write all letters, and even some large companies have one employee write all "official apology letters."[45] One such person was

nominally in charge of the personnel section, whose practical use to the organization in this function had long since been evaluated as counterproductive. Yet he was the only person out of some two hundred who had the necessary background to write one of those polite letters in which, given the vagaries of Japanese society, the slightest slip of grammar could lose the company several prestige points. Mr. Imamura was also a master at handling complaints and apologizing. Most Japanese groups contain within them an apologizer, useful for occasions when a soft, well-spoken answer can turn away a lot of wrath. Since Imamura's company sold household appliances, through the agency of some one thousand fast-talking salesmen, the old man often had some very angry customers to soothe. He rarely failed. Bathed in the polite polysyllables of Imamura's gentle phrases, relaxed by the utterly ambiguous wanderings of his honorifics, refreshed by the flattering balm of his concern for the other party's health, living arrangements, and future familial prosperity, the most irate complainant would generally go away happy, his order uncanceled.[46]

Even sales letters use this approach, according to Hanada and Shima:

Japanese sales letters cannot be so vivid, personal, aggressive, high-pitched, or hard-sell as American letters. Instead of declaring from the very beginning, "I have a very good proposition or a very good product to offer," the traditional Japanese way is to begin a letter with customary greetings, etc., and then: "By the way, our humble company has recently developed a new product, and we are submitting a sample for your kind inspection," or some such modest statement.[47]

A typical salesman's report, by the way, demonstrates as much about the Japanese way of conducting business as it does about their method of writing reports. Imai provides this example:

I visited one of our important customers this afternoon, although I had no particular business to discuss with him. I talked briefly with his wife and played with their five-year-old boy. I also gave the boy some toys before coming back to the office. I believe that the time I spent was quite productive.[48]

Informal System

The informal system of communication in the Japanese firm includes the grapevine, as it does in the American corporation; however, in Japan, the informal system is also comprised of *habatsu*, or cliques.

Yoshino reports that because the traditional culture of Japan included no notions of the large organization, Japanese tended to feel uncomfortably isolated in them. In response, the Japanese created "narrow social groupings offering particularistic and emotional ties within the impersonal formal organization."[49]

Although a part of the informal system, *habatsu* are highly goal oriented—the major goal being to enhance their own power and influence in the organization. Membership in *habatsu* is not the result of random associations as it is in American informal groups. It is based on a specific common unchangeable tie, such as place of birth or school. Membership is also nonoverlapping, unlike the American system, which allows employees to belong to several informal groups. Members of a *habatsu* are drawn from various management levels, and the *habatsu* themselves are hierarchically organized.

Habatsu have their own highly effective network of communication. They can be very beneficial or deleterious to an organization's operations. They benefit by bypassing an occasional blockage in vertical communication. They also provide lateral communication with a high level of trust.[50]

On the other hand, their approval is required in extreme cases before a new policy can be implemented. Also, inter-*habatsu* rivalries develop; and the outcome may present a morale problem for those members of *habatsu* which are not dominant.

NOTES

1. Hirota, "History Told in Communications Development," p. 32.
2. Ibid.

3. Ibid., p. 33.

4. Ibid., p. 34.

5. Ibid.

6. Emanuel, "Productivity Improvement—Japanese Style," p. 3.

7. Vogel, *Japan as Number 1*, p. 43.

8. Ibid., p. 51.

9. Tadao, "Escape from Cultural Isolation," in *The Silent Power*, ed. Japan Center for International Exchange, pp. 26–27.

10. Clark, *The Japanese Company*, p. 129.

11. Imai, *16 Ways to Avoid Saying No*, pp. 88–89.

12. Stephens, "Visions: The Rising Sun of Productivity," p. 5.

13. Sheldon, *Enjoy Japan*, p. 63.

14. Imai, *16 Ways to Avoid Saying No*, p. 103.

15. Bairy, "Motivational Forces in Japanese Life," in *The Japanese Employee*, ed. Ballon, p. 54.

16. Japan External Trade Organization, *How to Succeed in Japan*, p. 210.

17. Gibney, *Japan*, pp. 193–94.

18. Ibid., p. 194.

19. Furstenberg, *Why the Japanese Have Been So Successful in Business*, p. 32.

20. Emanuel, "Productivity Improvement—Japanese Style," p. 3.

21. Hewins, *The Japanese Miracle Men*, pp. 228–29.

22. Stephens, "Visions," p. 8.

23. Rohlen, *For Harmony and Strength*, pp. 56–57.

24. Hewins, *The Japanese Miracle Men*, p. 282.

25. Nakane, *Japanese Society*, pp. 145–46.

26. Pascale and Athos, *The Art of Japanese Management*, pp. 130–31.

27. Craig, "Functional and Dysfunctional Aspects of Government Bureaucracy," in *Modern Japanese Organization and Decision-Making*, ed. Vogel, p. 23.

28. Pascale and Athos, *The Art of Japanese Management*, pp. 131–32.

29. Ibid., p. 112.

30. Craig, "Functional and Dysfunctional Aspects of Government Bureaucracy," p. 24.

31. Furstenberg, *Why the Japanese Have Been So Successful in Business*, p. 72.

32. Rohlen, *For Harmony and Strength*, p. 101.

33. Clark, *The Japanese Company*, p. 181.

34. Rohlen, *For Harmony and Strength*, p. 101.

35. Marsh and Mannari, *Modernization and the Japanese Factory*, p. 255.

36. van Helvoort, *The Japanese Working Man*, p. 120.

37. Pascale and Athos, *The Art of Japanese Management*, p. 55.

38. Ibid.

39. Gray, "Japan, Corporate Strategies for the 1980s," p. 29.

40. Furstenberg, *Why the Japanese Have Been So Successful in Business*, pp. 57–58.

41. Gray, "Japan, Corporate Strategies for the 1980s," p. 45.

42. Haneda and Shima, "Japanese Communication Behavior as Reflected in Letter Writing," p. 23.

43. Gibney, *Japan*, p. 152.

44. Tanako, as presented in Johnston, "Business Communication in Japan," pp. 66–67.

45. De Mente, *How to Do Business in Japan*, p. 28.

46. Gibney, *Japan*, p. 152.

47. Haneda and Shima, "Japanese Communication Behavior as Reflected in Letter Writing," pp. 25–26.

48. Imai, *16 Ways to Avoid Saying No*, p. 43.

49. Yoshino, *Japan's Managerial System*, p. 208.

50. Craig, "Functional and Dysfunctional Aspects of Government Bureaucracy," p. 14.

PART II

THE UNITED STATES AND THE AMERICAN CORPORATION

7

Communication in the American Corporation

Communication, defined previously as transferring thought from one individual to another, is important in all human activity. Berlo reports that the average American spends about 70 percent of waking hours communicating verbally—listening, speaking, reading, and writing, in that order. Each person spends about eleven hours a day, every day, performing verbal communication behaviors.[1] A good portion of that time is spent on the job, where communication is intensified and expanded.

American executives devote 94 percent of their time in communication-related activities, according to George Plotzke, market manager of AT&T's technology group. Oral communication accounts for 69 percent of that time, with 53 percent spent in face-to-face meetings and 16 percent on the telephone. Dealing with written material and mail accounts for 25 percent of their time, and problem solving, planning, and idea work account for 3 percent. Middle managers spend somewhat less time communicating—80 percent for middle managers and 70 percent for first-line managers.[2]

Although communication is thus crucial to organizational life, its importance has been all but overlooked until recently in the history of organizations. After a brief look at the history of communication in the American corporation, we look at the typical corporate communication system, formal and informal, and at the communication policy which should be the basis of organizational communication programs.

A BRIEF HISTORY

In the early nineteenth century, when numerous companies were experiencing the kind of expansion that required greater control by fewer people, an approach that became known as scientific management arose. Frederick W. Taylor originated the techniques in *Principles of Scientific Management*, published in 1911, a book that systematized the work place for greater productivity and profitability. Prior to this, explain Rogers and Agarwala-Rogers, was the "development of a body of management principles by the managers of businesses and industries and by professors at the business schools in the United States universities, influenced somewhat by European authors like Henri Fayol. Most of these principles were very simple by today's standards, such as the admonition to 'plan ahead.' "[3]

Another theorist who contributed considerably to this school was Frank Gilbreth, whose time and motion studies prompted him to prepare a list of seventeen therbligs (his name spelled backward with an "s" added and the "th" reversed), which included the motions that permitted any job to be performed most efficiently. His wife, Lillian, in addition to giving him twelve children—the book *Cheaper by the Dozen* was written about their family by one of the daughters—wrote *The Psychology of Management* in 1914, thus beginning, many believe, the field of industrial psychology.

The scientific management school was successful. So well, in fact, did these theorists succeed that they turned the human operators of the machinery into just another interchangeable part. The employees' humanness was ignored, an attitude that unfortunately remains in many American corporations today.

In 1927, Harvard University Researchers Elton Mayo, Fritz Roethlisberger, and William Dickson went to the Hawthorne Works of Western Electric Company in Illinois to test some of Taylor's ideas. They increased the lighting in a room into which some workers had been moved, and, as expected, productivity increased. They increased the number of breaks in the day, and productivity increased. They lengthened the lunch break, and productivity increased. They were pleased with the results.

Then something strange happened. When they reduced the lighting in the room, productivity increased. When they reduced the number of breaks in the day, productivity increased. When they shortened the lunch break, productivity increased. Some other part of the job than the controlled variables was making the difference. What was it? They decided, after much study, that it was the human factor. For the first time the employees were being attended to like human beings; it didn't matter that the changes were negative. Thus began the human relations school of management thinking.

The human relations school focuses on the human element rather than the mechanical operations of the plant, on interrelationships of people rather than machines, on human needs rather than job requirements.

Douglas McGregor in *The Human Side of Enterprise* applied the term *Theory X* to the scientific management school and *Theory Y* to the human relations school. Theory X assumptions are:

1. The average human being has an inherent dislike of work and will avoid it if he can.
2. Because of this human characteristic of dislike of work, most people must be coerced, controlled, directed, threatened with punishment to get them to put forth adequate effort toward the achievement of organizational objectives.
3. The average human being prefers to be directed, wishes to avoid responsibility, has relatively little ambition, wants security above all.[4]

Theory Y assumptions are:

1. The expenditure of physical and mental effort in work is as natural as play or rest. The average human being does not inherently dislike work.
2. External control and the threat of punishment are not the only means for bringing about effort toward organizational objectives. Man will exercise self-direction and self-control in the service of objectives to which he is committed.
3. Commitment to objectives is a function of the rewards associated with their achievement. The most significant of such rewards, e.g., the satisfaction of ego and self-actualization needs, can be direct products of effort directed toward organizational objectives.
4. The average human being learns, under proper conditions, not only to accept but to seek responsibility. Avoidance of responsibility, lack of ambition, and emphasis on security are generally consequences of experience, not inherent human characteristics.
5. The capacity to exercise a relatively high degree of imagination, ingenuity, and creativity in the solution of organizational problems is widely, not narrowly, distributed in the population.
6. Under the conditions of modern industrial life, the intellectual potentialities of the average human being are only partially utilized.[5]

In the 1960s and 1970s, it became apparent that in certain situations the scientific management approach worked well; in others, the human relations approach was best. So a new system of thinking emerged. The systems school viewed the organization as a system of interacting and interdependent parts of a whole. It is concerned with the parts only insofar as they affect the whole. "Systems theory," say Daniel Katz and Robert Kahn in *The Social Psychology of Organizations*, "is basically concerned with problems of relationships of structure, and of interdependence rather than with the constant attributes of objects."[6] Communication in the systems school is recognized as an important function in the co-ordination of the independent parts of the system.

Structure

Before World War II, very little attention was paid to communication problems in organizations. Barnard first presented a serious discussion of the communication duties of the business executive. The Hawthorne studies are considered the first attempt to confront problems of employee communication.[7]

In the 1940s, books were written with titles such as *Sharing Information with Employees* by Alexander Heron (1942) and *Effective Communication in Industry* by Paul Pigors (1949). German psychologist Kurt Lewin, recognizing the value of two-way communication, conducted extensive communication research studies on the subject. The American Business Writing Association, the first such professional organization in the field, was formed.

In the 1950s, attention turned to choice of effective media, written or oral, and the respective advantages and disadvantages of each. Particular methods began to be recommended for communicating information from management to employees: employee handbooks, company newspapers and magazines, and bulletin boards. Some experts recommended supplementing these written forms with oral channels, particularly involving first-line supervisors, who were seen as key communicators in the organization.

Also in the 1950s, methods of upward communication received great attention: attitude surveys, suggestion systems, and interviews among them. Management began to realize that employees have ideas for improvement of their own work methods, the basis for the quality circle, which is growing in use and popularity today.

Researchers at this time suggested that the corporate climate created by management could improve or impede communication effectiveness in an organization. To create a positive atmosphere, management was encouraged to build a spirit of interpersonal trust and confidence and to use feedback continuously.

Beginning in the 1960s and continuing until the present there has been an explosion of material on organizational communication from the point of view of numerous other disciplines: psychology, sociology, anthropology, linguistics, social psychology, communication theory, and information technology. These discuss communication not as a linear process but in the context of a changing environment in which communication is an interactive series of behaviors fraught with error. Special attention began to be paid to informal communication, communication

Table 3
Importance of Job Elements, as Seen by Employees and Foremen

Job Element	Employees' Rating	Foremen's Rating
Appreciation of work done	1	8
Feeling "in" on things (full information)	2	10
Help on personal problems	3	9
Job security (steady work)	4	2
Good wages	5	1
Interesting work (belief in importance of job)	6	5
Promotion	7	3
Management loyalty to workers	8	6
Good working conditions	9	4
Tactful disciplining (respectful treatment)	10	7

Source: Merrihue, *Managing by Communication*, p. 42.

barriers, nonverbal communication, and international and intercultural communication.

Willard V. Merrihue reported on one such study which compared the subjects employees considered important with those their foremen thought important. The startling results are shown in Table 3. The top three subjects on the employees' list are lowest on the foremen's list.[8]

In the 1980s, communication is taking on an ever-increasing importance. Figure 4 shows the staff of present day communication departments.

Arnold Brown, president of Weiner, Edrich, Brown, Inc., New York, said this in an article in the *Futurist*:

Human history has been a record of movement from physical power to mental power. Hunting skills were pre-eminent first, then strength and fighting skill, then the ability to accumulate and control wealth. Now we are moving into an age when power resides not in size or weapons or property but in information.

The people who control information—control access to it, control understanding of it, control interpretation of it—are the people who will be the gatekeepers of power in the new age. Their skills will be communication skills. People who recognize this and seek to acquire and perfect skills in communication will be able to survive—and thrive—in the coming communication age.[9]

An article, "Work Won't Be the Same Again," in *Fortune*, June 28, 1982, begins; "The U.S. is well launched on the voyage from the industrial age into the information age."[10] Dr. Howard Hess, corporate

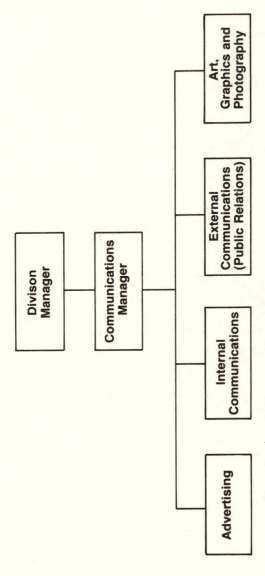

Figure 4. A typical communication department includes at least these sections.

psychiatrist of Western Electric Company, said in addressing the International Association of Business Communicators: "As we move from the industrial age to the information age, management must realize that survival depends on more democracy and better communication in the workplace."[11]

So in the short span of one generation, communication in organizations has progressed from a footnote mention in pre–World War II days to a chapter in the systems school of management of the 1960s and 1970s to the whole book in the 1980s and into the Information Age.

John Bailey, executive director of the International Association of Business Communicators, said in the preface to *Inside Organizational Communication*:

Organizational communication is somewhat akin to the actress who, after spending years in stock, finally lands a Broadway part. She is acclaimed as a surprising new talent, an "overnight" sensation—although she was developing and polishing her talent for years.

Organizational communication has existed for four hundred years. Yet today, almost overnight, communicators are recognized as prime problem solvers, and communication is regarded as a necessity for *all* organizations—large or small, profit or nonprofit, private or public.[12]

Proof that the message is now being heard in American corporations are articles to that effect in corporate publications. Rohm and Haas of Philadelphia recently published the answers of five newly appointed managers to the question, What is the most important message you would give right now to the people in your department? Here in their entirety are the answers:

New Area Manager: I think that the message I'd want to get across has to do with communication. If anybody has a problem, I'd like them to feel free and comfortable about coming into my office and talking about it. I want them to sit down and put everything on the table, to say, "This is my problem, I don't like this, let's talk about it." There's no reason for somebody to feel frustrated in a job when something's bothering him.

Assistant Area Manager: Most of the managers I have seen who are really good are the ones who have open lines of communication, whether with an hourly operator who's just started, or an engineer working in the area, or whoever. People should feel comfortable going to a manager and telling him what they truthfully think without having to mince words or worry about what he says. I'd like all the people working for me to feel they could just stop in when they're passing through the unit. And if they had a gripe, I'd listen to them and get back to them with an answer of some sort, even if it wasn't exactly the answer they wanted.

Manager of Maintenance, Utilities and Stores: The most important aspect is communications. You don't have to be a genius—all you have to be is willing to listen. You'd be amazed at how much better people feel just by getting something off their chest. You owe them an answer, but if they can just talk about what's bothering them, they feel 100 percent better. Even if you have to say "no, and this is why no," they still feel like they've accomplished something, and their outlook changes.

Supervisor of Pilot Plant Operations: For me, supervision is very new. But I feel that if I can open lines of communication both ways—from me to the people who work for me, and from them to me—I'll learn about what goes on in the organization so much more quickly, and I'll be able to do my job a lot better and faster. And I'd like to get to know everyone, to be able to talk to them about the Eagles game, for instance, and not feel that I'm only allowed to talk to them about batches and recordkeeping and business.

Assistant Area Manager: There's something unique in my move to Bristol, compared with that of the other new managers. I come to the job with a lot of field sales and marketing experience, and four years of close-to-plant experience, but no hands-on plant contact. Having worked at the grassroots level with customers, at the operations level with the marketing guys—the people who make selling and pricing decisions—I'm really looking forward to this opportunity to work in the plant, which is the heart of it. I hope to be able to learn the inside plant operations quickly, and good communications will be all the more important for me.[13]

But in efforts to communicate effectively, both business and government produce about 9,700 pages per second of memos, letters, reports, and other materials.[14]

One company reported that home-office employees spend $85,000 per year on postage (not including the cost of freight) and made 5 million Xerox copies a year at a cost of up to six cents a copy. That company reported these paperwork problems of American companies:

- Handling of paperwork and information accounts for 90 percent of all office work.
- Most offices waste about 65 cents per dollar spent on handling records.
- Nineteen of twenty field documents more than five years old are never looked at again.
- 65 percent of all records should be destroyed, 25 should be sent to a records center, and only 10 percent should be retained in the office more than a year.[15]

Printed matter distributed to employees has been estimated to be 215 million copies at any one time, about four times the total daily circulation of daily newspapers in the United States.[16]

Discussing this deluge of written materials in the average corporation, the *iabc news* offered some interesting facts:

- The production, processing, and distribution of information comprises nearly one half of the GNP of the United States.

- Businesses are spending approximately $660 billion a day on office communication. But approximately 80 to 85 percent of this amount is spent on people-related expenses.

- Thirty-one billion original documents and 630 billion pieces of mail, at an average cost of $6.07 a letter, were generated by businesses in 1980.

"By the year 1990," the *news* predicts in the same article, "nearly half of the nation's work force will be employed in the creation, transmission and management of the copious information flow."[17]

Good communicating is the indispensable element to a successful company, and poor communication is at best a provision for lower achievement and at worst for complete failure. Good communication, of course, means open, free-flowing communication. Chris Argyris investigated this subject and found that companies that do not encourage open communication elicit defensiveness and the concealment of important facts needed for effective decision making. Argyris also concluded that lack of openness in communicating reduced employee commitment to organizational goals.[18]

Companies most likely to discourage open communicating are those following scientific management principles. Their communicating is poor, limited to passing directives and commands down the management chain. Rogers and Agarwala-Rogers explain that, in the scientific management school, "communication was to be formal, hierarchical, and planned; its purpose was to get the work done, to increase productivity and efficiency. In sum, Taylorism viewed communication as one-sided and vertical (top-down) and task-related."[19]

The human relations school paid more attention to communication. It knew that good communication improved employee morale and performance. Still it viewed communication as a process for transmitting messages in the organization which, when they went awry, interfered with authority and productivity.

It was the systems school which perceived the importance of communication in the organization. When there are interacting subsystems in the whole, communication between and within each of them becomes extremely important. Communication was viewed as a dynamic element in the formation and operation of the organization. Additional comparisons of communication in the three schools of management thinking as presented by Rogers and Agarwala-Rogers are shown on Table 4.

Gerald Goldhaber has distinguished Theory X and Theory Y companies with regard to their communicating. The Theory X manager behaves this way:

Table 4

Comparison of the Nature of Organizational Communication as Seen by the Three Schools of Organizational Behavior

	Scientific Management School	Human Relations School	Systems School
Importance of communication	Relatively unimportant, and largely restricted to downward communication from management to workers.	Relatively important, but mainly limited to peer communication; some attention to communication of needs from workers to management.	Very important; communication is considered the cement that holds the units in an organization together.
Purpose of communication	To relay orders and information about work tasks, and to achieve obedience and coordination in carrying out such work.	To satisfy workers' needs, to provide for lateral interaction among peers in work groups, and to facilitate the participation of members in organizational decision making. A high degree of receiver orientation in communication from management.	To control and coordinate, and to provide information to decision makers; and to adjust the organization to changes in its environment.
Direction of communication flows	Downward (vertical), from management to workers, in order to persuade or convince them to follow instructions.	Horizontal among peers who belong to informal work groups; vertical between workers and management (1) to assess worker needs, and (2) to make possible participatory decision making.	All directions within the system, including downward and upward across hierarchical levels, and across the organization's boundary with the environment.
Main communication problems thought to exist	Breakdowns in communication due to (1) bypassing a hierarchical level, and (2) a too-large span of control.	Rumors, which are communicated through the "grapevine"; a partially ineffective formal communication structure that is thus supplemented by informal communication.	Overload, distortion, and omission; unresponsiveness to negative feedback.

Source: Rogers and Agarwala-Rogers, *Communication in Organizations*, p. 56.

1. Most messages will flow in a downward direction from the top down through the rest of the organization.
2. Decision making will be concentrated in the hands of a few people toward the top of the organization.
3. Upward communication will be limited to suggestion boxes, grapevines, and "spy systems" (employees who secretly report information about other employees to the manager).
4. Little interaction will take place with his employees and always with fear and distrust.
5. Downward communication will be limited to informative messages and announcements of decisions, thus creating conditions for the grapevine to prosper as a means of supplementing the inadequate messages from above.
6. Since upward communication is almost nonexistent, decision making will often be based on partial and often inaccurate information.[20]

The inevitable result is lack of trust and understanding and an atmosphere of fear. This is not true in the Theory Y organization, in which these communication behaviors are present:

1. Messages travel up, down, and across the organization.
2. Decision making is spread throughout the entire organization. Even important decisions involve inputs from members at *all* levels of the line organization.
3. Since feedback is encouraged in an upward direction—since management "listens"—no supplemental upward system is required.
4. Frequent, honest interaction takes place with employees in an atmosphere of confidence and trust.
5. The flow of messages downward is usually sufficient to satisfy the needs of employees.
6. Decision making is based upon messages from all levels of the organization, thus improving the accuracy and quality of the decisions.[21]

Goldhaber feels all of these are conducive to open communication and an atmosphere of trust and growth.

FORMAL AND INFORMAL SYSTEMS

Every business organization has two systems of communication: formal and informal. The formal system, shown in Figure 5, follows the chain of command. Authority is delegated from one level of the organization to another according to a strict code which includes communication procedures.

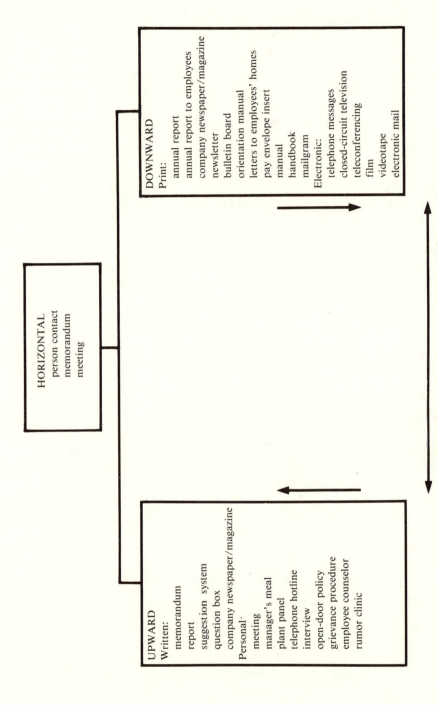

Figure 5. The formal system of communication in the American corporation has changed in recent years with the emergence of electronic media.

The informal organization is found in social relationships of employees. It is neither required nor controlled by management. An informal communication system generally arises in a corporation as a dynamic, variable force running across organizational lines and rapidly changing course. Employees refer to this communication network as the grapevine and to messages it carries as rumors.

Most people misunderstand the relative importance of these systems. "It is erroneous," says Davis, "to consider the chain of command as *the* communication system because it is only one of many influences. Indeed, procedural and social factors are even more important."[22] Thayer stated, "The command function of communication is as pertinent to informal relations as it is to formal relations, although in ways which are probably not as apparent. Informal relations which persist over time...are founded upon mutually understood relationships."[23]

The formal system of communication in the American corporation is described by the directional flow of information through channels: downward, upward, and horizontal. Information is defined as knowledge that contains an element of surprise. If it didn't, why would anyone want it?[24] A channel is the means through which the message travels from the source to the destination.[25]

A superior communicates with his subordinates in downward communication. Channels for downward communication are usually numerous and opportunities for using them unlimited because it is through them that the leaders of the organization tell others whatever it is felt they need to know about the organization. Downward communication is the most studied form of communication in the American business organization.

In upward communication, the members of the organization communicate with their leaders; it provides feedback to management of work being done in the firm. Channels for upward communication are usually fewer than those for downward communication. Apparently there is less need to hear what members of the organization have to say than to say things to them.

Finally, lateral or horizontal communication is that between persons of the same level in the organization. Least attention is paid to this type of communication, even though indications are that more communicating is done horizontally in a business organization than in either the downward or upward direction.

In addition, organizations cannot avoid informal communication between members. The informal system provides additional channels over which members send and receive messages.

Also part of the corporate communication network are communications into the organization in the form of letters, telephone calls, and visits to the company by outsiders, and communications out of the company in the form of letters, telephone calls, and visits outside by employees.

Specific channels of communication take different forms based on the organization and the country in which that organization is located. The communication program in the American business organization is designed for speed and efficiency. As Figure 5 shows, more emphasis is placed on downward communication channels.

Personal contact plays an important part in all three types of communication, though it seems to predominate in lateral communication. Memos are a part of everyday life, but they seem to be more a lateral and upward communication form than downward communication. Important as forms of upward communication are reports, since the primary purpose of that form of communication is reporting to superiors about work of the organization, and interviews of all kinds.

Horizontal communication, usually for the purpose of coordinating work between lateral units in the organization, has few channels: personal contact, memos, and meetings. Finally, downward communication, which both directs employees in their work and apprises them of important company information, receives the most attention in American firms. The most important piece of business communication, the annual report, is included here because most companies use it to communicate with employees and other important publics.

Downward communication is the most common form in American organizations because those at the top have the facilities and status for initiating communication. They also have a greater need to do so and are certainly less inhibited about taking such action.

Messages expand as they move down the management chain. An initial idea of the president or vice-president grows because lower-level executives add the means to achieve an assignment, for example.

Sometimes written messages are issued by top executives to all levels of the organization. Although this presents the kind of distortion that takes place when oral messages are sent down the line, employees are conditioned to believe that communications should come through their immediate supervisors. When they don't, employees quickly begin to lose respect for the supervisors.

The effectiveness of upward communication is directly dependent on the effectiveness of downward communication. Employees today want more than directions in downward communication. They want information on products, services, benefits, competition, and the future of this company whose existence is intertwined with their own. As the amount of information employees receive increases, they tend to want more.

In the organizational hierarchy, the chief executive officer and first-line supervisor make an effort to communicate well. Between them are middle managers, however, most of whom fail to recognize communication as an aspect of their jobs and, as a result, communicate poorly.

Lower-middle managers—from department heads down—are the poorest communicators in any organization. It is in part not their fault in that they receive little information on corporate policies, yet they are expected to explain those policies to subordinates.[26] This was documented in a study in which a message issued by the board of directors was only 20 percent complete by the time it reached the rank and file:[27]

Board of directors	100%
Vice-presidents	63%
General supervisors	56%
Plant managers	40%
General foremen	30%
Workers	20%

The manager who is unable to communicate properly has been called "the most fragile link in the organizational communication system."[28] Since communication is the most important function of management, the whole organization is jeopardized by the uncommunicative manager. Good managers are by nature good communicators who are able to use media that let them communicate and who therefore manage better.[29]

There are numerous other barriers to communication in American business organizations, too many to try to cover here. Some have to do with the nature of the communication; for example, each specialty in the organization has its own special language, which impedes communication between members of different groups.[30]

Other barriers have to do with the culture in general. One is the English language. There are about 800,000 words in the English language, some 800 of which are used in daily conversations. Because the 800 words have 14,000 meanings in total, we have trouble interpreting messages as they are intended.[31]

In some organizations, employees believe it is safer *not* to communicate (and in some companies it is). Sometimes communications, particularly those going up the line, are summarily shut off. Some managers believe it is the subordinates' duty to communicate with them rather than vice versa.[32]

Somewhat related to this is the inability of most Americans to listen well. Very few Americans have learned to concentrate on listening, which is wasteful because studies have shown that we spend 40 to 60 percent of our working day listening[33] and we do it at about 25 percent efficiency.[34]

Another reason we listen poorly on the average is because of our hearing and speaking capabilities. We are able to speak at the rate of

125 words per minute and be understood; if we speak faster, it is gibberish. However, we can listen at a rate four times faster. The result of the discrepancy is that we lose interest and tune out what is being said.

Efforts are being made in organizations today to overcome these and other problems in communicating. Partly because of the emphasis on productivity, communication has become the focus of managerial attention.

The least studied form of corporation communication is lateral communication—that between employees on the same management level. Often it is a tedious process in which a message must be given to your superior, who relays it to the individual on his level to whom your destination reports, who in turn sends it down to that person.

Katz and Kahn point out the importance of horizontal communication in relation to management style. In an authoritarian system, information becomes the property of select groups and can be used to control people at lower levels. In this system there is little horizontal communication between groups. The division executive, for example, knows about his department heads and their respective areas, but each of them knows little or nothing about one another's areas. That leaves the division executive in a powerful position to manipulate and control them as he wishes.[35]

For those who report to the same superior, the process is simpler. It simply involves getting the employees together in meetings and conferences weekly to allow them to communicate with one another about what they are working on.

In addition to that formal system of communication, the American corporation has an informal system, the grapevine. We think of the grapevine as supplementing the formal system, which misleads because studies have shown that more than half and sometimes as much as 85 percent of information circulating in an organization is being transmitted on the grapevine.

According to Keith Davis of Arizona State University, the term *grapevine* can be traced back to the Civil War custom of hanging telegraph lines loosely from tree to tree like a grapevine. Messages were often garbled, and false information was attributed to the grapevine.[36]

Davis has also shown that information on the grapevine moves in clusters. That is, one person tells three or four others, only some of whom pass it along. That grouping is called a cluster; the whole process is called a cluster chain. By the time information reaches the fourth cluster, Davis says, it is only 5 percent complete. Overall, however, information passed along this informal network is from 75 to 95 percent accurate.[37]

Nonverbal communication theorists estimate that 93 percent of the emotional content of a verbal message sent orally is transmitted via nonverbal channels.[38] Nonverbal communication in the business organization includes clothing, space, time, and touching. Voice tones also convey messages nonverbally, independent of the words being said. Exactly the same words can be said in ways that nonverbally suggest whether the speaker is pleased or displeased, sad or excited, depressed or enthusiastic.

If the male employee wishes to communicate competency and authority, he should wear a gray or dark blue suit, according to John Molloy in *Dress for Success*. Never should a man wear a green suit, and brown suits are acceptable only in certain areas of the country, such as California. The female employee, covered by Molloy in *The Woman's Dress for Success Book*, should decide whether she wishes to concentrate on the bedroom or the boardroom. If the latter, she must emulate male dress as much as possible. She must never accentuate her sexuality by wearing a sweater or a pantsuit. Instead, two-piece, conservative suits should be her daily dress.

Space and control of personal space communicate. At Bell Laboratories, nonsupervisory personnel had offices—usually shared with at least one other person—with clear glass in the door. The lower half of the glass in the doors of the private offices of supervisors was frosted so that you had to stand on tiptoes to see in. Department heads had all of the glass in their office doors frosted so that you couldn't see inside but you could still hear what was going on in there if you listened carefully. Executive directors had a wooden door to their offices; you couldn't see inside or hear what was going on in there.

To improve productivity, some designers advocate an "open landscape system," which has been used widely in Germany and Japan. In it, there are no enclosed offices; the appearance of private offices is achieved through use of panels, partitions, furniture, and accessories. There are no floor-to-ceiling separations of any kind. Middle managers oppose the system. Private offices, to them, are a status symbol.

A Stanford Research study showed that in 1977, 18 percent of American offices had open plan systems. In that year, 65 percent of new office buildings used the system. The National Office Products Association, which commissioned the study, predicts that by 1989 half of the offices in the United States will use the open plan.[39] The open plan is more productive because it is so flexible. It can be altered to accommodate any combination of departments, communication flow, or work routine.

There are two aspects of nonverbal communication that should be understood. One is that it is impossible not to communicate. Nonverbal communication cues are always being received. Even if you shut yourself up at home and try not seeing anyone you are communicating. All behavior contains message value.[40] Also, when there is a conflict between a verbal message and a nonverbal one, you should believe the nonverbal one, which can't be fabricated as can the verbal message.

These important facts are overlooked by most American businesspersons, who communicate verbally rather badly and have almost no comprehension of nonverbal messages. The result is a loss of much of any message received.

Some companies are beginning to do something about teaching employees how to intercept nonverbal messages. Salesmen at Midland Mutual Life Insurance Company are being taught how to read body language when communicating with potential customers. Knowing what the prospect is saying can make the difference between a sale and a disappointment. They are being told, for example, that a person touching the nose probably doesn't believe what you are saying. A good sign, on the other hand, is touching the policy, an indication the prospect wants to own it.[41]

COMMUNICATION POLICY

The basis for the communication system of a business organization is the corporate communication policy, preferably in written form. The communication policy should express a set of objectives management wishes to achieve in and through its communication program and should include guidelines to be followed in decision making about communication issues.[42] Its value to an organization is obvious; however, many companies do not have one, at least in written form. The danger there is that each manager is then free to create a policy for himself or herself.

Part of a survey I recently conducted of Fortune 500 companies on the subject of their corporate communication policies revealed that only half of the 111 respondents have a written communication policy:

56 yes	50.4%
53 no	47.8%
2 no answer	1.8%

Interestingly, they had previously been asked whether they felt their companies' communication programs were well defined, and they answered differently:

80 yes	72.1%
24 no	21.6%
4 not sure	3.6%
3 no answer	2.7%

Some respondents felt their unwritten communication policies are well defined. Some explained why. James H. Mayes, director of publications, Standard Oil Company (Indiana), said this:

As you will note, we do not now have a written communication policy. For many years, we did have. What we found was simply this: To be meaningful, a communication policy must look ahead several years, and be tied closely to the operating and financial goals of the company it is designed to serve. Otherwise, it becomes merely a platitudinous, and often times self-serving, statement of the obvious. In years gone by, we labored mightily to create a policy which we felt tied communication goals to corporate goals. After some experimentation, we found that a five-year plan, revised annually, fit our pistol about right.

Then came the '73–'74 oil embargo, a rapid downturn in the petroleum industry's public image, and—for us—a departmental reorganization and new leadership. All this was happening simultaneously, and in the ensuing confusion our communication policy was overlooked for a period of time. When we again took a cold, hard look at our written communications statement, we realized that our policy—actually more a program, perhaps—was largely lacking in value insofar as keeping our communication in tune with company objectives. Frankly, we let it die a quiet death, and do not believe that we have ever been the worse for having done so.

During those years that we *did* have a written policy, I was very much the advocate. I can recall having given talks to IABC groups in which I maintained that a communications program without written objectives was no program at all. And I still believe that written policies can be extremely valuable in those companies where management must be persuaded that good communications are necessary to the achievement of their corporate goals. The oil industry learned this the hard way, and I doubt that we will ever again be faced with the necessity of selling our management on the idea of communicating.

Today, Standard Oil and its Amoco subsidiaries communicate with a variety of audiences through a variety of verbal and written media. We have employee publications in each of our major field locations (some 30 of them), a tabloid for General Office employees, another for our annuitants, and a flagship magazine that goes to all our employees worldwide. We also publish a shareholder magazine that goes to all our employees as well as shareholders; all employees receive the annual report and quarterly financial reports. We have a magazine for our dealers and a tabloid for our jobber organization. We have an effective speakers' program through which our employees are trained to speak to the public, special audio-visual programs dealing with public issues affecting the company and industry, and communication experts who address district (field) level employees at least once each year.

Communications activities are given direction by the General Office, but considerable latitude is given field locations in developing and implementing communication programs that will be best received by their respective audiences. For example, a monthly *Communicators' Digest* is prepared in the General Office for the direction and information of our field communicators. Each of the field publications are critiqued on a regular basis, and plaudits (or constructive criticism) are given routinely. Every other year we bring all our communications people together for a two-and-a-half-day workshop seminar that reviews writing, editing, and production techniques. We also publish our own stylebook.

I've most likely omitted some aspects of our communications program, but the point I'm attempting to make is that ours is a fairly sophisticated and comprehensive program, well established and running smoothly—all without "benefit" of a written communications policy.[43]

W. E. Wilson, a special assistant in corporate marketing of Hyster Company, Portland, Oregon, said about his company's communications program that formalized communication with employees has been spotty and the subject of much discussion. Technical analysis would rate it poor, Wilson explained, but an attitude exists which transcends the information-distribution process normally termed communications.

Six years ago the company experienced the kind of readjustment, he said, which reached epidemic proportions for American businesses in the mid-seventies. Problems were both internal and external, so marketing created a program called "Turnaround" to dramatize for dealers and their salesmen the need to approach the marketplace with positive, enthusiastic modes and moods.

Company officers then made the theme a rallying cry to persuade employees to improve productivity. In the process, they formed a team, including the president, which met and talked with all but a handful of the company's 6,000 U.S. employees, in about three weeks. That meant travel to Kentucky, Alabama, Illinois, and Indiana, going nonstop to catch swing and graveyard shifts, when employees are available, in groups of 50 to 75 people. The response was great, and the program turned out to be one of the best communication devices ever—primarily because it was genuine and management was completely open about the company and its current position.

The important point, Wilson stressed, is that the program wasn't part of an overall communications plan; instead it responded to the "need to know" on the part of employees, dealers, and others with a personal stake in the company's fortunes. While the proper response to a situation is not considered a substitute for regular communication, that attitude is necessary for successful execution of either.

Wilson said the company is attempting another effort to publish a satisfactory vehicle for employee communications. It is expected to be one which will barely scratch the surface of the information the company might profitably communicate; however, with a worldwide audience, and policies which of necessity are fractionated by localized procedures between different countries and even between different American areas, the company feels it has few alternatives. Wilson sees the ideal as a separate publication for each plant city, but the company finds that too costly.[44]

The experiences of those companies prove persuasively that it is possible to carry on communications programs successfully without a written communication policy. Here are some equally convincing views from companies which follow the guidelines of such a policy. First, Donald A.

Easterly, general manager, Corporate Communications, Armco, Inc., Middletown, Ohio, states this about his company's approach:

Our company's basic communications policy rests upon the Armco Policies, which were formally promulgated by the Board of Directors in 1919, and formally reaffirmed in 1969.

Improved internal communications and greater emphasis on Armco Policies as our management fundamentals are among our continuing objectives for the company during this decade. Both objectives have been reinforced by establishment of an Armco Education Center effective July 1, 1981. When our Education Center achieves full operational status, training can be provided for up to 4,000 supervisory-level employees, with Armco Policies and Culture a fundamental theme.

In addition, our Corporate Communications Department provides business unit managers and communicators with manuals which outline procedures for establishing plant newsletters, newspapers, and other internal communications tools, as well as providing specific guidelines for dealing with news media.[45]

The response by Robert Edward Brown, manager of business communications, W. R. Grace & Company, stated a fact of corporate life which I noticed to be true when I was in industry and which several writers on the subject corroborate: the top man sets the tone for the whole organization in terms of quantity and openness of communication:

The communications policy of W. R. Grace & Co. really originates with its Chief Executive Officer, Mr. J. Peter Grace. Because Mr. Grace is not only an extraordinarily energetic businessman but an executive who concerns himself with broad issues of political and economic policy, he generates many ideas for speeches, advertisements, and other forms of communications. In addition to Mr. Grace, others at Grace are also original thinkers; obviously every notion could not originate with our CEO.... The company communicates to its own employees through several media, including a number of periodical company publications such as a newsletter, a magazine, and a daily gathering of newspaper stories on Grace operations and activities.[46]

David Orman, manager, Employee Communication, Atlantic Richfield Company, said this very succinctly about his company's communication policy:

Atlantic Richfield has long maintained the belief that informed employees who take pride in their company, their jobs, their fellow employees, and themselves are better workers, more loyal spokespersons for the Company and the industry, happier human beings, and better able to contribute to the profitability of the company.[47]

The manager of employee communication at Western Electric, Emmett Nathan, similarly expressed his company's communication objectives:

It is our goal to promote, through open communication with our employees, customers, and outsiders, a better understanding of our purpose, responsibilities, and actions. Thus, we will help the company maintain its reputation as a business worthy of trust.

It is our goal to monitor and appraise, on a regular basis, the effectiveness of our communications and take action as necessary.[48]

James B. O'Connell, director of internal communications at IBM, responded this way to an inquiry about communication from a former student of mine at California State University, Sacramento:

Our communication philosophy is guided by a basic management belief in respect for the individual. We believe each person is entitled to timely, accurate information about the company, and we try to give people the opportunity to offer their opinions, complaints, and suggestions about management actions.

The best form of communication, we think, is person to person. Consequently, we place great emphasis on meetings—between manager and employee, and larger groups, as appropriate. We supplement this with a wide variety of media, including posted news bulletins, publications, and videotapes.

We feel upward communications is equally important. To accomplish this, we encourage open discussion between managers and employees. We also conduct regular opinion surveys and offer Speak Up and the Open Door.[49]

The Burlington Industries, Inc., Employee Handbook has this to say about communication:

Keeping each other informed is an important job for all of us at Burlington. We will make every effort to keep you up-to-date on matters that affect you and your job. But communication is a two-way street. Your questions, your ideas, and comments are important to the company, too.

Day-to-day, your supervisor is the one who should keep you informed. If you have a question, ask your supervisor. He or she will either answer your question, find the answer, or put you in touch with someone who does know.

Your plant bulletin boards are an important source of information, and you should make it a habit to check them at least once a day.

In addition to bulletin boards, Burlington uses a variety of methods to keep you informed, including departmental and plant meetings, a company newspaper called *The Burlington Look*, plus audiovisual programs such as films, videotapes, and sound/slide shows. Occasionally, you may receive a letter at your home from plant management or a special brochure about company programs and benefits.

You are encouraged to let management know what's on your mind. Listening is part of the job of every supervisor and manager in Burlington. The open door policy means you can talk with anyone in management, and most meetings set aside a special time for questions and answers. You are also invited to send any comments, suggestions or story ideas to the editor of *The Burlington Look* or to your personnel manager.[50]

There is evidence to suggest that the use of written communication policies causes use of "proactive" rather than "reactive" methods of management.[51] There is also some proof that the written policy increases employee participation in communication programs.

General Motors Corporation lists, as part of its written communication policy, these reasons for creating a strong "corporate-wide internal communications program":

In today's critical business and social environment, effective two-way communications between management and employees is needed if we are to have the full support of the entire General Motors team—both on and off the job—in several key areas:

- Better communications will encourage our employees to make a greater contribution to our organizational goals simply because they will have a clearer understanding of these goals and what they mean to their own well-being.
- More effective communications will stimulate increased ideas from employees to help us run the business more efficiently.
- Better communications also will help secure wider support for the corporation's stand on important national and local issues because employees will have the necessary background and facts. As a result, they will be better prepared to defend our positions in contacts with friends, neighbors, and government officials.[52]

Included in "A Handbook for Xerox Managers" is this comment:

Xerox believes that open communications among all levels of employees is essential to the effective operation of the company. The basic intent of our communications programs is to provide Xerox people with the information they need to perform their jobs effectively and to understand the mission and direction of the company and their operating unit.

Xerox also guarantees employees the freedom to express ideas and concerns about their jobs and work environment to management without fear of any adverse effect on job status and working relationships.[53]

The handbook also provides these specific suggestions for managers:

Responsibility for the success of the Xerox communications program is vested in all Xerox managers.

Communications leadership in any Xerox organization is the responsibility of that organization's senior management.

All Xerox managers are responsible to their own managers and to their people for communicating information on the state of business, the tasks and goals of the organization, and the progress of the organization's work.

Xerox managers owe it to their subordinates to pass employee concerns and questions upward and to press for timely and responsive answers.

Xerox managers are responsible to their employees for candid communication regarding the individual's performance and career aspirations, and for resolving misunderstandings of Xerox policy and its applications.

Employee self-esteem, as well as the quality of work life, can only be protected through continuing interpersonal and intergroup communication between employees and management.

It is the responsibility of the senior manager of each Xerox operating unit to maintain an appropriate employee communications program for the organization.

In their communications with their people, all managers have an obligation to be forthright and timely in discussing objectives, results, problems, difficulties, and opportunities.

Make sure your people are aware of and have access to formal company information sources. These include *Xerox World*, our monthly newspaper; *Agenda*, an information journal for managers; periodicals published by the operating groups; and specialized functional publications. Proprietary information should be handled with care, but may be shared with people if it helps them to do their jobs more effectively.

Respond to queries from employees honestly and promptly. If you can't answer a question, be prepared to say, "I don't know the answer, but I'll try to get it for you." Then follow through with a response.

You should support the Open Door Policy. In brief, the policy states that employee concerns that cannot be resolved with the immediate supervisor can be referred to higher management at any level within the company—including the chairman and president.[54]

Atlantic Richfield, in a book entitled *Policies and Public Thoughts*, states its "Policy on Relationships with Employees," including this about communication:

Promote continuous, two-way communications between employees and management....But formal communications programs can't do it all. We must all become listeners and communicators, and it is especially in the supervisor–employee relationship where effective two-way communication must begin. The company is earnestly working on ways to improve daily face-to-face, one-on-one communication of this type—with emphasis on the phrase "two-way."[55]

As shown above and in the additional sample of a communication policy in the Appendix, the written communication policy is best when it is written for the company's present needs and is projected into the future. Ready-written, form policies could not do much more than state general, virtually useless policies.

Most written communication policy statements, however, include a need for regular, open, two-way communication; list some subjects that should and should not be covered; and state who is responsible for carrying out the program—sometimes a corporate communications manager and sometimes all individual managers and supervisors of the company.

Respondents in the survey mentioned earlier were also asked how employees were apprised of the communication policy, if they had one. The order of preference was this:

Regular corporate publications	19
Policy manual	12
Through managers and supervisors	10
Meetings	4
Special periodicals	4

Alarming here are responses that state, "Employees don't have to be aware of this policy," and "Employees do not see the policy. They see the execution of the policy." Other companies make the mistake of withholding this important policy only from employees below the supervisory level.

NOTES

1. Berlo, *The Process of Communication*, p. 1.
2. Tortoriello, Blatt, and DeWine, *Communication in the Organization*, p. 105.
3. Rogers and Agarwala-Rogers, *Communication in Organizations*, p. 29.
4. McGregor, *The Human Side of Enterprise*, as cited in Wren, *The Evolution of Management Thought*, p. 449.
5. Ibid., p. 450.
6. Katz and Kahn, *The Social Psychology of Organizations*, p. 18.
7. Tortoriello, Blatt, and DeWine, *Communication in the Organization*, p. 34.
8. Merrihue, *Managing by Communication*, p. 42.
9. Brown, *The Futurist*, p. 5.
10. Main, "Work Won't Be the Same Again," p. 58.
11. "Don't Let Technology Defeat Productivity," p. 1.
12. Baily, Preface, in *Inside Organizational Communication*, ed. Reuss and Silvis, p. xi.
13. "Good Communication Is Important to These Five," p. 8.
14. Moskowitz, Katz, and Levering, *Everybody's Business*, p. 444.
15. "Paperwork 'Life Cycle' Consumes Time, Dollars," p. 3.
16. Deutsch, *The Human Resources Revolution*, p. 132.
17. "Frenetic, Automated Future Awaits Communicators," p. 1.
18. Housel and Davis, "The Reduction of Upward Organization Distortion." p. 53.
19. Rogers and Agarwala-Rogers, *Communication in Organizations*, p. 34.
20. Goldhaber, *Organizational Communication*, p. 60.
21. Ibid., p. 61.
22. Davis, "Management Communication," p. 49.

23. Thayer, *Communication and Communication Systems*, p. 218.

24. Martino, *Information Systems*, p. 37.

25. Rogers and Agarwala-Rogers, *Communication in Organizations*, p. 12.

26. Brush, "Internal Communications and the New Technology," p. 12.

27. Killian, *Managing by Design*, p. 255.

28. Schneider, Donaghy, and Newman, *Organizational Communication*, p. 54.

29. Brush, "Internal Communications and the New Technology," p. 12.

30. Treece, *Communication for Business and the Professions*, p. 19.

31. Coffin, "Communications for Profitability," in *Communications Downward and Upward*, ed. McNamara, p. 10.

32. Bassett, *The New Face of Communication*, p. 93.

33. Treece, *Communication for Business and the Professions*, p. 99.

34. Wood, "The Give-and-Take of Communication," p. 26.

35. Katz and Kahn, *The Social Psychology of Organizations*, p. 244.

36. Davis, *Human Behavior at Work*, p. 335.

37. Davis, "Care and Cultivation of the Grapevine," p. 46.

38. Hanneman and McEwen, *Communication and Behavior*, p. iv.

39. Bauder, " 'Open Plan' Advocated for Offices," p. B-1.

40. Robbins and Jones, *Effective Communication for Today's Manager*, p. 53.

41. "Elsewhere," *Communication World*, June 1982, p. 20.

42. Timm, *Managerial Communication*, p. 44.

43. Mayes, June 25, 1981, letter.

44. Wilson, comments on questionnaire.

45. Easterly, comments on questionnaire.

46. Brown, June 19, 1981, letter, and comments on questionnaire.

47. Orman, June 17, 1981, letter.

48. Nathan, June 19, 1981, letter.

49. O'Connell, March 16, 1978, letter.

50. "Communication," pp. 10–11.

51. "What Goes with a Formal Communication Policy?" p. 13.

52. General Motors Corporate Communication Policy.

53. "Communications," p. 22.

54. Ibid.

55. "Policy on Relations with Employees," p. 3.

8

Downward Communication in the American Corporation: Print

Downward communication moves from superior to subordinate, whether from the chairman to all employees of the company or from one superior to one subordinate. It is the predominant form of communication in American corporations. In this chapter we discuss print channels of downward communication.

More media carry more messages down the management chart than carry them upward or horizontally combined. That is not to say that formal communications in the business organization are mostly downward or even vertical. Most are horizontal, as noted previously. However most formal ones are downward, as one writer notes: "It is obvious that the bulk of communication in most organizations is downward—directing, instructing, explaining, and the like. The passing on of orders, policies, and plans is the backbone of managerial communication."[1] Katz and Kahn list five purposes of downward communication:

1. Specific task directive: job instructions.
2. Information designed to produce understanding of the task and its relations to other organizational tasks: job rationale.
3. Information about organizational procedures and practices.
4. Feedback to the subordinate about his performance.
5. Information of an ideological character to inculcate a sense of mission: indoctrination of goals.[2]

The day is past in America when items one through three dominate downward communication. Directing is important, but it is no longer

Table 5
Comparison of Employees' Current and Preferred Sources of Information

Current Source of Information		Preferred Source of Information	
%	Source	%	Source
77.5	Grapevine	64.3	Own supervisor
48.0	Bulletin board	57.3	Company newspaper
38.7	Company newspaper	44.5	Interoffice memo
35.1	Interoffice memo	40.2	Employee handbook/ pamphlet
34.2	Employee handbook/ pamphlet	37.6	Bulletin board
32.9	TV, radio, newspaper	36.1	Letter to employees' homes
32.8	Own supervisor	35.4	Top company executive
19.5	Small group meeting	34.6	Small group meeting
19.1	Annual report	14.7	Annual report
12.9	Letter to employees' homes	8.0	TV, radio, newspaper
6.6	Company magazine	6.2	Company magazine
4.6	Top company executive	5.7	Grapevine
3.8	Company news sheet	2.9	Company news sheet

Source: "How Do We Rate: Here's What You Said," p. 2.

the only purpose of information sent down the organizational chart, nor is it even the predominant purpose.

The information employees are requiring to know from management is changing rapidly because they are today a younger, better-educated work force. Among subjects they want to know are facts about new and improved products, fringe benefit programs, sales successes, work of other departments and divisions, status of company products, business trends, competition, and the company's stand on union issues.[3]

Channels available to management for communicating with subordinates are numerous and quite diverse. The primary problem with media in downward communication is their one-way nature, which could be overcome with a comparably strong upward communication system. As we'll see, that is not the case in most American companies.

Another problem is that management frequently misunderstands employee preferences in information sources, as they do employees' attitudes toward various job elements, mentioned in the previous chapter. Table 5 shows sources of information preferred by General Tire Company employees, compared to those they actually have. The survey that determined that is described in an article in *General-ly Speaking*:

A vast majority (77.5 percent) of our employees say that they receive their information from the grapevine. When asked where they would like to get the information from, they rated grapevine at the bottom of the list. The bulletin

Table 6
Subjects About Their Company That Interest Employees

Rank	Subject	Combined Very Interested/ Interested Responses
1	Organizational plans for the future	95.3%
2	Productivity improvement	90.3%
3	Personnel policies and practices	89.8%
4	Job-related information	89.2%
5	Job advancement opportunities	87.9%
6	Effect of external events on my job	87.8%
7	How my job fits into the organization	85.4%
8	Operations outside of my department or division	85.1%
9	How we're doing vs. the competition	83.0%
10	Personnel changes and promotions	81.4%
11	Organizational community involvement	81.3%
12	Organizational stand on current issues	79.5%
13	How the organization uses its profit	78.4%
14	Advertising/promotional plans	77.2%
15	Financial results	76.4%
16	Human interest stories about other employees	70.4%
17	Personal news (birthdays, anniversaries, etc.)	57.0%

Source: "How Are We Doing?" p. 7.

board system is mentioned as the second most popular vehicle of current information sources, followed by *General-ly Speaking* and other forms of print communication. Top company executives and small group meetings are listed by about a third of the respondents, and TV, radio, and newspapers are rated at the bottom of the list. The grapevine is rated last as a preferred source.[4]

In a survey of 32,000 employees of 26 organizations representing nine industry groups in 1982, the International Association of Business Communicators (IABC) determined, as shown in Table 6, what it is employees wish to know. The future and productivity were highest on the list. Personal news, which many companies emphasize heavily, was last.[5]

Some companies, responding to the author's Fortune 500 survey discussed in Chapter 7, listed their downward media. General Motors Manager of Internal Communication Jerry T. Robbins listed these:

- *GM Today*: This monthly, eight-page tabloid is mailed directly to the homes of all employees. With a circulation of approximately 450,000,

GM Today covers corporate and industry business news, technological and product developments, unusual employee achievements, and newsworthy divisional and staff activities.

- *GM Daily Newsline*: Provides a summary of top news stories on GM, the auto industry, and the economy. Information is transmitted daily to GM locations across the United States through a computer system. A daily tape-recorded telephone message also provides the same information for employees.

- *International Newswire*: Includes highlights of international automotive and business stories. Transmitted daily to GM locations overseas.

- *Information Briefs*: Six to eight pages of printed and graphic materials mailed every two weeks to local GM communicators. The materials, bite-size format, are not duplicated elsewhere and are used extensively in local publications.

- *Inside Information*: A monthly, four-page, idea-sharing publication for GM communicators.

- *Issue Update*: Excerpts on selected subjects from executive speeches. Mailed bimonthly to local communicators and members of management.[6]

Similarly, Gordon C. Hamilton, director of public relations services for Texaco, Inc., provided this information:

- *Texaco Star*: Quarterly for stockholders as well as employees and opinion leaders.
- *Texaco Topics*: Bimonthly, for employees.
- *Texaco Marketer*: Quarterly, for retailers and wholesalers.
- *Forum*: Quarterly, for retired employees.
- *Texaco Times*: Monthly, for employees at executive offices.[7]

Hamilton noted that Texaco also sends annual and interim reports to stockholders, employees, and opinion leaders.

In a letter to one of my former students, Kathleen Hyland, director, Public Relations and Advertising, Kaiser Steel, said this about that company's downward communication:

We communicate regularly with our employees—the good news and the bad—via a monthly newspaper, *The Ingot*. This is mailed to the homes of most of our employees, so that their families are presumed to be our readers as well. In one mine location where we have no home addresses for our miners, the paper is distributed at the pay windows, and at our Oakland headquarters office, it is delivered to our employees' desks. . . .

We also publish weekly newsletters at the Fontana Works and at the Oakland headquarters, since the bulk of our employees are located at these two locations. Consequently, the majority of our employees receive at least two routine company publications: the monthly newspaper and the weekly newsletter.

In addition, we post press releases on bulletin boards at all company locations, and we reprint or excerpt in our own publications items about the company which have appeared in the local or national news media. Our policy is to tell our employees everything we tell the press.

We have experimented with daily telephone news programs both at Fontana and at Oakland but after careful study, discontinued these at both locations. The expense was not justified by evident employee interest. For example, calls to the news program at Fontana averaged 200 calls daily—whether the program featured health tips from the plant doctor or news of the company's having filed lawsuits challenging certain environmental regulations. And that's at a location with approximately 8,000 employees.

We also routinely circulate to our management personnel reprints of speeches made by senior members of management and, again, reprint the speeches, in part or in total, in *The Ingot* for the benefit of all our employees.

And, of course, we have the capability of sending letters to our employees' homes. In the recent past, this communications vehicle has been used to send Christmas greetings and news of improvements in the company's employee benefits programs.[8]

James Ferrell, general manager of Hewlett-Packard Company's Manufacturing Division, said this about downward communication in a letter to a student:

The major difficulties encountered in downward communication is utilizing the various layers under you. There is the risk that the message may never reach the lower level.

If you choose to communicate directly, there is the problem assuring that you do not alienate the layers between yourself and the person you are communicating with. You must also be careful of what you say so as not to countermand or cause confusion from what more immediate supervisors have said.[9]

Several writers, like Marshall McLuhan in *The Medium Is the Massage*, have explained how media influence the receiver's perceptions of the message. Douglas Brush asserts, "A ten-minute videotape of a chief executive officer announcing a new corporate policy imparts hundreds of times more information than an audiotape of that same message, which contains hundreds of times more information than a printed text of the message."[10]

The remainder of this chapter will discuss print media used for downward communication purposes. Electronic media will be discussed in the following chapter.

ANNUAL REPORT

Owners of an American corporation are the shareholders, a public the corporation reaches primarily through the annual report, quarterly reports, and the annual meeting. Acknowledged to be the most important of these and the single most important piece of business communication issued by a corporation, the annual report is presented by some companies to employees, among many other publics, including the government and shareholders.

" 'Ten years ago, annual reports were tools of a company's financial department, produced for shareholders and the financial community. Today, they serve as multi-purpose documents,' said Charles Tisdall, president of Tisdall, Clark and Partners, a public relations firm in Toronto."[11]

It is the item in which companies invest the most time and money. Production lead time is nine months, so that a report to be issued in March is begun the previous June. By law, an annual report must be issued 120 days after the end of the fiscal year, but it must also be delivered to shareholders with or prior to delivery of proxy material, which is due at least ten days before the annual meeting. It is felt that shareholders need time to read and understand the contents prior to being asked to vote on important corporate matters at the annual meeting.

As financial editor at Pennsylvania Power & Light Company, I was responsible for the annual report. So urgent was the date of distribution that I made a critical path method chart after learning from the legal department what the distribution date would be. We began in June for a mid-March distribution.

Annual reports include a narrative of the company's progress, if any, in the year and financial tables showing the same thing. At PP&L, I wrote the narrative. Subsequent revisions by the vice-presidents, executive vice-presidents, and president left little that I recognized when the final version was printed.

We then decided what photographs were needed to accompany the text and scheduled them to be taken by our own staff of photographers. We arranged for needed artwork: charts, graphs, drawings, and so forth, and we lined up the printer for a rush job.

The troublesome aspect of scheduling the annual report production was the late availability of financial figures at fiscal year's end. No matter how much we were able to accomplish in advance, there was still much to be done as the deadline date approached. Some companies overcome this handicap by publishing two different booklets: one for the narrative section and another for the financial pages. The narrative can be printed and ready by the time the financial information is ready for printing. Each can then be used for distribution to different publics later as needed.

As a downward communications medium, the annual report emphasizes major points that top management wants to convey. Some companies distribute the report to all employees. The 1981 annual report of the New Brunswick Telephone Company was sent to all employees rather than just those enrolled in the company's stock plan. "An informed employee is a better employee," said Kenneth Cox, chairman and president. In a letter to employees Cox said: "Even though you are not a shareholder, I think it is important you become aware of NBTel's financial performance and the issues facing the company in coming years."[12]

Subjects covered in annual reports that employees also need to know about are executive changes, equal opportunity employment programs and other socially responsible efforts, and current affairs of the company in its markets.

An *iabc news* article stated: "More and more reports are becoming selling pieces for a company's products and services. . . . They are used for marketing public relations, even job recruiting."[13] Wheelabrator-Frye, Inc., of Hampton, New Hampshire, produces each year "An Annual Report for Young People." And companies such as IBM, General Motors Corporation, and AT&T produce annual reports for the blind on audio cassette or record, often with an accompanying braille book.[14]

Many companies are opting for a video annual report. First to innovate in this way was the multinational Emhart Corporation, Farmington, Connecticut, in 1981. Video versions of the annual report are now standard fare for Emhart shareholders.

The company's video experimentation started in 1979, when it beamed a 26-minute highlight digest of its annual meeting to some 10,000 shareholders in the eight states with the highest shareholder population. Some 200 cable TV stations carried the program, relayed from the East Coast via Westar I satellite in geostationary orbit 22,300 miles up. In 1980, the company sent a two-minute news preview of its current annual report to 100 commercial television station business news editors, again using the Westar I satellite as the relay point.

Today the company routinely sends fifteen- to twenty-minute video color cassettes of the annual report to about 300 shareholders, some 50 college and university business schools in the United States, the United Kingdom and Europe—and to approximately 200 corporate and financial executives who request a tape. The company estimates that its audience runs around 3,000 at the present time.

Yet another key use of the video annual reports has been via the company's own in-house network, which embraces 32 locations in eleven countries. Screenings are arranged for employees and/or managers to view the highlights of the past year's activities. The TV reviews have proven to be a pivotal communications asset for the company as it works to create a corporate unity among its 30,000 employees, half of them non-American and including 24 nationalities.[15]

Responses to such telecasts have been negative for some companies because of an overly literal transfer to the film version of the written annual report. The video medium enables the communicator to do a great deal more than is possible with the printed page, however, in the way of personal presentations by executives and the like.

ANNUAL REPORT TO EMPLOYEES

Some companies send copies of the annual report to employees. Others prepare a separate annual report to employees and distribute that instead. Usually, because of obvious differences in quality between the annual report and the annual report to employees, the employees feel somewhat slighted and the medium fails.

The stepchildren of annual reports, annual reports to employees "remain inferior because companies simply do not want to spend as much money on employees as they do on shareholders," said Eileen Golab of the International Association of Business Communicators. Walter Anderson, editor of the *Editor's Newsletter*, said, "Without doubt, it's a rapidly growing communication area, but corporations don't have a really clear idea of *what* they want to communicate. About 50 percent don't even include financial data."[16] This is inconceivable in the document that is supposed to present annual-report content to employees.

A *Ford World* article explained the annual report to employees this way:

"Think of an annual report as a basic form of communication about the health of a company," he [Ford's chief financial officer, Executive Vice-President Will Caldwell] says. "Stockholders are its principal constituents, as are employees, suppliers, dealers, and the financial community."

Typically, Ford's report has three key sections: management's message, reports on each company operation, and the financial section.

"Certainly one should read the message to shareholders to capture its spirit," Caldwell advises. "See if management is confident, enthusiastic, depressed, discouraged or whatever....

"The financial community reads the financial section very carefully, but it's also very important to read and understand the footnotes in context," he adds. "Ten or fifteen years ago profits or losses from foreign exchange, for example, were practically nonevents, but not today. Without understanding the footnotes, one might interpret results from two different companies quite differently from what they are."[17]

Some companies include the annual report to employees in a special issue of the company magazine or newspaper. In the April 1982 issue of *The Springs Bulletin*, Springs Mills, Inc., of Fort Mill, South Carolina, seven pages (of twelve) were devoted to an annual report to employees. It is filled with large pictures, all black and white, of employees and the same kind of text and charts and graphs one expects to find in an annual report.

Similarly, the *Schering-Plough World* of the Schering-Plough Corporation of Kenilworth, New Jersey, covered the annual report to employees in eight of twelve pages of its March 1982 issue. Again it was filled with excellent pictures and text; however, like *The Springs Bulletin*, it has nothing close to the opulence of a regular annual report.

Several corporations devote entire issues of the house publication to an annual report to employees:

- *AlcoaNews*, Aluminum Corporation of America, Pittsburgh, March 1982.
- *fyi*, SCM Corporation, New York, special edition.
- *Lever Standard*, Lever Brothers Company, New York, March 5, 1981.

Among companies which followed the more conventional technique of issuing a special document as an annual report to employees was Nabisco, Inc., of East Hanover, New Jersey, which used simple, direct language to explain how the sales dollar was distributed. The twelve-page report discussed what percentages were spent on employee benefits, dividends to shareholders, advertising, supplies and services, taxes, and so on. Each page included a picture of an employee removing a slice from a pie chart, until the chart comes full circle with "reinvested earnings."[18]

Another company using this approach was Johns-Manville of Denver, which showed employees doing the talking in the annual report to employees. Double-page spreads with handsome black-and-white photographs review the company and life in general from the points of view of a new sales representative, an employee who rejoined the company after a long layoff, a mechanic who recently celebrated his twenty-fifth anniversary with the company, a working mother who is going back to school, and a retired plant manager. Four pages of financial charts and letters from the CEO and president complete the sixteen-page, two-color report. A supplement to the report is a copy of "Understanding Financial Statements," prepared by the New York Stock Exchange.[19]

COMPANY NEWSPAPER/MAGAZINE

Probably the most common form of downward communication in American corporations is a magazine or newspaper. These slick, carefully prepared, professional publications contain messages from top executives, company news, feature stories and general information about employees—marriages, engagements, births, retirements, vacations, and so on. Although the trend is reportedly away from including the latter in such publications, a review of them seems to reveal the opposite. In fact, some companies have introduced entire publications recently which are devoted entirely to news of employees.

When a company has plants in different regions of the country and employees move from one to another, this section of the company publication is particularly welcomed. At Dixie Cup, employees didn't wait for distribution of the *Dixie News* to their offices. Many of them came to my office on publication day to pick up a copy just for this sort of news. A great deal of interest in the company was generated by what many experts consider wasted space in the house publication.

How does a company learn what its employees want to know about the company? It conducts readership surveys of its company magazine or newspaper. For example, R.J. Reynolds Industries, Inc., of Winston-Salem, North Carolina, conducted one for *RJR World*. This is what it learned:

Readers of *RJR World* find the publication a valuable source of information about R.J. Reynolds companies.... About 22 percent of the 5,531 employees and retirees who were sent the questionnaire responded to questions on the content and appearance of the publication.... The survey indicated that nearly all employees take the time to read *RJR World*, with 54 percent reading half or more of each issue. Another 37 percent say they select articles of special interest to read. Only 7 percent say they "skim" through the publication. Overall, *RJR World*'s content and appearance received an 89 percent rating of "excellent" or "good.". . . Employees view *RJR World* as their most valuable source of information about the company. A total of 92 percent rated the publication "very informative" or "somewhat informative" for news about their own company and other operating companies.... About 95 percent of respondents "strongly agreed" or "somewhat agreed" that *RJR World* makes them aware of the various business interests of the company and its broad geographic reach. Survey responses also indicated strong positive attitudes toward the company as a whole. About 90 percent of employees agreed that *RJR World* helps make them proud of the company for which they work.[20]

Emhart Corporation of Farmington, Connecticut, performed a worldwide survey on *Emhart News* by inserting questionnaires in the June 1981 issue. "The *News* was rated either good or excellent by 74 percent of the readers. Some 67 percent reported they read most or all of each issue." Other results were:

- 82 percent of the readers said they found the *News* as easy or easier to read than their local hometown daily newspapers.
- 77 percent said they rated the *News* good or excellent in conveying what they believed to be accurate information.

- 74 percent scored the *News* as good or excellent in conveying useful information about Emhart's worldwide operations and people.

- 54 percent said they wanted to see more "people" stories in the *News*, while 33 percent want more "product" stories. "Financial" stories were only requested by 11 percent.

- Lowest rating was in the category of how often the *News* was read by members of the employee's family. Only 41 percent of employees occasionally or always bring the paper home.[21]

With a better-educated readership, such publications are being forced to cover more serious subjects as feature material. "Suddenly money, financing, and economics are hot topics in organizational publications," reports an article in *iabc news*. "Communicators throughout the United States and Canada are tackling economic issues in terms of how they affect their organization, its employees and their families."[22]

One company found it necessary to include in its publication this message to management: "Supervisors should feel free to use this material for discussion with peers and subordinates." Although anything that encourages communication is certainly commendable, that message included in the publication's masthead seems proof that communication skills in the American corporation are at an elementary level. Supervisors shouldn't have to be told that.

Company publications today have joined the trend toward frankness, focusing on genuine company issues and avoiding propaganda.[23] A survey conducted by Syracuse University found that the company publication staff is enjoying a new independence in the organization from the public relations and personnel functions with which they have historically been connected.[24]

El Paso Electric Company's newspaper *Epeople* conducted a readership survey and found that its readers wanted more stories about people. Next most popular were stories about company policies and changes and employee benefits. Least read were stories about utility or other energy-related topics and anniversary/birthday news. As a source of information about the company, *Epeople* ranked behind memos and letters, bulletin boards, and individual supervisors. The response rate of the survey, mailed to 900 employees, was 25 percent.[25]

Occidental Life replaced its eight-page bimonthly, *The Company Paper*, with *You*, a twelve-page monthly that will focus on the individual experiences and cooperative efforts of the employees. Final issue of *The Company Paper* commented, "Zeroing in on the individual is the best way to show where the strong, positive, and vital growth of a company comes from."[26]

The Ralston Purina Magazine, a two-color bimonthly, is mailed to about

23,000 employees and friends of that company. It contains company- and people-related articles and uses photos liberally.[27]

New Jersey Bell Magazine is a quarterly that reaches 40,000 active and retired employees and selected outside audiences. The four-color publication contains company news and articles on issues within and outside the company which affect employees.[28]

Arcospark is published weekly for Atlantic Richfield Company employees. It contains company and industry news and articles about employees and their jobs.[29]

Some companies are using marketing techniques to try to create interest. One company offers cents-off coupons for company products in its publication. *The Dispatch*, the monthly employee publication of the National Distillers and Chemical Corporation, offers cents-off coupons or a special purchase price on consumer products in each issue. The program is a means of introducing employees to the products of various divisions in the diversified company.[30]

Another technique being used to create interest in the company publication is to charge a small subscription fee for it. Research has shown that employees are willing to pay for the information contained in the house magazine or newspaper. This has been documented in a study of British companies.

A survey of British Association of Industrial Editors showed that 10 percent of British house journals are paid for. Most cost only a few pence, about five cents, which are deducted from the employee's paycheck. That money, along with advertising revenues, offset production costs and are believed to release the publications from management's control.[31]

NEWSLETTER

For special purposes, consultants have long published newsletters for special interest groups. American companies have begun to follow the practice, sometimes even charging a subscription fee.

QDP Report is a new monthly newsletter of Q.D.P., Inc., which presents worldwide developments in quality and productivity improvement programs. Each issue contains 40 to 70 news items, case studies and features of developments and innovations companies use to achieve success in product quality and worker productivity.[32]

Carpenter News, a newsletter of Carpenter Technology Corporation, expanded its coverage with its July 1981 issue to include local news on the two inside pages while continuing to cover corporate news on the outside pages. The change was the result of employee feedback, which indicated a desire for more localized news.[33]

R. J. Reynolds Industries, Inc., publishes *Management Advisory*, a twice-monthly newsletter intended to "develop a sense of family" among the company's 1,200 middle- and upper-level managers worldwide, according to Peter Allen, manager of internal communication. "The R. J. Reynolds companies include tobacco, shipping, oil, and food. Company managers, especially those in foreign locations, often are expected to know something about them all. *Management Advisory* tries to give an overview of the entire organization," Allen explained.[34]

Peter Earle, public affairs planner for Dofasco, Inc., of Hamilton, Ontario, describes his company's *Management Newsletter* as a typewritten publication that "doesn't include a lot of different articles. It is issued monthly from the office of the president to keep 900 first-line managers current on things we think they should know."[35] The newsletter in this company, as in others, supplements a general employee publication, a bulletin board program, and regular meetings among employees.

BULLETIN BOARD

An inexpensive and highly visible form of downward communication, the bulletin board is used to supplement other media. It enjoys high credibility among employees because information posted on it is usually timely and accurate.

From management's standpoint, bulletin boards are desirable because they are flexible and easy to maintain. More important, notices placed on them are read! More than any other medium, the bulletin board allows the company to announce news in printed form quickly.[36]

A survey of 90 percent of the 3,000 employees of Southern Company Services of Atlanta, Georgia, found that its information boards rank second only to the company's monthly publication in readership and credibility among employees. Topics on company boards range from electric utility industry–related business and company news to feature stories and health tips. Stories are coordinated with the company's telephone newsline to avoid duplication.

News and cartoons are changed daily at the company's 43 boards; other items remain on them for from two days to a week. When major events occur in a business day, they are posted as a "Flash" or a "Bulletin." Boards are located near elevators and restrooms so that employees will see them often. The felt boards are covered with Plexiglas.[37]

Bulletin boards at Suncor, Inc., of Toronto, it has been determined, have higher readership than all company publications. Some 80 to 90 percent of employees read items placed on bulletin boards. The boards supplement the weekly employee newsletter, *Newsline*. Special bulletins are posted until publication of the next week's edition of *Newsline*, which carries further details. The newsletter itself is posted in one corner of the boards.[38]

Items posted on bulletin boards at Transaction Technology, Inc., Los Angeles, include company news, job promotions, and news clips of articles on the computer industry or Citibank, the parent company. Other subjects are lists of new employees and notification of recreational activities. The most popular items are photographs taken and submitted by employees, which are enlarged to eight-by-ten-inch color prints and posted with the photographer's name and information on the type of camera and film used. Boards are changed every week, and hot items are posted if something occurs during the week.[39]

Needless to say, there is a proper method of operating a bulletin board program. The boards should be covered and locked so that employees cannot remove items or arbitrarily post items. The name of the person in charge of the program should be indicated on each board so an employee wishing to have an item posted knows who to see about it. Employees should also be told how to obtain copies of posted items. All boards should be similar in design and placed at eye level in well-traveled areas. Items should be short and easily legible.

Bailey Control Company has started a "Know Your Customer" campaign using bulletin boards. The company posts information about important customers, including recent orders, equipment supplied, and key requirements like quality, price, and delivery. More than 2,300 employees in the United States have access to these postings, which are prepared by the public relations department. The marketing department uses the postings to let customers know they are important to Bailey.[40]

OTHER METHODS

Others among the many forms of downward communication in use in American businesses today are the orientation manual, letters to employees' homes, pay envelope inserts, manuals, handbooks, and mailgrams.

Orientation Manual

The orientation manual is usually the first official contact management has with an employee. It is presented to him or her on the first day of work. It contains company rules and policies; information of facilities such as restrooms, supply rooms, and cafeterias; information on benefits; credit union information; and a history of the company. It is intended to be read and kept for future reference. Often it is in looseleaf form for easy changing of outdated pages.

Letters to Employees' Homes

Letters are sometimes sent to employees' homes, mainly to involve the employee's family in his or her job. Studies have shown that when a spouse is involved in the employee's job, the employee is more interested, too.

There are two types of such letters. One is written to a specific employee for a purpose of congratulating, supporting, encouraging, and so on. The other is general and is written to all employees. Some companies send periodic letters from the president as part of their management–employee relations. More often the letter from the president is in response to a particular situation, and it is only written when the need arises. Though an effective way to communicate with employees, these letters should never scold or complain, tell the employee how well he or she is being treated by management, provide the employee with conclusions or opinions instead of facts, or try to influence the employee's political beliefs or actions. A better usage is to communicate a particular employee's value to the company by informing him or her that the paycheck is going to be increased, for example.

Pay Envelope Insert

The pay envelope insert is a sure way to reach all employees; however, if overdone, the technique loses its value. Messages to all employees should be inserted in pay envelopes infrequently to have communicating value. A better use is to communicate with individual employees, explaining that this is the check which has been increased as a result of the raise he received recently, of which he was informed by letter.

Manual

A manual is an integrated system of instructions for reference mainly. A company manual contains a company's basic operating practices, policies, and procedures.

The manual is usually looseleaf rather than bound for easy updating. Its value is that it has a high degree of authority, is formal, legalistic, and systematized, and is a highly formal presentation intended for a limited audience.

Handbook

The handbook is less authoritative, formal, and rigidly controlled than the manual. It is usually pocket-sized and intended for training, ready reference, or dissemination of general information. A manager's handbook, for example, provides each manager with a reference guide for operations of his department. It contains confidential data on department personnel, standard work practices, production schedules, control reports, and departmental objectives.

Mailgram

Mailgram and telegram messages are useful when speed, economy, and a sense of urgency are important. The telegram, as everyone knows, is sent via Western Union with cost depending on length of message. The fastest type of public message service, the telegram is guaranteed to be delivered in five hours. Phone delivery is guaranteed in two hours with a written copy sent in the mail.

The Mailgram was introduced in 1970; it is a cooperative program between Western Union and the Postal Service for delivery of mail in one day. The message is sent by microwave and satellite network to the post office near the recipient's location. There the message is typed and inserted into a distinctive blue and white envelope for delivery overnight.

NOTES

1. Robbins and Jones, *Effective Communication for Today's Manager*, p. 267.
2. Katz and Kahn, *The Social Psychology of Organizations*, p. 239.
3. Deutsch, *The Human Resources Revolution*, p. 135.
4. "How Do We Rate: Here's What You Said," p. 2.
5. "How Are We Doing?" p. 7.
6. Robbins, July 1, 1981, letter.
7. Hamilton, June 19, 1981, letter.
8. Hyland, March 6, 1978, letter.
9. Ferrell, March 10, 1978, letter.
10. Brush, "Internal Communications and the New Technology," pp. 10–11.
11. "Annual Reports Help Sell Organizations," p. 1.
12. "Elsewhere," *iabc news*, May 1982, p. 18.
13. "Annual Reports Help Sell Organizations," p. 1.
14. "Corporations Expand Shareholder Communication," p. 3.
15. "Telecast Annual Report," p. 6.
16. "Employee Annual Reports Rarely Shine," p. 1.
17. "Annual Report: A 'Must' to Read," p. 8.
18. "Employee Annual Reports Grow Up," p. 6.
19. Ibid.
20. "Employee Response Strong to RJR World Readership Survey," p. 10.
21. "Worldwide Survey Profiles Emhart News Readership," p. 4.
22. "Organizational Publications Tackle Economic Issues," p. 10.
23. Deutsch, *The Human Resources Revolution*, p. 131.
24. Ibid., p. 132.
25. "Elsewhere," *iabc news*, January 1982, p. 6.

26. "Elsewhere," *iabc news*, November 1981, p. 14.

27. Emig, "Matching Media with Audience and Message," in *Inside Organizational Communication*, ed. Reuss and Silvis, p. 96.

28. Ibid.

29. Ibid., p. 98.

30. "Elsewhere," *iabc news*, January 1981, p. 16.

31. Aspery, "Would Readers Pay for Your Publication?" pp. 38–39.

32. "Elsewhere," *iabc news*, April 1982, p. 22.

33. "Newsletter Expanded and Localized," p. 1.

34. "Internal Publications Keep Managers Informed." p. 3.

35. Ibid.

36. Anderson, "Bulletin Boards, Exhibits, Hotlines," in *Inside Organizational Communication*, ed. Reuss and Silvis, p. 157.

37. "Bulletin Boards Produce Quick Information," p. 6.

38. Ibid.

39. Ibid.

40. "Elsewhere," *iabc news*, April 1982, p. 16.

9

Downward Communication in the American Corporation: Electronic

Both the oldest, the newest, and, some feel, the most exciting techniques of downward communication are electronic. The growth of the telephone paralleled that of the corporation, at least in America. And modern methods of film making and teleconferencing are rapidly revolutionizing corporate communication today.

Old methods of "talking to" employees through primarily print media have become inadequate. More and more companies are using audiovisual techniques to achieve the same thing more quickly and cheaply.

A survey of its members conducted for the International Association of Business Communicators by the University of Kansas showed that 90 percent of the 406 respondents publish a magazine or newspaper, some more than one, and 57 percent use bulletin boards. About 70 percent use videotapes, and 53 percent are beginning to use other methods such as teleconferencing. Films are used by 44 percent and audiotapes by 38 percent. One-quarter of the respondents maintain telephone hotlines.[1]

"*New Jersey Bell Magazine* is part of that company's overall multimedia program, which includes daily and weekly news programs on closed-circuit television, a weekly employee newspaper, and a twice-monthly management newsletter. Also news bulletins, closed-circuit TV programs, face-to-face discussions, and seminars are all used on an 'as-needed' basis."[2]

Caterpillar Tractor Company wanted to communicate a message to employees in its East Peoria, Illinois, plant to reinforce the concept of quality workmanship. It would also improve communication between management and the hourly employees. While the accepted method a few years ago would have been a special issue of the plant newspaper,

Caterpillar used a 50-minute audio-visual presentation shown around the clock to all shifts at the plant entitled, "You Make the Difference."[3]

The trend today is toward a great deal of diversity in corporate communication programs. In this chapter we discuss the electronic forms of downward communication.

TELEPHONE MESSAGE

The telephone is useful as a channel of communication for two-way exchanges of messages that require immediate responses to ideas. Another common use for the telephone is to reply to a question where no written response is required. Studies show that 60 percent of the people who make telephone calls leave a message, and only about a third of those leave more than just their name and number. So 20 percent get the job done with that one call.[4]

To counteract that, some companies use the voice message service. A *Hercules Mixer* article described that program this way:

Voice Message provides its users with an electronic "box" in which spoken messages can be retrieved when the intended recipient finds it convenient. Safeguards and dial commands protect communication privacy and make it possible to send the same message to more than one person, respond automatically to a sender's message, have messages transmitted outside the Hercules telephone system, or transfer a message to a third party.

Simply put, the system gives the caller command of transmitting the message and gives the recipient command of receiving it.

VMS enhances communication efficiency and increases productivity because:

- It is available 24 hours a day, 7 days a week, from the office, the home, or a remote location. Communication is independent of the recipient's or your location.
- It allows for immediate reply/redirect, which enables the user to handle messages only once.[5]

Increasingly popular in recent years, particularly in companies with employees widely dispersed, is use of a telephone system of communication. The companies make available to employees recorded messages of general company information such as facts on benefits or job openings. Other companies use telephones for suggestion or question systems; for questions, a personal reply is given the next day.

The primary consideration in using this procedure is cost for telephone lines and equipment. Cost is usually more than justified by speed and simplicity of the method. Even though employees consider the reporting honest and appreciate the human connection of the announcements, new information is constantly needed to keep callers interested, making the procedure demanding on communicators' time.

DuPont has a telephone newsline system with a recorded message on company news, emergency weather, and traffic information.[6] San Diego Gas & Electric Company has recently introduced a similar system, as described in its *News Meter Digest*:

News about SDG&E and the energy industry is available on a daily basis on SDG&E's NewsLine, a tape-recorded service provided by Employee Communications Section of the Corporate Communications Department.... NewsLine, which is in service Monday through Friday during the 8 A.M. to 5 P.M. work day, has the capability of being updated at any time to bring employees late-breaking developments on news affecting the company."[7]

Chrysler Corporation has a phone information system, which adds background sounds such as a trial of a new engine to supplement the announcer's voice. Taped messages are changed three times each day. In three years, Chrysler expanded to nineteen telephone lines, handling an average of 18,000 calls a week at a cost of $200 a month, excluding salaries.[8]

Western Electric Company uses a phone information system at plants across the country. It has determined that these are advantageous in carrying up-to-the-minute news, circulating important information swiftly in an emergency, opposing the rumor mill, and boosting employee morale.[9]

At General Electric's Re-entry and Environmental Systems Division's headquarters building in Philadelphia, a telephone system (Dial 6) provides a recorded message, changed daily, of the latest information on division business, closing GE stock and mutual fund prices, and, three times a week, an answer to an employee's question. Each message ends with an invitation to call another number and ask a question. Answers are given immediately, and those of general interest are included in the telephone tape.

This program forced the division to improve other communication channels. For example, managers complained that employees were receiving information from Dial 6 before the managers could answer their questions about it. So the division's *Management Newsletter* began to provide details on subjects a day before they were broadcast on Dial 6.[10]

Atlantic Richfield provides a telephone information system at each plant. The company's "Statement of Policy on Relationships with Employees" states:

Through programs such as Dial 3000 in Philadelphia, Dial 5000 in Dallas, Dial Info at Cherry Point, and Dial Offer in Los Angeles, the company solicits employees' opinions and answers their questions. This opportunity for two-way communication is also available through the Infone and Letters section of the *ArcoSpark*.[11]

General Telephone of Illinois/Wisconsin, to establish better employee communication, developed "WAT's Happening," an employee call-in telephone line, and "Speak Up!" a confidential write-in question-and-answer program. According to the *General News*, the company publication, "WAT's Happening" helps get the latest company news to all employees within minutes. The all-time high number of calls so far is 1,626 in one day. "Speak Up," which averages 150 inquiries a year, is designed to answer those nagging questions employees can't ask supervisors. Employees are assured complete confidentiality.[12]

For companies using the recorded-message system, the length of the message is from two to three minutes, with rotary access handling five callers at a time. Messages are changed daily or weekly and usually can be dialed 24 hours each day. Almost all systems include a call counter.[13]

CLOSED-CIRCUIT TELEVISION

Television has had an enormous impact on how we see the world, how we perceive and internalize information, and what we believe. Information is more readily accepted when it is presented in an audio-visual form simply because this is the way most of us are used to receiving it. Television has also limited our attention span because we are used to a continual reawakening of interest every few minutes.[14]

More and more companies are turning to broadcast media to communicate with employees, but most of them use broadcast media to supplement and not to replace printed media. Today some 300 major companies use the television format regularly.[15] These companies use television in a number of different ways, including news shows.

Bethlehem Steel Company does two news programs a day: "Nine Minutes" and "Nine Minutes Plus." New England Mutual Life Insurance has a video program that substitutes for the company magazine.[16] Xerox's "Private Network"—one of the oldest tape networks in existence—was started in 1973. In the first year, the use of videotape saved 20 percent of what conventional methods would have cost. Now the network, operating out of Rochester, has 300 Sony U-matic systems installed at 200 locations throughout the United States. Primary audience is 22,000, with potential audience of the company's entire work force of 65,000.[17]

Television was originally used only for training purposes, but companies increasingly use it for downward communicating. AT&T, Smith-

Kline Corporation, and First National Bank have covered their annual meetings on in-house television. Dana Corporation of Toledo, Ohio, broadcasts continuously to all top managers its marketing results, the leading economic indicators, balance sheet ratios, the company's cash balance, comparison sales and profit performance with forecasts and last year's results. GE has a closed-circuit television network in 35 major cities, mostly hotel meeting rooms, to save the expense of company-wide conferences.[18]

Another company which taped its annual meeting was Emhart Corporation. It taped the two-and-a-half-hour program and edited it down to a 25-minute tape, adding video clips of plant scenes. Then the company offered it in cassette form to shareholders. The result has been a screening not only by 2,000 shareholders in 23 cities but also by management and employees in 21 U.S. cities and eight foreign nations.[19]

Advantages of closed-circuit television are its reliability and dependability in daily use and its ease of operation. On the other hand, infrequency of use make it expensive and impractical for many corporations.

TELECONFERENCING

Teleconferencing is two-way communication by both video and audio equipment between persons at different locations (see Figures 6 and 7). The system has visual aid transmitting capabilities as well. This system of communication was begun in the 1950s, but it was not economically feasible for most companies to use until just recently. The value to a company today is its savings in time and money for those employees who would otherwise have to travel to distant locations to attend such meetings or conferences. It does, however, eliminate the valuable informal contact between the participants.

In the late 1960s, we used teleconferencing for meetings of the editorial board of *The Bell System Technical Journal* at Bell Laboratories. I was assistant editor, my boss was editor. We met monthly via teleconferencing with members of the editorial board, who were at the company's three New Jersey locations: Murray Hill, Holmdel, and Whippany.

The cameras were sound-activated so that the moment a person at any one of the three plants started to speak, his image appeared on all the screens. A great deal of work was accomplished at those meetings at near the level of efficiency of a personal conference.

Realizing its cost-saving potential, numerous companies have begun to use teleconferencing. Ford Motor Company recently installed a universal conferencing system (UCS) that can link up to 28 company locations anywhere in the world. All it requires is dialing into the universal conferencing bridge, which is the heart of the system. Employees use electronic blackboards to convey diagrams to television screens at all

Figure 6. The QUORUM Teleconferencing Microphone and Loudspeaker, introduced in April 1982, frees participants from the constraints of conventional microphones. The vertical product houses sensitive microphones that reduce echo and extraneous noises. (Reproduced with permission of AT&T.)

Figure 7. Picturephone Meeting Service, a video teleconferencing service, is provided by the Bell System. (Reproduced with permission of AT&T).

locations. The images can be altered or erased at any of the participating plants.[20]

Atlantic Richfield Company has installed a nationwide teleconferencing system, called ARCOvision. It began in 1982 at company headquarters in Los Angeles and offices in Denver and Philadelphia. Within a year, offices in Dallas, Houston, and Anchorage were added.

The system, projected to save the company $5 million annually, was designed by researchers from the Annenberg School of Communication at the University of Southern California. They interviewed 150 ARCO managers and distributed questionnaires to 1,000 managers and professionals. Findings were verified through telephone interviews with one-third of the respondents.

Findings indicated that most company meetings include a maximum of twelve people at any given site, and most presenters use audio-visual aids. In addition to formal meetings, the system can be used for informal sessions to discuss blueprints or other documents. During presentations, one screen projects the image of the presenter, while the second one displays graphics.[21]

Reliance Insurance Company recently used a two-way video teleconference via Picturephone Meeting Service for a long-distance job interview. The Detroit-to-Philadelphia interview by Picturephone realized a 50 percent savings in travel costs. The company has signed a letter of intent to participate in a network of up to 40 earth stations linking company offices across the United States. The network will provide high-speed data transmission capability, full audio-visual teleconferences, and facsimile transmission. The network is expected to save the company $4 million over the next ten years.[22]

General Electric Information Services Company of Rockville, Maryland, recently used an interactive video teleconference to announce a major reorganization of the company's national sales department. The audience of 1,600 employees in 23 cities, using Holiday Inn's Hi-Net system, is believed to have been the largest employee communication teleconference presenting the same message at the same time. Estimates are that bringing the employees together in one city would have cost over a half-million dollars. With the teleconference, the message was sent at one-third that cost, including video production, travel, food, and beverage.

Shell Concada, Ltd., of Toronto, Ontario, recently purchased about fifteen hours of satellite time for a trial teleconference link between offices in Toronto and Calgary, Alberta. It succeeded so well that a proposal for a permanent system is under consideration. The main use for the system will be business meetings with perhaps three or four people involved at each end. They plan to use it for training via teleconferencing and for special occasions such as national sales meetings.[23]

An article in the Hercules Incorporated *Mixer* explained the variety of teleconferencing systems in use today:

There are now three different kinds of teleconferencing being used at Hercules. All of them utilize standard telephone connections.

"Audio conferencing, which often takes the form of a conference call, enables many people at different locations to participate in a telephone conversation at the same time," [Reid L.] Nurenberg [director of advanced office systems] explained. "Audio conferences are simple to arrange and allow for the instant transfer of information.

"The second kind of teleconferencing at Hercules is the electronic blackboard. This is an audio/graphics mechanism which provides a powerful problem-solving, information-sharing tool for researchers and technical designers. Graphic images, such as equations, can be transmitted to a TV monitor at different locations," Nurenberg said.

Used like ordinary blackboards, electronic blackboards integrate surface-sensitive boards, two telephone lines, and standard TV monitors. Chalk strokes are converted to digital data for transmission and are received as images on a video monitor at the other location.

"Graphics drawn on the transmitters' blackboards are clearly displayed on the receivers' TV monitors. The audio portion is transmitted simultaneously on another telephone line, and both the audio and video portions may be recorded and played back with any standard stereo/audio tape recorder. For permanent record, copies of the information on the blackboard may be obtained by connecting a custom-designed printer to the television monitor," said Nurenberg.

Video conferencing is the third teleconference installation at Hercules. It is similar to the network television system . . . it enables people to meet long distance, using video monitors, without losing the valuable advantage of face-to-face communication. . . .

The savings are impressive. For a four-hour meeting in San Francisco requiring the attendance of the Home Office employees, the approximate cost in terms of air fare, lodging, and related expenses would be $2,250. The trip would take approximately 60 hours altogether.

The same meeting . . . could be conducted via the video-conferencing network for $440 and would take only 14 hours of work time to be set up and conducted. The $440 is based on the use of five telephone lines (one audio and four video) for four hours at a cost of $22 an hour for each line. . . .

According to Nurenberg, there are essentially two kinds of video conferencing. . . . They are the slow-scan system, which transmits a still picture every 30 seconds, and the full-motion system, which transmits action pictures. The company is presently using the slow-scan system because of the low cost ($22 per line per hour) compared with $3,000 to $4,000 per hour for full-action video. . . .

Although it transmits still pictures, slow-scan video allows the conference participants to view almost anything—outdoor settings, a flip chart or blackboard, people, objects, or printed documents. It can even be used to look through a microscope. Copies of transmitted information can also be made with this system, which adds to its versatility. . . .

In addition to saving time and money, video conferencing also increases information recall. Studies have shown that the amount of information retained by a person over a period of time is increased when visual and audio techniques are used. For example, after three hours, participants in an oral presentation retain about 70 percent of the information, compared with 85 percent when visuals and audio-tape are used. After three days, the participants' retention rate drops to 10 percent for the oral presentation; in an audio-visual presentation it is 65 percent.

Aside from the obvious savings in time and money, how will teleconferencing benefit business? Among other things, it will increase productivity. The current nationwide slump in productivity is attributable largely to existing office routines and service-oriented activities. A management expert for Booz, Allen & Hamilton, Inc., a New York-based consulting firm, asserts: "Most managers and professionals spend 18 to 30 percent of their time doing what we term less productive tasks—seeking information, seeking people, scheduling. At Hercules, all of these can be reduced through AOS [advanced office systems]."[24]

Specialized uses of teleconferencing include sales meetings and editorial conferences. Hewlett Packard is one company which uses the medium for sales purposes:

HP's first video teleconference was a four-hour product training session for members of the instrument and computers sales force.... The audiences, meeting in specially equipped Holiday Inn conference rooms, had several opportunities throughout the show to ask questions via telephone to an on-camera panel of experts.

Soaring air fares and hotel rates have made video conferencing a logical alternative to in-person gatherings. "When compared to the traditional method of taking the trainers on the road to the sales force, our costs for the teleconference were about half," said Marika Ruumet of HP-TV and producer of the program.

The logistics for a video conference are complex. Meeting rooms must be booked for groups ranging from as small as 6 to as large as 100. Meals must be ordered and telephones installed. Microwave and satellite links must be scheduled and tested to carry the audio and video signals 22,000 miles into space and back to earth. Prerecorded segments of the program must be edited and timed. Dress rehearsals for the show must be staged.

HP's first video conference was labeled a great success, despite some transmission problems with a repeater station feeding the video signal to the satellite part of the program. "Based on feedback from the attendees and the local coordinators, the overall rating of the program came out higher than a regular new product training hour," said Bob Lindsay, coordinator of the program from the computer marketing group.[25]

It was the editorial staff of *Xerox World* which used teleconferencing for a staff meeting between employees in Stamford and the editor of the company's BSG Edition in Xerox Square. "Through an experimental teleconferencing technique which started last month between the two locations, we were able to review the design of the April issue via a simplified form of closed-circuit TV—all without traveling," said an article in the May 1981 edition of the company newspaper. They transmitted the first page first to show the art director how the artwork and text came together. Then they zoomed in on certain sections to show more detail. Changes were discussed. The program was being tested for cost savings with the thought of extending it to Dallas and the West Coast, "if the savings prove out."[26]

A survey on teleconferencing conducted by the International Association of Business Communicators of participants in a teleconference on new communication techniques determined how respondents feel the method is beneficial. Training and status reporting are handled well by the teleconference; negotiation and conflict resolution are not. A questionnaire was mailed to 1,200 attendees of the conference, and 67 percent responded. Only 21 percent said their companies presently use teleconferencing, but 48 percent said their companies are considering it.[27]

Survey results suggested these guidelines for using the teleconference:

- Determine whether one-way or two-way transmission is best by knowing the quality of the interaction required.
- Punctuate the presentation with on-site discussion and questions.
- Choose speakers who are comfortable with and skilled at television presentations.
- Design a format that encourages interaction by limiting the number of sites, providing a local resource/discussion leader, and encouraging discussion among presenters.
- Provide supporting print materials.
- Focus time on fewer topics; favor intensity over diversity.
- Keep transmission time under two hours.[28]

Adele Q. Brown, director of marketing for the JMP Videoconference Group of New York, has said that an affirmative response to six of the following questions means that your company would benefit from teleconferencing.:

1. Are your target audiences scattered across the country or abroad?
2. Do you have a total target audience of 200 persons or more?
3. Can your aggregate audience size be grouped into per location/site sizes of 25 people or more?
4. Is feedback from your viewing audience of critical importance to those presenting the information and those listening on the network?

5. Is the information you have to impart technical, detailed, or full of facts and figures?

6. Do you need to illustrate salient points through role-plays, location shots, still photographs, product demonstrations, or other graphic aids?

7. Do your speakers need to retain a strong and visible presence among your audience?

8. Is your meeting objective one of productivity, motivation, or training?

9. Do your information and communication needs require more frequently scheduled meetings among your target audience than you currently hold?

10. Is your meeting longer than one hour, including a time period for questions from your audience?

11. Do you have at least a two-month planning period before your scheduled meeting?

12. Does your message need to be disseminated quickly, have visual support, and require interaction?

13. Can you estimate the costs involved in displacing key personnel when they are traveling?[29]

Teleconferencing doesn't eliminate all employee travel. Personal meetings are often needed, as are trips to locations for work with equipment or materials. However, the teleconference does reduce the need to travel considerably and does increase company savings.

FILM

Another technique that is gaining in usage is the film. It provides an immediacy to certain situations that is unavailable in other media. It combines all the elements of communication: movement, color, language, drama, and humans.

San Diego Gas and Electric Company produced what is believed to be the first utility-produced safety film, *Danger...Handle with Care*, a 25-minute film which stars seventeen employees and an accident-prone cartoon character. It was made to comply with Public Utility Commission requirements to provide local safety personnel with information on gas and electric accident or safety problems. Used in safety workshops, the film was shot in ten days.[30]

Xerox films an interview with its president to inform employees of problems facing the company.[31]

The catch in using films is that humans tend to compare industrial films with those they've seen in the theater or on television. They overlook a crude chart or slide show, but a movie is viewed differently in more ways than one. Minimum cost for a good film is $150,000.

Ford Motor Company has produced a safety film, *Messages*, featuring employees who have suffered disabling on-the-job injuries: one lost both legs in a railway accident; another lost an arm and shoulder in a conveyer accident; the third lost a hand in a small-press accident. An article in *Ford World* described the film:

> In the film, each man tells about his accident and how it has affected his life. Then their wives talk about the effects on the family. "We decided to make the film because we wanted to make a strong statement about safety," explains Dale Gray, corporate safety manager. "It had to somehow get across the message that safety is not something that can be taken for granted—it requires the full-time attention and commitment of everyone.[32]

The film is being distributed in either 16mm film or videotape for showing to all employees.

VIDEOTAPE

Videotape offers several advantages over other media: the end product is usually of professional quality, electronic editing and special effects can be used, and wide distribution is possible with playback capability during showing. It is easy and inexpensive for personal use, fast and flexible production is possible regardless of content, and the television medium has high viewer credibility. On the other hand, it is a one-way medium permitting no feedback, and it requires a large investment, which inhibits investment of further technological advances.

San Diego Gas and Electric Company produced a film which it uses in orientation of new employees. The nineteen-minute videotape, *Heartbeat of the City*, which describes the role of the company in San Diego and neighboring communities, was named Public Relations Film of the Year by the Public Relations Society of America in November 1982.[33]

Exxon, Travelers Insurance, Bell Telephone, John Hancock, and several other large companies use their own facilities and personnel to prepare regular newscasts.[34] At Exxon's New York headquarters, employees can view a twice-monthly in-depth interview and feature called "Exxon Conversations." Programs have looked at profits, the corporation's search for oil in the Atlantic, and regulations.[35]

Standard Oil Company of California sends each month a 30-minute color video cassette to its many operations. They feature management people discussing significant issues and topics relating to the company. Each costs about $500 to produce. The cassettes are sent to 28 domestic and foreign locations.[36]

DuPont uses videotapes of monthly programs of company news for informal noontime viewing by employees.[37] And AMAX of Greenwich, Connecticut, makes available to employees for use in the home, civic club, or school video cassette programs about the company. For example, "AMAX Story" is an overview of the company—its products, operating divisions, projects, and locations. "Let's Build a Mine" describes AMAX's development of the Henderson mine, considered a model of environmentally sound planning and management.[38]

ELECTRONIC MAIL

An emerging technology that is revolutionizing one area of communication is the sending of messages electronically. Companies use teletypewriters, among other means, to send messages rapidly to one or more persons at other locations. This is the fastest, cheapest, and most efficient means for communicating when the need is immediate and a written record desirable. Although impersonal and one-way, the system of communication allows a time flexibility available in few other systems. A danger is overusing it to send trivial messages.

Companies such as Hewlett-Packard, Palo Alto, California, Citibank of New York, and Johns-Manville Corporation of Denver use it to communicate with their branch offices.[39]

Facsimile equipment has a special light, which scans the material, converting images to electronic pulses. These travel over conventional telephone lines from the sender's office to the receiver's office. There they are converted into sound pulses by placing the telephone receiver into a special acoustical coupler on the facsimile machine. This reverses the "send" process. Incoming pulses are converted back into a visual image of the original. A light etches the image onto a sheet of paper.

A facsimile machine that sends and receives letters in as few as 30 seconds on unattended machines is being used in some companies. The machines used to take four to six minutes to transmit one page. New units skip white space on the page while using standard analog methods of transmission. Other machines convert messages to digital form and compress it for easy transmission.

AMAX recently introduced an interconnection of company word-processing equipment through an internal teletypewriter system to send messages between plants (see Figures 8 and 9).

The system's main function is to send and receive messages electronically. "Instead of getting messages of AMAX's familiar green telex form, they are sent to us from word-processing terminals around the company. We assign them proper headings and transmit," says Rosanne [telecommunications supervisor]. The feature eliminates retyping messages, reduces typographical errors, and increases productivity.

One of the system's advantages, say telex operators . . . is that the machine can be programmed to send messages any time of day. "If we can't get a line at 5 p.m., which is the peak hour for telex communications, we can program the

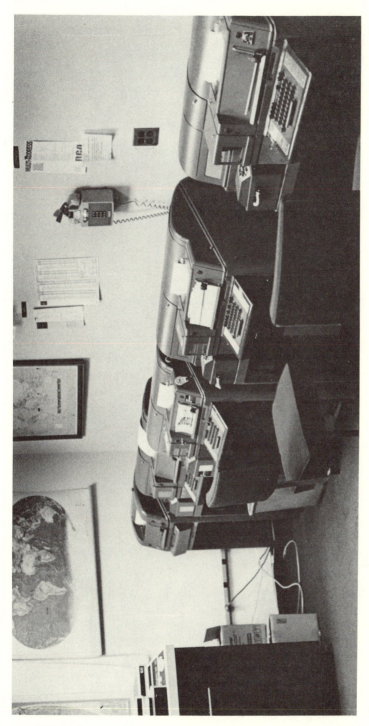

Figures 8 and 9. Before and after views of the transformation at AMAX Inc., Greenwich, Connecticut, of World War II-vintage teletypewriting machines to a state-of-the-art telecommunication system. (Photographs courtesy of AMAX Inc.)

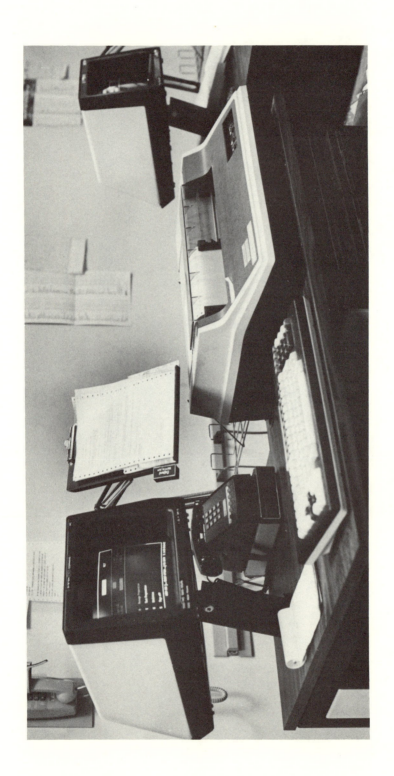

machine to try again at 8 P.M. or any other convenient time," says Virginia [an operator].

The system is also able to send a message to several different locations with minimum operator assistance. "A message going to fifteen or twenty places is assigned various telex numbers and carrier routings. The text is merged with the address list, and the machine, programmed by us to send, dispatches it to each location," says Rosanne. The old mechanical machines required operators to run a paper tape to each location.

These features, plus the addition of a private line to AMAX offices in Australia and Japan, have already reduced the company's monthly telexing costs.

The system's initial success encouraged its expansion, and now many terminals at the center are connected to it. "We receive messages from Digital and Wang processors and are working on connecting Micom," says Rosanne. "Seventy percent of outgoing messages are processed electronically. As everyone becomes aware of what this system can do, that number should grow."[40]

Firestone is introducing a similar system in its Administrative Message Network (AMNET). It will serve the company worldwide. "Any user will be able to send a message to any Firestone location worldwide, but more important the system is cost effective," said an article in *Firestone nonskid*, the company publication.[41]

The U.S. Post Office introduced electronic mail service in 1982. The postal service hoped in the beginning to handle 12 million pieces of mail electronically the first year, a mere dent in the 110 billion pieces of surface mail it handles annually. The service delivers in 24 hours in 95 percent of the cases to any place in the country. In contrast, local mail is delivered now in 24 hours in 95 percent of cases, in 48 hours in 88 percent of mail sent up to 600 miles away, and in 72 hours or more in 89 percent of cases beyond that.[42]

Just how would one go about posting a letter electronically? Assuming you've got a sufficiently big volume of mail, step one is to transfer your outgoing mail, with a computer, onto a suitable storage medium, such as magnetic tape or floppy disc. The data is then transmitted via telephone lines from the mailer to one of the "serving post offices" (SPOs) designated by the customer. The electronic message is then turned into an enveloped letter and delivered by a letter carrier as first-class mail.[43]

Principal users of the Electronic Computer Originated Mail System (E-COM) will be medium- to small-sized companies, public utilities, and any company that sends out computer-generated mail—bills, statements, and notices—in large volume. Today more than 60 percent of the mail sent in the United States is generated by computer for which tapes are sent to a company's mailroom. E-COM could intercept those tapes and do the job better, even at 26 cents per single-page letter.[44]

Communication System (Comsys) has been in use in Hewlett-Packard for over a decade. Almost every HP sales and manufacturing office in the United States, Canada, and overseas is equipped with Comsys and uses it regularly for sales, product orders, financial information, shipping, and delivery functions. Brad Whitworth, internal communication editor, calls it the best time-saver ever. "There's a savings in mailing time and preparation since letters don't have to be typed by the sender and retyped by a secretary. I can key a message in at 9 A.M., have it in our Geneva office in the next hour, and have a confirmation copy back on my desk by noon."[45]

Electronic mail service is offered to small companies by independent communication service companies.

One, CompuServe, Columbus, Ohio, has more than 20,000 customers in the United States and Canada using its EMAIL service and is adding new customers at the rate of 200 a week, according to Richard Baker, editorial director for CompuServe.

EMAIL customers may send messages to each other anywhere in the United States or Canada on any brand of personal computer in the home or office. All they need to do is direct the message to the people they want by indicating the receiver's user ID number. The message is forwarded and stored in the receiver's electronic mailbox. The next time the computer is accessed, the receiver will be notified that a message awaits that can be retrieved on the screen.

EMAIL customers pay an initial, one-time fee of $29.95 and $5 an hour for use. Customers have access to all of CompuServe's computer services for that cost, which, in addition to the electronic mail services, include the Associated Press news wire, electronic editions of eleven major newspapers, the latest information on the stock market, electronic games, shopping, and banking. But the electronic mail system is one of the heaviest uses of CompuServe, said Baker.

One of the special features of EMAIL is the citizen's band simulator. Based on the concept of a citizen's band radio, it allows many speakers to communicate via the computer at once.[46]

Electronic methods of communicating are changing both the nature of business communication in America today and the world of the American corporation itself.

NOTES

1. "Media Use Survey Shows AV Popularity Nudging Print," p. 13.
2. Emig, "Matching Media with Audience and Message," in *Inside Organizational Communication*, ed. Reuss and Silvis, p. 99.
3. Deutsch, *The Human Resources Revolution*, p. 130.
4. Donnelly, "Productivity at the Top," p. 5.
5. "Advanced Office Systems," p. 7.
6. Farinelli, "Fine Tuning Employee Communications," p. 23.
7. "Want Company Information? Dial 2001, or Read FYI Flyers," p. 4.

8. Heyal, *How to Communicate Better with Workers*, p. 378.
9. Whitburn, "An Experimental Telephone Information System," pp. 33–34.
10. Caplan, "Dial 6," pp. 12–13.
11. "Statement of Policy on Relationship with Employees," p. 3.
12. "Elsewhere," *iabc news*, September 1981, p. 12.
13. "Script for the New Trends Session," p. 5.
14. Schwartz, "Want to Plan Livelier Meetings?" p. 18.
15. Hunter, "Organizational Video Use Booms," p. 19.
16. Deutsch, *The Human Resources Revolution*, p. 138.
17. Ibid., p. 139.
18. "Script for the New Trends Session," pp. 2–3.
19. "Satellite Helps Emhart Reach Shareholders," p. 15.
20. "Try Teleconferencing," p. 13.
21. Holtz, "ARCO Installs Internal Teleconferencing System," p. 19.
22. "Elsewhere," *iabc news*, May 1982, p. 18.
23. "Teleconferences Can Cut Communications Costs," p. 9.
24. Mooney, "Getting It All Together," pp. 4–7.
25. "Live from Palo Alto," p. 8.
26. "Sharing Ideas and Information via Television," p. 4.
27. "New Survey Supports Technology," pp. 1, 11.
28. "Survey Suggests Teleconference Guidelines," p. 10.
29. "Six Yesses Mean You Could Use Teleconferencing for Meetings," p. 5.
30. "Employees Star in New Fire-Police Safety Film," p. 1.
31. Farinelli, "Fine Tuning Employee Communication," p. 23.
32. "3 Employees Send 'Messages' in Film," p. 17.
33. "Orientation Film Wins Top Honor in Competition," p. 2.
34. Swindle, *The Business Communicator*, p. 6.
35. Emig, "Matching Media with Audience and Message," p. 100.
36. Deutsch, *The Human Resources Revolution*, p. 138.
37. Farinelli, "Fine Tuning Employee Communication," p. 23.
38. "Videotapes Now Available for Home Use," p. 6.
39. "Electronic Mail Speeds Communication," p. 11.
40. "From Telex to Telecommunications," pp. 2–3.
41. "Telegraph System Can Reach 1000 Locations," p. 3A.
42. "Very Special Delivery," p. 17.
43. Ibid.
44. Ibid., pp. 17–18.
45. "Electronic Mail Speeds Communication," p. 11.
46. Ibid.

10

Upward Communication in the American Corporation

Upward communication is the transmission of information from subordinate to superior, not necessarily one's immediate supervisor. Oral reporting of performance to a supervisor is the most common form of upward communication.

The importance of upward communication is that it provides management with information that is unavailable otherwise, as users of quality circles have discovered. The impressions of the persons "on the front line" and data on their experiences are important to management planning and decision making. Most American managers have only recently begun to realize this.

An employee communication effectiveness survey conducted by the International Association of Business Communicators and Towers, Perrin, Forster and Crosby, Inc., polled 45,000 employees in 40 U.S. and Canadian companies. It found that of the top five major sources of information preferred by employees, four involve face-to-face communication with the immediate supervisor in small group meetings, with top executives and in orientation programs. Lacking in most organizations, according to the survey results, are "formal upward communication programs. Only 55 percent of the survey respondents said their firm's management both talks and listens. As a major current source of information, upward communication programs were ranked last among fifteen possible choices."[1]

THEORY

The effectiveness of upward communication varies directly with the effectiveness of downward communication. Drucker regards upward communication as more important than the downward flow of information:

> Downward communications cannot work and do not work. They come *after* upward communications have successfully been established. They are reaction rather than action, response rather than initiative....The upward communication must first be focused on something that both recipient and emitter can perceive, focused on something that is common to both of them.[2]

William Scholz states:

> Probably the greatest single contribution to improving the atmosphere for good upward communication is the existence of consistent, articulate, and forthright downward communication. Unless the downward communication in an organization sets the tone and establishes the permissive atmosphere, it is absolutely unrealistic to expect that any significant degree of helpful upward communication will take place.[3]

"Permissive atmosphere" refers to a receptivity and accessibility to higher management by their subordinates.

Conversely, it is important for management to realize that adequate downward and horizontal communication depends on good upward communication. Only if the circuit is complete can the organization function properly. "To encourage horizontal communication," states Richard W. Hall, "the department head must play no favorites, demand no special recognition for himself. He must keep the information flowing circularly through his department and vertically from his own to higher sources. He must genuinely want his people to know, respect, and communicate with each other."[4]

Pigors explains the importance of upward communication to the whole organization: "Only if free communication is invited from every level within the enterprise, as well as from the union, can there be expression of meaning as a whole by all who are in a position to contribute to organizational efficiency."[5]

Scholz further reported that the proper atmosphere for upward communication is more than the statement by higher management that it is desirable or welcome. What is needed is evidence that opportunities for upward communication exist and will be improved, that upward communication will be paid attention to, that the skills of all involved in upward communication will be sharpened to eliminate distortion and speed transmission, and that employees' ideas are important factors in the success of the business.[6]

Even more important than the right atmosphere is a conscientious effort by managers to encourage upward communications. Ernest Dale explains:

It is sometimes said that communication is a major part of a manager's job, and so it is.... If he cannot get them [subordinates] to talk freely to him, he may be kept in ignorance of some of the things he should know about—to say nothing of the possibility that he may miss hearing some good ideas. But achieving good communication is clearly part of the directing function, in which the manager attempts to ensure that each of his subordinates contributes as much as he is able to the success of the whole corporation.[7]

Upward communication, then, is important in the two-way flow of communication of corporate information that is similar to an electrical circuit. Says Davis:

The message of the sender is taken by the receiver, who makes a response which is transmitted back to the sender. If the circuit is broken by a poor upward flow, then management loses the following benefits:

1. Stimulation of employee interest and participation.
2. Receipt and use of valuable employee ideas.
3. Reevaluation of how downward communication is accepted.
4. Encouragement to management to understand employee problems and views.
5. More and better information for better evaluation and decision making.[8]

Scholz lists five functions of upward communication of which only number five above is repeated. The others are:

1. It helps employees relieve the pressures and frustrations of the work situation.
2. It enhances employees' sense of participation in the enterprise.
3. It serves as a measure of the effectiveness of downward communication.
4. As a bonus, it suggests more rewarding uses of downward communication for the future.[9]

Earl Planty and William Machaver have suggested that upward communication should include the following:

1. Present employee activities: highlights of their work, achievements, progress, and future job plans.
2. Information on unsolved problems on which employees need help or may require aid in the future.
3. Suggestions for improvements in their own departments or in the company as a whole.
4. Employee attitudes and opinions about their job, their associates, and their company.[10]

Of the content of upward communication, Drucker says:

> One cannot communicate downward anything connected with understanding, let alone with motivation. This requires communication upward, from those who perceive to those who want to reach their perception.... Instead of starting out with what I, that is, the executive, want to get across, the executive should start out by finding out what subordinates want to know, are interested in, are, in other words, receptive to.[11]

Planty and Machaver also suggest that if upward communication is to be successful, these principles must be present:

1. Coverage must be systematic and balanced.
    a. Upward communication must be planned.
    b. It must provide for continuity.
2. The flow of communication must be directed.
    a. It should move step by step up the organization.
    b. It should stop when it reaches the person who can take action on the condition mentioned.
3. Listening must be sensitive and objective.
    a. Listening must try to get employees' ideas and interpretations on the basics of what they think, not what management wants them to think.
    b. Supervisors must seek to get actual, not stated, reasons for complaints.
    c. Superiors must realize that anything they hear has passed through a sieve to win communicator approval.
    d. A superior's body language is as important as words in encouraging or discouraging free upward communication.
    e. Ideas from below must be accepted without condescension.
    f. Superiors must not select only those communications they want to hear and the communicators they want to hear from.
4. Listening must imply action.
    a. Corrective action must be taken. The complaint does not end by letting employees "blow off steam."
    b. Superiors should not agree with employees or appear to do so unless they intend to take corrective action.[12]

Of these principles, numbers three and four are extremely important to good upward communication. They describe the primary element of good corporate communication: listening. Dr. Paul Rankin of Ohio State University reported that we spend 70 percent of the day in verbal communication, which in turn is divided this way: 9 percent of the time writing; 16 percent reading; 30 percent speaking; and 45 percent listening.[13] The important revelation that almost half of verbal communicating is listening should cause us to pay greater attention on this aspect of communication. According to Percy A. Field, listening shows these characteristics:

1. Listening skills vary greatly among individuals.
2. There is a deterioration in listening attention from kindergarten through high school.
3. Males are better listeners than females.
4. People listen much faster than they talk.
5. Listening takes energy.
6. Listening skills can be improved greatly.
7. There are many obstacles to effective listening.
8. On the average, people listen at a low level of efficiency.
9. Bad listening habits result in an emphasis on the faults and a decrease in listening ability.
10. Men are attracted to women who listen interestingly.
11. Listening skills can be taught.
12. The average person remembers very little of what he takes in.[14]

Walter Wiesman calls the supervisor "a listener, a receiver...an interpreter...part of an 'early warning system'...information channel...feedback medium."[15] Zelko and O'Brien list these responsibilities of a manager as receiver:

1. He must attune himself to the sender. This means developing a positive attitude of wanting to understand.
2. He must try to receive, no matter how poorly the message is sent. A rambling letter or disjointed conversation makes receiving difficult, but he must try to receive the message.
3. He must evaluate and analyze as he receives. He will need to look beyond the message for hidden meaning.
4. He must receive objectively.
5. He must be ready to receive at any time.
6. He must take appropriate action on what he receives. If he can't bring about a suggested change, he should tell the sender why.[16]

Top management is obligated to keep all managers, supervisors, and foremen informed. Pigors reports, however, that each man in one of these positions serves as a "communications center." He is both a "transmitter of information and orders downward, and an important receiving station for communication up the line." Pigors states that the manager is often disqualified from transmitting meaning in either direction because he "lacks adequate information about the ideas and purposes of higher management."[17] This is only one of several barriers to good upward communication.

Barriers

The most prevalent barriers to good upward communication in the business organization include these as listed by several authors, including Merrihue:

1. Faulty organization with too many levels.
2. Specialization of task functions, fundamental to all organizations. This has the effect of complicating and thus perplexing the exchange of information in organizations.
3. The filter effect.
4. The tendency of associates to surround the head man with a "brass curtain."
5. Unfavorable climate for upward communication created by the head man.
6. Failure to act on receipt of bad news from below.
7. Regarding critical comment by employees as a healthy blowing off of steam.
8. Lack of confidence by employees in the motives and integrity of their top management.
9. Lack of understanding from top management of the true objectives or needs of the employees.
10. Poor listening habits at every level.
11. Lack of formalized mechanisms for getting employees' reactions, questions, and ideas.[18]

A few of these deserve closer attention.

Too Many Levels

In a large company, the chain of command from top to bottom consists on the average of from six to ten persons. That in itself becomes a barrier to good communication and creates closely related barriers.

Going up the chain of command seems longer than coming down because upward information travels slowly. It is subject to more delay, filtering, and dilution. The condition worsens as the size of the company increases, as Davis reports: "As the firm grows, the management levels increase in number, while the worker levels remain stationary. Communication problems are aggravated by these additional levels because the chain of command is lengthened and complicated."[19]

Status

William H. Read states, "The structuring of groups into hierarchies automatically introduces restraints against free communication, particularly criticism and aggressively toned comments by low-status members toward those in high-status positions."[20]

H. A. Simon and his colleagues report that, in contacts between individuals of different status, "communication from the superior to the subordinate generally takes places more easily than communication from the subordinate to the superior."[21] Although this seems natural and obvious, it has not been recognized in many business organizations until recently. Businesses today are studying upward communication, its structure, and methods of improving it. They have found this to be the situation:

> A suggestion coming from a person of low status will not usually be treated with the same respect and seriousness as one coming from a person of high status....A major reason for discounting the communication of low-status persons is the psychological immaturity of high-status persons....A suggestion stemming from a humble source may be regarded, consciously or unconsciously, as an affront to their position and a challenge to their unfailing wisdom.[22]

A study of the Opinion Research Corporation showed that there is a difference of opinion between managers and workers on the effectiveness of executive action on employee complaints and suggestions. The population was composed of 101 supervisors and 609 other employees of four companies. Eighty-six percent of the supervisors said they "almost always" or "usually" take prompt action on employees' ideas, complaints, and problems. But only 24 percent of the nonsupervisory employees rated their supervisors "good" on their ability to handle employee questions and complaints.[23]

Wiesman says that for a manager or supervisor to be considered a respected upward channel of information by subordinates, higher management must demonstrate that it accepts him as a member of management. Such acceptance is greatly diminished when supervisors are, for example, paid by the hour while the rest of management is salaried. The basis a supervisor needs to function as a key communicator is provided largely by the attitudes and actions of top management.[24]

Filter Effect

Filtering occurs because each level is reluctant to take a problem upward. To do so is considered an admission of failure. Each level therefore delays information about a problem in an effort to decide how to solve it. If the problem can't be solved, then at least the information concerning it can be filtered before it is passed on. By the time this has taken place at several levels, the original communication may be hardly recognizable.

Read reports on research findings which prove the instrumentality of upward communication:

"Lows" behave toward "highs" in a manner designed to maximize good relations and minimize feelings of unease.... Pleasant matters are more likely to be communicated upward than unpleasant ones, achievements are more likely to be passed upward than information about errors or difficulties.... Screening of information passed upward is likely to be at a maximum when the information content is of a type which might reflect negatively upon the competence and thus, indirectly, upon the security or progress of members of the subordinate level.[25]

Schuyler Hoslett states the problem this way:

It is well known that the subordinate tends to tell his superior what the latter is interested in, not to disclose what he doesn't want to hear, and to cover up problems and mistakes which may reflect on the subordinate. He tends to tell the boss those things which will enhance his position and indicate his success in meeting the problems of the day. This creates distortion in the upward flow of communication matched by distortion in the downward flow.[26]

Read says that accurate upward communication was least likely to occur when a subordinate had a strong desire for advancement and when he mistrusted his supervisor.[27] Read also observed that research conducted by "Kelly (1951), Thibaut (1950), and Back, et al. (1950), have shown that selective screening of information from low-to-high status members... serves as a 'psychological substitute' for actual movement upward on the part of aspiring low-status members."[28]

Myopic Manager

Probably the greatest barrier to good upward communication involves the manager who does not recognize any or all of the other barriers to good upward communication. Davis describes him this way:

His status and prestige at the plant are different from the workers'. He probably talks differently and dresses differently. He can freely call a worker to his desk or walk to his work station, but the worker is not equally free to call in his manager. The worker usually lacks the ability to express himself as clearly as the manager, who is better trained and has more practice in communication skills.... Just as the worker lacks technical assistance, he also usually lacks the use of certain media such as plant magazines, public address systems, and meetings. The worker is further impeded because he is talking to a man with whose work and responsibilities he is not familiar. The result is that very little upward communication occurs unless management positively encourages it.[29]

Encouraging Good Upward Communication

What techniques are available to executives inclined toward encouraging upward communication? Merrihue[30] and Scholz[31] each present a list of possibilities, depending on the company's size. A composite list would center on two issues: structure and accountability.

Structure

The structure of the company must be such that it encourages good downward, horizontal, and upward communication. A large measure of this is an intangible. "Somehow an 'atmosphere of approval' for communication must be created, to such a degree that the parties will mutually accept criticism, welcome suggestions, and admit to problems," says Hoslett, "meeting these situations without trading on their formal positions of authority and responsibility. For unless this kind of relationship can be developed, effective communication cannot take place."[32]

Accountability

Merrihue suggests that each successive level of management should be made responsible and held accountable for effective two-way communication.[33] This includes motivating each manager to accept and discharge his responsibility for upward communication by encouraging him to use these techniques.

Good upward communication is becoming the sine qua non of effective management as corporate size increases, business technology expands, and more and more American companies adopt the quality circle. It is a mutually reinforcing process: good upward communication improves management, and effective management provides channels for good upward communication.

W. H. Weiss quotes Rensis Likert, director of the University of Michigan's Institute for Social Research: "It is significant that when we look at organizations today, we find that the greater the group loyalty, the better the supervisor is informed about the attitude, point of view, and situation of his subordinates. Upward communication as well as downward communication is performed significantly better."[34] There is thus a strong relationship between upward communication and work attitude.

Planty and Machaver list these results of an effective upward communication program:

1. Management gets an improved picture of the work, accomplishments, problems, plans, attitudes, and feelings of subordinates at all levels.

2. Before becoming deeply involved, management spots individuals, policies, actions, or assignments which are likely to cause trouble.

3. By helping lower echelons of supervision to improve their selection of those things that are to be communicated upward, management gets them to do a more systematic and useful job of reporting.

4. By welcoming upward communication, management strengthens the only

device for tapping the ideas and help of its subordinates. This gives management a better answer to its problems and eases its own responsibility.

5. By opening the channels upward, management helps the easy flow and acceptance of communications down. Good listening makes good listeners.[35]

The final point above seems to be a key to good upward communication in the business organization. Planty and Machaver agree:

There are many values...that accrue to those managers who listen willingly, who urge their subordinates to talk freely and honestly. Upward communication reveals to them the degree to which ideas passed down are accepted. In addition, it stimulates employees to participate in the operation of their department or unit and, therefore, encourages them to defend the decisions and support the policies cooperatively developed with management. The opportunity for upward communication also encourages employees to contribute valuable ideas for improving departmental or company efficiency. Finally, it is through upward communication that executives and administrators learn to avert the many explosive situations which arise daily in industry.[36]

Unlike the organizational structure of the church, school, union, or government, that of industry is essentially authoritarian. That makes it even more necessary in industry that subordinates be given opportunities to express their views and make their influence felt.

EMPLOYEE ATTITUDE SURVEY

The employee attitude survey is one of the most commonly used and most effective techniques of upward communication. It provides anonymity for the respondent and an opportunity for management to obtain information about selected topics. Through open-ended questions, the employee can express his opinion on anything related to the company. It is considered vital that the results of the survey be reported back to the employee and that he be told in advance that this will occur to ensure his full cooperation. Surveys should be repeated at appropriate intervals to enable management to establish and evaluate trends and to gauge the effectiveness of downward communication.

Joyce Gildea and Myron Emanuel state this about the employee attitude survey:

The communications effort attached to increasing employee performance in any area begins with an exploration of employees' knowledge and perceptions about the current status of that area. Usually, this takes the form of an employee survey. If, for example, reduced waste and improved quality have been established as the organization's goals for an eighteen-month period, the nature and sources of existing waste and quality problems need to be probed from the vantage point of employees at various levels.

The data describing the specific problems are, of course, available from the company's own records. But only employees can enliven the statistics and give dimension to the patterns the numbers may reveal. Their attitudes toward management, their perceptions of the human relations climate, and their expectations ("What's in it for me?") can form the building blocks of a communications approach that will reach and motivate them.[37]

A questionnaire survey is taken regularly at Sandoz. Topics covered include working conditions, employee benefits, salaries, and relations with supervisors. Intent of the survey is to measure overall employee satisfaction and to help identify problem areas within the company.

Bendix conducted an employee survey and reported these results:

The large majority of Bendix employees report a strong sense of loyalty to the company, according to a 1981 opinion survey commissioned by the corporation.

The study, conducted by Yankelovich, Skelly and White, also reported that, given a choice, employees would select Bendix again as a place to work.

More than 2,000 questionnaires were mailed to a random sample of Bendix employees, of which 896—44 percent—responded to the survey. Other major findings included:

- Credibility of Bendix's information is extremely high; more than eight of ten respondents always or usually believe Bendix's communications to employees.
- Bendix's diversification and broad product line are seen as the company's main strengths.
- Bendix is most often described as a major supplier to the worldwide automobile industry and/or a company with impressive financial performance.
- A majority of Bendix employees say it's extremely or very important to know a great deal about the company. Six of ten employees believe the company tries to keep them fully informed or provides information to the extent possible.

Generally, Bendix employees would like to see improvement in both "upward" and "downward" communications. Specifically, they would like more information about competitors, new product developments, future plans for various locations, and technological changes affecting jobs.

The study also reported more than three of five Bendix employees say they are satisfied with their jobs, while one of four reported they would like more opportunities for growth.[38]

Ethyl Corporation's employee attitude survey yielded these results:

Ethyl employees want to know about their company, and they want to hear it from their supervisors and plant managers. They also want to hear both sides of the story on issues that affect the company, and not just the company position. . . .

These were just some of the conclusions of a company-wide communication survey conducted last fall. About 4,700 employees at thirteen locations throughout the United States and Canada were asked their opinions on 75 questions. The Corporate Communications Department initiated the survey in an attempt to identify the communications needs of Ethyl employees. An independent consulting firm, Towers, Perrin, Forster and Crosby, and the International Association of Business Communicators collected and tabulated the nearly 2,000 responses and provided the company with an analysis of the results. . . .

Currently, according to the survey, employees get most of their information from their supervisors, through the "grapevine," and from plant bulletin boards.

While they would prefer to continue getting information from their immediate supervisors, employees like to have small group meetings at which they can share ideas and ask questions. Employees apparently would like to hear more often from the top management of the company.

The "grapevine" did not fare as well among preferred sources. Most employees, according to the survey results, would rather not rely on this type of information. Ethyl employees seem to desire first-hand communications.

As to subjects employees want to know more about, they were given seventeen choices. Ethyl employees ranked highest the desire to know more of Ethyl's plans for the future and how they as employees figure in such plans. Close behind was the desire to know how Ethyl is doing versus the competition. Other interests rated high were: "how-to" information related to the job, how Ethyl can improve productivity, and general personnel policies and practices including benefits and salary administration.[39]

National-Standard Company of Niles, Michigan, conducted its first employee opinion survey in the summer of 1981. When the results were announced in *The Shop Rag*, a quarterly tabloid publishing its first issue, the headline said, "Communication Stinks!" The results called for changes, and the company responded immediately.

Of the 505 employees in National-Standard's three Niles plants, 81 percent gave poor marks to the company's upward communication process, or lack of one. "This is the first time I have ever been asked for an opinion," one employee commented. Another said, "They listen, but don't fix the things that we have discussed and agreed need to be fixed."

In addition, 72 percent of the employees responded negatively to management communication downward, and 64 percent faulted company leadership. "They do a lot of things without any explanation at all, and this gets rumors started and workers mad," an employee said. . . .

"It takes good communication to make an organization work," said Mike Savitske, Niles operations manager. "If we don't have it, we'd better do something about it. And the sooner the better. . . ."

On seeing the survey results, Savitske formed a seven-person task force, con-

sisting of plant managers and union leaders, to tackle the communication problem. After lengthy and sometimes heated discussions, a plan of action emerged.
Basics were reviewed in a letter sent to employees' homes on June 18, and
discussed at greater length in the first issue of *The Shop Rag*, which appeared in
July....

In August, the company initiated "The Daily Wire," a newsgram that includes
"Serving National-Standard Employees Since 1981" in the flag. The daily bulletin, which serves as the basis of the company's new bulletin board program,
devoted its first issues to combating grapevine rumors of plant closings and a
company move to the Sunbelt. Other items covered personal employee news.

"In setting up communication training programs for managers, we started
first with sessions in problem solving and interpretation of the survey results,"
said Christensen [president of the consulting firm that conducted the survey].
"Those were followed by a formal program in interactive management. We also
established a high school equivalency program for the 100 or so employees
without high school diplomas."

"State of the business" meetings started this fall, with managers, union officials,
and randomly selected groups of employees. The intention of the meetings,
according to Savitske, is "to get the facts out there where people can see and
discuss them."

The National-Standard experience provides an interesting parallel with IABC's
1981 Employee Communication Effectiveness Survey, which was conducted by
Towers, Perrin, Forster and Crosby, New York City.

The more than 45,000 U.S. and Canadian employees polled in the survey
indicated that the immediate supervisor and the office grapevine were the major
current sources of organizational information, with top executives in twelfth
place. Their major *preferred* sources of information, in descending order, were
the immediate supervisor, small group meetings, and top executives.[40]

Ford Motor Company conducts a survey of salaried employees every
two or three years to learn their attitudes and opinions. Asked in an
interview published in *Ford World* whether employees see the survey as
an effective way of communicating with management, John Stewart,
manager of education and personnel research, Personnel and Organization Staff, answered,

While they think it is a good way to communicate, they are not optimistic about
actions forthcoming from the survey. This is disappointing because following
the 1978 survey, many actions were taken to respond to local issues. We think
the answer to this situation may be to do a better job of communicating actions
that are taken in response to survey findings.

In the survey, 4,000 Ford employees from all over the United States
were invited to participate after they were selected at random by computers using social security numbers. Almost 80 percent of them completed the 198 questions in the survey, which reportedly took 45 minutes
to an hour to do. Completed forms were deposited in sealed boxes,

which were shipped to Data Decisions, a survey processing firm in Edina, Minnesota, for tabulation. Statistical reports were sent to Ford's Education and Personnel Research Department in world headquarters for analysis. Results were compared to those from previous surveys in 1978, 1976, and 1973. Findings were summarized in a report which went to the Policy and Strategy Committee and, on request, to division and staff management. A four-page survey report was also published in a supplement to the company newspaper, *Ford World*.[41]

NOTES

1. "Meetings Are Versatile Communication Tools," p. 7.
2. Drucker, *Technology, Management and Society*, p. 19.
3. Scholz, *Communication in the Business Organization*, p. 61.
4. Hall, "When a Champ Is a Loser," p. 50.
5. Pigors, *Effective Communication in Industry*, p. 3.
6. Scholz, *Communication in the Business Organization*, pp. 61–62.
7. Dale, *Management Theory and Practice*, p. 6.
8. Davis, *Human Relations in Business*, p. 259.
9. Scholz, *Communication in the Business Organization*, p. 61.
10. Planty and Machaver, "Upward Communication," in *Business and Industrial Communication*, ed. Redding and Sanborn, p. 359.
11. Drucker, *Technology, Management and Society*, p. 16.
12. Planty and Machaver, "Upward Communication," p. 362.
13. Rankin, as cited in Nichols, "Listening is Good Business," p. 2.
14. Field, "The Receiving End of Communication—Listening," in *Managerial Control Through Communication*, ed. Vardaman and Halterman, p. 167.
15. Wiesman, "Effective Communication," p. 724.
16. Zelko and O'Brien, *Management–Employee Communication in Action*, p. 152.
17. Pigors, *Effective Communication in Business*, p. 63.
18. Merrihue, *Managing by Communication*, p. 195.
19. Davis, "Management Communication and the Grapevine," p. 43.
20. Read, "Upward Communication in Industrial Hierarchies," p. 71.
21. Simon, Smithburg, and Thompson, *Public Administration*, p. 235.
22. Ibid., p. 236.
23. Heyal, *How to Communicate Better with Workers*, p. 72.
24. Wiesman, "Effective Communication," p. 725.
25. Read, "Upward Communication in Industrial Hierarchies," p. 71.
26. Hoslett, "Overcoming the Barriers to Communication," pp. 188–89.
27. Read, "Upward Communication in Industrial Hierarchies," p. 71.
28. Ibid.
29. Davis, *Human Relations in Business*, p. 260.
30. Merrihue, *Managing by Communication*, pp. 196–97.
31. Scholz, *Communication in the Business Organization*, pp. 61–62.
32. Hoslett, "Overcoming the Barriers to Communication." p. 189.
33. Merrihue, *Managing by Communication*, p. 197.
34. Weiss, "Breaking the Fear Barrier," p. 64.

35. Planty and Machaver, "Upward Communication," p. 370.

36. Ibid., p. 350.

37. Gildea and Emanuel, "Internal Communications: The Impact on Productivity," p. 11.

38. "Feedback," p. 13.

39. "Survey Indicates Employees Want More 'First-hand' Data," p. 4.

40. "The Shop Rag Improves Communication," *iabc news*, December 1981, p. 7.

41. "Salaried Survey," pp. 1–4.

11

Upward Communication in the American Corporation: Written

Upward communication is the weakest link in the communication system of the average American corporation. Not only do employees lack adequate facilities for sending messages up the management chart, but they are given no incentive whatsoever to try to do it using those facilities that are available to them. In this chapter, we will examine the possibilities for employees to communicate their thoughts in writing to their superiors. Both employees and manageient need to know about these channels, and managers need to pay attention when employees use them with the understanding that using them, as stated in Chapter 10, implies action.

One problem, of course, with written communication of all kinds is keeping them in already full file cabinets. An article in *New Jersey Bell* noted, "In the American business world, it's estimated that 50 million file drawers contain more than 250 billion pieces of paper."[1]

One company that has begun to do something about it is Rohm and Haas Company of Philadelphia, which recently conducted a "Dump Your Documents" campaign. As described in the company newspaper, the campaign was conducted like this:

Simple guidelines were prepared for the "dumpers": the principal target was company confidential documents that were no longer needed, but private and unclassified documents were accepted, too. A hot-line consulting service was set up to help employees interpret the nuances of the guidelines. Research Services provided an ample supply of fiber drums and secured them for transport as they were filled.

"The Spring House [the company's Research Center] effort was an unqualified success," says James Burke, manager of corporate security and research security officer. "Our files are now lean and mean." The crash "weight-loss" program netted more than 100 55-gallon drums full of extraneous paper over the five collection days, says Burke. Numerous B-reports were also returned to Research Records for destruction; some of these documents had previously been reported lost.[2]

Every organization should follow some similar program to clean out files periodically.

MEMORANDUM

The most common form of upward communication in written form is the ubiquitous memorandum. That's the purpose of a memorandum: to convey messages between employees of the same organization. It is internal, as opposed to letters, which are external. The form of the memorandum can be anything from a multipage formal message to a written note on a small piece of paper.

"Memos are especially useful if there is the possibility that information communicated verbally may be forgotten or misunderstood.... A memo is an effective method of expressing appreciation and building good morale within an organization."[3]

REPORT

Another common form of upward communication in an organization is the report. It takes almost unlimited form, depending on who prepares it for whom and for what purpose. A report may be long or short; anything that is six pages or more in length is considered a long report.

The report may be informational, just presenting facts; analytical, analyzing and interpreting those facts for the reader; or persuasive, going one step further and urging the reader to take a definite position on the subject. Reports may be formal, usually equated with the long report, or informal, the short version. It is the latter that proliferate in most American corporations, causing many employees to feel besieged with information—information overload.

Reports are also differentiated by destination—internal or external; by frequency of appearance—annual, quarterly, monthly, and so on; by source—auditor's, salesman's, or any other employee's. The great majority of reports in any business organization are prepared by employees and presented to superiors, usually for decision-making purposes.

At Sandoz Company of Hanover, New Jersey, all divisions and sections submit periodic reports to top management. Although those are written, the preferred policy is the oral report, which provides personal contact and saves time and money. This policy holds where there is little numerical or statistical data required. Should such figures be required, memos or reports are appropriate. The philosophy behind encouraging oral reporting is to reduce distortion as much as possible and encourage interactions between managers and subordinates.

Within the category of the short report, literally hundreds are prepared daily in every business organization: periodic reports, progress reports, memo reports, letter reports, inspection reports, suggestion reports, recommendation reports, proposals, abstracts, minutes, and on and on and on. The most important part in controlling its reporting system is for a company to audit its communications periodically to make sure that all written documents, particularly these kinds of reports, have a legitimate reason for continuing and have not been replaced by other means of communications.

SUGGESTION SYSTEM

The suggestion system is an upward communication process through which employees who see a way to improve their work procedures pass that information up the management chain. This is one of the oldest and most widely used of the formal devices for upward communication.

In the early 1880s, an Englishman named Denny ran an organization that built ships. He let his employees know that if any of them had ideas on how to improve their work to let him know. That is considered the start of today's formal suggestion system.

A few years later, the Yale and Towne Manufacturing Company installed a suggestion box. But the first formal system was that of the National Cash Register Company. It was begun in 1896 and followed two years later by one at the Eastman Kodak Company, which, because it is still operating, is the oldest continuous suggestion system in the United States.

During World War I, suggestion systems received a boost by the government's encouragement of ideas from companies providing war material on how to do the work faster. They were asked to solicit their employees' ideas.

On July 27, 1942, 35 administrators met in Chicago to explore methods, advantages, and values of suggestion systems. They voted to establish a clearinghouse through which organizations could benefit from others' experience. The National Association of Suggestion Systems (NASS) was founded on August 2, 1942. Current membership is nearly 750 firms and organizations representing close to 12 million employees. Ideas are exchanged through periodicals, seminars, and an annual conference.[4]

In suggestion system operations, boxes are placed throughout the organization in high traffic areas, and employees are free to place questions or suggestions in them. Monetary rewards are offered to the employee for the adoption of any suggestion. The suggestor of an idea which saves the company money receives a reward of a certain percentage of the savings in the first year. Supervisors are ineligible. Suitable forms are provided at conveniently located suggestion boxes to facilitate employee participation. In many instances dissatisfaction is the basis for suggestions. By consistently considering the ideas presented as worthy of adoption, management creates a constructive upward communication medium. With the growth of quality circles in American companies, the suggestion system, largely the same procedure but on an individual basis, is experiencing a resurgence of interest and support from management.

Ford World reported in its July 1982 issue that in 1981 23,563 employees in the United States and Canada submitted about 40,000 ideas and earned more than $5.8 million for the 10,000 ideas accepted. Ford saved an estimated $53.9 million from suggested ideas. Employees received one-sixth of the saving to the company of their idea—up to a maximum of $6,000, plus a Ford vehicle. Ford managers participate in the Management Proposal Plan, which awards from $100 to the price of a new car for ideas. James Emanuel, corporate suggestions program coordinator, calls it "one of the best vehicles I can think of for upward communication to management." The program has been in operation at Ford since 1947.[5]

Yes, there are risks in such a program as the suggestion system. Employees may make suggestions that top management rejects, resulting in lower morale. Management may wonder why the suggestor's supervisor never thought of the idea suggested. The suggestion system may result in change, good or bad, all of which humans resist. Jobs may even be eliminated because of the suggestion. So to benefit the company as it is supposed to, the suggestion system must be properly managed. One company that does an excellent job of that is Sonoco Products Company of Hartsville, South Carolina. Full-page, even two-page coverage in the company newspaper, *Sonoco News*, is frequently given to the subject of the suggestions system and how it works.

Just how good that company's program as compared to those of other companies was discussed in an article, "Suggestion Systems: Ours vs. Theirs," in *Sonoco News*. It reviewed a survey conducted by the National Association of Suggestions Systems of Chicago:

In 1980, the NASS conducted a survey among its members to arrive at a "national average," whereby a company could compare how well its suggestion program was working versus other similar programs. Let me show you just how well Sonoco's Suggestion System "stacks up" against the NASS national average.

In Hartsville, we have approximately 1,800 persons eligible to participate in our program—so let's compare total suggestions submitted per 100 eligible employees. Sonoco averages 21 suggestions per 100 eligible employees. The national average is only 14!... We are proud to say that in 1980, 169 suggestions were accepted, or 45 percent of those reviewed by the Suggestion Committee. The national average is only 26 percent acceptable.... Quoting the nationl average, processing time is 130 working days. This is about six and a half months.... We average 31 working days as the turn-around from the date the idea was received to first committee action.... NASS's national average award is $169. Sonoco is only slightly behind with $153 average award.... One company paid an employee a whopping $75,000 for an idea, which was the highest award paid in 1980 among the companies.... Many of our people enjoy "initial" awards for their suggestions. These awards are given as a portion of expected savings for the year and sometimes given even before an idea is completely implemented.... As much as 54 percent of the companies pay *no* initial award.... In the survey, 49 percent of the companies have a *lower* minimum award than Sonoco (which is $15). And Sonoco has *no* maximum award amount—along with 14 percent of the companies surveyed.... Sonoco awards 50 percent of the first year's net savings. As much as 96 percent of the companies pay less than 31 percent of the annual net savings. And only 4 percent pay between 31 and 50 percent of the annual net savings. No companies pay more than 50 percent.[6]

Two months later, the same company in the same publication explained how the suggestion system works in the article, "This Is What Happens to Your Suggestions":

Almost 400 suggestions have been dropped into suggestion boxes throughout the Hartsville plant this year. And if one of these suggestions is yours, you've probably wondered at one time or another what happens to it along the way.... A suggestion is checked for complete information such as clock numbers, department name, supervisor, etc. It is recorded and a number assigned. A copy of the suggestion is mailed back to the suggestor as an acknowledgment. Then the suggestion is studied for content to determine what areas, processes, or equipment are involved.... A follow-up status sheet is prepared for each suggestion. This sheet keeps track of investigation activity, all contacts made with evaluators and suggestors, letting us know when follow-ups are due.... Now that the idea is understood an evaluator can be assigned to investigate the suggestion. Many of these evaluators work within departmental idea committees.... Under *normal* conditions an idea is investigated promptly and the evaluation submitted to the Suggestion Committee for final review. The committee reviews the idea along with the evaluation report and a decision made to accept or reject. The suggestion is finalized, and the suggestor is notified within one week of the committee's decision.[7]

The article continues by explaining delays: "When an evaluation has been delayed, the importance of communication is stressed. Every attempt is made to keep suggestors informed when a delay is expected." Reasons for delays listed in the article were:

1. When suggestions involve more than one department, they are assigned to several evaluators.

2. Some ideas require a trial. Installation and trial can take six months to a year depending on delays. Some ideas require purchase of materials or new equipment before installation is possible for a trial. Often budgeted funds are not available for these purchases.

3. Some installations must be made during shutdown of machinery.

4. Suggestions involving changes to existing machinery are often difficult to evaluate. Engineering study and review is necessary which takes time.

5. Ideas involving manufacture of new products, new methods, new ventures, or new equipment all require research.

6. Calculations involve cost studies and comparisons, verification of cost–savings figures, collection of data, and historical data. These all take time.

Finally, the article plugs the communication function of the system and asks for employee participation: "Our Suggestion System opens a channel through which your ideas are communicated to management, presenting an opportunity to identify and solve problems and to share in the resulting savings. Your suggestions are important contributions to our company—submit them today and enjoy the rewards tomorrow."[8]

The first article in this excellent series of three, all part of a strong, ongoing effort to support the program, introduced the members of the suggestion committee and explained exactly how that committee works:

At Sonoco, the suggestion system functions through a group of employees whose responsibility lies in reviewing all suggestions for evaluation and award. The seven-member committee representing production and management is responsible for deciding the eligibility of suggestions and/or the employees submitting the suggestions, to determine the value of each suggestion and set the amount of award according to company policy.

All decisions made by the committee are final. However, employees may request to the committee that accepted or nonadopted suggestions be reopened, if new or additional information can be presented. The committee at its discretion may review its decision, and frequently does.

Committee members serve two-year, staggered terms so that half the members go off the committee each year, providing a committee of veteran members along with new members, bringing together experience and freshness.

The Suggestion Committee meets at least once every two weeks. If all suggestions cannot be reviewed at a regular meeting, a special meeting is called to complete the agenda.[9]

In April 1982, *Sonoco News* summarized the suggestion system program for the previous year. Over 200 employees shared in nearly $40,000 for the year. The top award mentioned was $4,350. It seems the same people keep making suggestions and meeting with great success. Two individuals had sixteen suggestions accepted; one, eleven; one, nine; and two, eight. Managers know that the same individuals continue to be the troublemakers in any shop or office; this shows that the opposite is also true. The reward received was "one-half of the first year's net savings for their ideas, plus a 20 percent bonus at year end."[10]

Bendix Corporation recently celebrated the thirtieth anniversary of the founding of its suggestion system.

In those 30 years, hourly nonexempt salaried employees have received approximately $2,750,000 in awards. These suggestions have saved the corporation, its employees, and stockholders more than $26 million. And that's a conservative estimate, since it is based only on the first-year savings resulting from an employee's suggestion....

The Bendix Suggestion Program is corporate-wide. Cash awards are based on an evenly applied formula—20 percent of the savings realized from the first year of implementation, less the cost of labor and materials to put the suggestion into effect....

Eliminating job frustrations, gaining financial rewards and management recognition are some of the reasons why the Bendix Suggestion Program has worked so well for the past 30 years.

"From a corporate point of view," says Bendix's corporate hourly employee relations manager, "there is really nothing like it. What other program can improve job satisfaction, increase communications between employees and management, and improve productivity—all while paying cash awards to our employees and saving the corporation and its stockholders millions of dollars each year?

"Most important, it shows that management is interested in and respects the individual employee as an important contributor. That alone ought to justify the suggestion program for another 30 years, at least."[11]

Other companies give ongoing coverage of the suggestion system in the publications. *Northrop News* of Northrop Corporation, Hawthorne, California, carries a regular column headed, "Ideas Pay off for Employees." The house publication of General Tire and Rubber Company of Akron, Ohio, *General-ly Speaking*, seems to carry one article per issue on the subject, usually at the top of the first page. One such article describes a special drawing from among all suggestions received for the period: "One name will be drawn for every 50 suggestions received. The first drawing will be for $100 and $50 for each 50 suggestions received thereafter. And, of course, adopted suggestions will receive the normal 20 percent of first-year savings and 30 percent on energy-related ideas."[12] Here's a system that rewards the mere submission of suggestions.

Another special campaign was that of the Gillette Company, reported in *Galaxy*:

A dozen employees received a total of approximately $6,000 for cost- or energy-saving ideas they submitted in the Gillette "Go for the Grand Slam" Suggestions Campaign. One hundred seventy-six suggestions were submitted by more than 100 employees . . . during the month-long spring promotion. The participants were competing for cash awards of 25 percent of the first year's estimated savings for implemented suggestions.[13]

So this program in which both company and employees gain, sometimes large amounts, receives a great deal of attention in corporate publications.

QUESTION BOX

Handled like suggestion boxes are other boxes intended for questions only. Signed questions are answered personally, usually in 24 hours; those unsigned are answered by a notice placed on the bulletin board. A standard form is usually used, and a special coordinator answers the questions.

Some companies follow a similar procedure but without the boxes:

Wisconsin Electric Power Company System wants to know what its employees are thinking. To find out, they devised "Write to Know," a new employee feedback program. Employees are encouraged to fill out "Write to Know" forms, which are on display at various work stations throughout the company. The forms are processed by the communications department and sent to the "person most qualified to give an answer." Employees' names are kept confidential and a reply is guaranteed within ten days.[14]

Delta Drilling Company established a program called "Contact" for a similar purpose: "to provide a direct channel through which employees can get answers to questions about the company. Questions or comments are submitted to a coordinator in the company's public relations department, who then forwards them anonymously to the appropriate manager and returns the answers to the employee within ten working days."[15]

COMPANY NEWSPAPER/MAGAZINE

Somewhat similar to those programs is use of the corporate newspaper or magazine, primarily its "Letters to the Editor" column, for upward communication. Some companies provide employees wider opportunities than that column to express their opinions.

American Airlines' employee publication runs a regular opinion and editorial page devoted mostly to employee questions about its policies and practices.[16] Southern California Edison Company has an "action reporter" in its biweekly newspaper to answer questions from employees about the company.[17]

CBS's *Columbine* includes a "What's the Answer?" column, which includes a form to be filled out with a question. Instructions state:

"What's the Answer?" is one of the most important features of *Columbine* because it can foster clearer communications throughout CBS. When you have a legitimate concern about CBS policy or events, we would like to hear from you. Won't you jot down your question in the space provided below and mail it in? We'll take care of finding out "What's the Answer?" If you wish, you need not include your name with your question.[18]

The *Gulf Oilmanac* does the same thing with a form, inserted in the publication, that folds into a postage-paid envelope. The column is "Write to Know" and the instructions state: "To participate, write your comment or question on the form, fill in the blanks on the reverse side, and mail (postage in the U.S. will be paid). The portion of the form containing your name is detached and held by the editor in strictest confidence until an answer is mailed to you at your home address. The name slip is then destroyed." Information to be filled in includes name, address, strategy center, and Gulf location. There is an additional note that asks the questioner to "check here if you do not want your letter published in *Gulf Oilmanac*." The "Write to Know" column is a two-page spread in each issue.[19]

The Consolidated Aluminum Quarterly in its second edition, published in the second quarter 1981, announced a new Q-Mailbox system.

Specially designed Q-Mailboxes will be available at all locations for your convenience in mailing contest entries, Q-Tips, etc., pertaining to the *Quarterly*. Contents of each mailbox will be collected regularly and sent to the editors. We're doing our best to present news in an interesting, attractive way with plenty of photos. We want you to tell us how we're doing so far and what you think about our newspaper. Tell it like it is! Just print or type your tips on the form below and drop it in one of the Q-Mailboxes. Thanks. We promise to read every one![20]

One company created a whole new publication to serve the purpose usually served by a letters to the editor column. A new two-color magapaper, *Avco News* supplements existing publications of Avco Financial Services. It is the first Avco paper devoted entirely to employee news. The first issue included a message from the chairman on why the company decided to publish and to encourage employees' participation in a "We Need a Name" contest. Information on employee accomplishments and employee-related programs and a request of all employees to offer hot tips for future issues were also included in that issue.[21]

Finally, Xerox Corporation uses a program called "Comment" to obtain employee questions, ideas, and opinions. A "two-way communication" program between employees and management, Comment asks employees to complete a form and submit it for managerial review. A company brochure cautions, however,

Comment can never replace the daily communication you have with your supervisor, who is there to help solve your problems and concerns. Indeed, that's generally where you should start. Comment should be used when your supervisor fails to give you a satisfactory response, or you have concerns that you want brought to the attention of top management, or you want the anonymity Comment ensures."[22]

So although American corporations are making some improvements in methods employees have to communicate with management, most have a great deal more to do. As stated previously, elaborate techniques for downward communication fail without equally elaborate means for upward communication.

NOTES

1. "Stemming the Paperwork Tide," p. 16.
2. "Document Dumping Leads to Leaner Files," p. 5.
3. Hennington, "Memorandums—An Effective Communication Tool for Management," p. 11.
4. "A Brief History of Suggestion Systems," p. 2.
5. "Cash in on Your Ideas," p. 10.
6. Funderburk, "Suggestion Systems: Ours vs. Theirs," p. 5.
7. "This Is What Happens to Your Suggestions," p. 5.
8. Ibid.
9. "Suggestion Committee Responsible to You," p. 10.
10. "1981 Top Suggestion Award Winners," p. 5.
11. "Suggestion Program Celebrates 30th," pp. 18–19.
12. "Suggestions Earn Extra $ in Contest," p. 1.
13. "Suggestion Campaign Winners Chosen," p. 9.
14. "Elsewhere," *iabc news*, August 1981, p. 6.
15. "Elsewhere," *iabc news*, November 1981, p. 16.
16. Farinelli, "Fine Tuning Employee Communications," p. 23.
17. Ibid.
18. "What's the Answer?" p. 19.
19. "Write to Know," pp. 18–19.
20. "From the Editors," p. 1.
21. "Elsewhere," *iabc news*, March 1982, p. 10.
22. "The Comment Program."

12

Upward Communication in the American Corporation: Personal

Most forms of upward communication in the American corporation are personal in nature, a superior and subordinate meeting face to face in casual conversation or the context of formal meeting. This chapter discusses these forms of corporate communication.

MEETING

Meetings are gatherings of preferably from eight to ten persons to discuss some area of the company's work. "The small working meeting is found everywhere in organizations. Its dimensions are few: it has a group of people, three or more; it has a purpose; and it has a function to perform that will contribute to the mission of the organization."[1]

"An estimated 11 million meetings of all kinds are conducted every day in the United States alone," according to Linda Roberts.[2] Pascale and Athos report that Harold Gineen, chief executive officer of International Telephone and Telegraph Company for two decades, and his top executives spent over three months each year in meetings![3]

"Of the great variety of meetings held in a typical organization, nearly all can serve as effective upward communication devices," says Scholz.[4] A problem is that at most such meetings the agenda is full of downward communicating, leaving little time for upward messages. Some companies plan meetings with up to half of the time devoted to opportunities for upward communication. In large-group meetings, upward communication can be facilitated by distributing an advance agenda and cards for employees to write out their questions.

Meetings may be held regularly, as in the case of weekly staff meetings, or irregularly, as in the case of a meeting to handle a problem. The term *meeting* as used in business includes several variations on the theme:

- Conference: a face-to-face meeting of people, usually to exchange information.
- Clinic: a training session on a particular skill or subject.
- Seminar: a training session in which experts share knowledge and experience.
- Workshop: a training session designed to give participants firsthand experience on a subject.

In informal meetings, the manager discusses something of current interest such as new orders or competition and encourages employees to discuss the subject. This form of meeting increases management's credibility.

Every meeting should have clearly defined objectives because each consumes valuable time. Legitimate reasons for calling a meeting are:

1. To receive reports from participants.
2. To reach a group judgment as the basis for a decision.
3. To discover, analyze, or solve a problem.
4. To gain acceptability for an idea, program, or decision.
5. To achieve a training objective.
6. To reconcile conflicting views.
7. To provide essential information for work guidance, or for the relief of insecurities or tensions.
8. To assure equal understanding by all present.
9. To obtain immediate reactions when speedy response to a problem is important.
10. To have an excuse for taking up a matter which has gotten stalled.
11. To advance the course of management, that is, to run the business.[5]

Of course, more than one of these reasons may require a meeting.

The specific ways that meetings are conducted are reflective of the individual organization. The *Supervisory Management* article, "You and I Have Simply Got to Stop Meeting This Way," includes this:

Every meeting is a microcosm, a condensed version of the values and style of the organization. If the meeting leader is also the boss, the relationships in the meeting will be those he permits or encourages, the tone and style like his own everyday style, its sense of organization like his, too. Regardless of his pledges and promises, his pep talks and slogans, every member of the meeting can "read" his boss's *behavior* and will act accordingly. More than anything else, the boss is a model whom his people emulate—at least in his presence.

If the meeting leader is not the boss, he or she tends to use the prevailing norms and attitudes of officials in the organization. Because of this tendency, a pattern develops in meetings throughout the organization, from those at the highest echelon to those at the first-line level of supervision.

In working toward a change for the better, then, meetings defy separate treatment because they are all contaminated by the organization's basic values and styles. They cannot, for example, force motion into an organization in which the overriding purpose is to preserve in perpetuity jobs, status, and the world in general as they are. Meetings are only a single instrument of the total organization.[6]

Given that, it was interesting to find in *The Gillette Company News* an article in which three executives express their opinions on "How to Conduct Productive Meetings." Robert Hinman, vice-president, Chairman's Office, said this:

In advance, distribute to all participants the materials to be covered at the meeting. Unless the meeting is purely a presentation for information purposes, limit the attendance to eight to twelve people; many people shy away from participating in large group discussions.

The meeting chairman should lead the discussion, ask questions, encourage all members to participate, and keep the meeting moving at a fast pace so interest doesn't lag.[7]

Hinman also recommended scheduling meetings for 45 minutes to an hour and telling participants how long the meeting is expected to last in the beginning. "That way anyone who must leave early can be sure to contribute his or her ideas early in the meeting before departing."

Robert Jenal, vice-president of GNA materials, management, and manufacturing had this to say:

Establish objectives, issue an agenda—including a starting and ending time—and make sure each participant is aware of what is expected of him or her in meeting objectives.

During the meeting, use audio-visual equipment where appropriate to illustrate ideas and summarize key points as the meeting progresses. At the end of the meeting, the chairman should make sure participants agree to their responsibilities, and he should issue minutes of the meeting, including participants' agreed-upon responsibilities.[8]

Finally, Fred Stephens, vice-president of GNA business relations, listed five essential aspects to a meeting:

1. Purpose: All participants should be informed in advance of the meeting's purpose so they can prepare their thoughts.

2. Place: The proper atmosphere and size of the meeting site contribute to establishing the right attitude among participants.

3. Involvement: The meeting should provide the opportunity for all participants to become involved, and the person who knows the most about a certain topic should be called upon to discuss it.

4. Excitement: Where appropriate, there should be an element of excitement built into the meeting.

5. Recap and action: A recap should be given at the end of the meeting, and agreed-upon actions should be confirmed and then put in writing.[9]

Several companies use meetings creatively in their overall communication programs. Xerox uses meetings of 1,500 to 2,000 employees for an employees annual meeting, presented a day after the shareholder's meeting. Xerox executives give employees the same information that the shareholders receive and then throw the floor open to a question-and-answer session.[10]

Xerox employees also have opportunities to ask questions at other internal meetings. Unit vice-presidents meet regularly with departmental representatives or even with entire departments of 40 to 50 employees to discuss business-related issues. Some vice-presidents meet employees over breakfast or lunch; some meet over coffee in the office; others get away from the company altogether to minimize interruptions.[11]

At Chase Manhattan Bank in New York City, Friday meetings have become the way to communicate with bank officials. Meetings feature three speakers: the treasury department representative, a senior bank officer, and a representative from a bank department who discusses business in his or her area.[12] Size of the meeting is usually 180 bank officers, including all those able to attend that day. Others receive the same information through a newsletter, which publishes highlights of the meeting. Primary purpose of the meetings is to make bank officers conversant with customers on subjects discussed. The meetings also promote horizontal communication in the bank.[13]

The February 1982 issue of the *Gifford-Hill Times* included an article, "Face-to-Face Meetings Boost Two-Way Communication," which expresses well the value of meetings to an organization:

June 28, 1979 was an exciting day for a group of Dallas' Gifford-Hillers as they arrived at the Louisville, Kentucky, Metal Building Products office. They were anxious to meet all the employees but were a little uncertain about what they might face.

They were participating in what was to become Gifford-Hill's most important communication program—face-to-face meetings. The purpose is to give people the opportunity to meet top management and to tell them what they think about the company.

Face-to-face was not conceived in a smoke-filled conference room. It was the brain child of several employees who responded to a Communication Department attitude survey in 1978.

"We want to meet top management," several said emphatically. "We have ideas that will help our company, and we want to give them to the top." They drove that message home. "Gifford-Hill hired our minds as well as our hands. We can contribute more."

They made sense. Top management listened and committed time for eight meetings in 1979. Results? "I'm overwhelmed with what I hear," says John R. Hill, Jr., chairman and chief executive officer. "People's candid comments are very helpful in making decisions to guide our company."

"The comments I hear tell me that Gillford-Hillers are very interested in their company," says Thomas B. Howard, Jr., president and chief operating officer. "The information gleaned from these meetings is helpful to me and is an indicator of the intense interest of employees in their company. I also enjoy the opportunity to visit with the people who are Gifford-Hill."

The meetings are simple. Usually Hill, Howard, and the product line group executive vice-president attend along with senior vice-presidents from the area being visited. The top officer starts with a five-to ten-minute state-of-the-company message.

He also tells how the people in the meeting are doing in terms of sales and goals. Then the meeting is opened for questions—no holds barred.

To keep channels open, several managers are holding local meetings which include divisional vice-presidents. People are communicating—speaking and listening.

More than 2,200 people have participated in face-to-face in seventeen locations. Local managers like them. "Everyone was pleased to meet top management," said one. "Our employees know they are important to the company," said another.... It's impossible for management to visit each location, but the general issues covered at meetings are printed in the *Gifford-Hill Times.*

"Face-to-face will be continued in 1982," says Hill. "Our goal is to help local managers have better open-door communication.

"Open, constructive communication is even more important to us in the 80's. We will rely on your comments and participation to cut costs, increase quality, service and productivity in this difficult time.

"Tom [Howard] and I strongly encourage you to discuss your ideas and suggestions about your job with your supervisor. No one knows your job better than you do, and you can make the difference."[14]

The lead article in the *Nalco News* of April 1982 was "Communication Meetings Reach Over 1,500 Employees," describing meetings similar to those held at Xerox:

For the third consecutive year, as part of an ongoing two-way communication program, Nalco President Tex Collins and several senior management officers met with employees in informal question-and-answer sessions.... At each meeting, employees were given a review of 1981 and the outlook for 1982.... Collins closed each meeting by touching on two points. He stressed the importance of the employee survey as part of Nalco's ongoing two-way communication program, thanking those who participated. "They tell me that our 70 percent response was a very good one," Collins commented, "but I can't help but wonder what the other 30 percent were thinking. We'd like to have everyone's ideas." Employees were encouraged to maintain communications on a regular basis—not just once every three years. "Regular department and plant meetings," Collins added, "offer another good opportunity for an exchange of ideas."

The article included a one-and-a-half-page presentation of questions and answers from the meetings.[15]

At Amoco Oil Company's Whiting Refinery, Whiting, Indiana, a series of meetings is the forum for a Foreman's Development program, reported in *Whiting Refinery News*:

A refinery program that has been a year in the making had its kickoff this month, as fourteen foremen and first-line supervisors gathered in the conference room of a local hotel for the first session of the Foremen's Development Program.

Its purpose, as described by Training Manager Bob Mecklin of Employee Relations, is to provide foremen with a broader understanding of "what makes the oil mill tick." He was close at hand when the group met to learn about certain fundamentals of refinery operation that extend beyond the scope of each foreman's own unit.

"The idea is to bring foremen closer to management," he says, "and to give an overview of operations at every level. We try to give employee specifics that will make his role as a supervisor easier."... Over the next year, about 250 foremen and first-level supervisors will receive the training in groups of about twelve to fifteen people.[16]

San Diego Gas and Electric Company uses frequent employee meetings for communicating. The meetings are covered in the company newspaper, *News Meter Digest*, including the more important questions asked by employees with answers given:

November 14, 1980. "Top Management Discusses Issues at Employee Meetings": Recently, company management began a series of meetings with employees, called "An Open Discussion with Top Management." The purpose of the meetings is to facilitate the discussion of key company issues between management and employees.[17]
December 12, 1980. "Some Answers on Company Finance, Rate Publicity, Interconnection": Meetings between SDG&E employees and members of the company's management team have continued to generate a large number of questions on various issues impacting on the company.[18]
July 17, 1981. "SDG&E Summer Power Reserves Good, Employees Told": [After

three questions] These questions and more were answered by the SDG&E Energy Speakers during two weeks of briefings conducted for company employees. *June 29–July 10*. The briefings, called Employee Update, reported on the summer power supply situation in SDG&E's service territory and throughout California, plus the status of licensing San Onofre Units 2 and 3 and the APS/SDG&E Interconnection.[19]

At Indiana Bell, group "rap" sessions are a means of two-way communication. Their purpose is to pass on information about a work group's operation—what the group is doing that is worth sharing with others in the company, what problems the work group is having in doing the job, and how operations might be improved.

Avon Products uses communication clinics to obtain face-to-face feedback in its communication program. Small groups of employees discuss what they like and dislike about current programs.

Employee briefings at New Orleans Public Service update the 2,800 employees on topics of current interest. Questions and answers appear in the employee tabloid as well as on flyers distributed to staff and posted on bulletin boards three times a month.[20]

Finally, a highly informal form of meeting is the huddle—a term created by Dr. V. Dallas Merell in *Huddling*. The huddle is a temporary, intimate, work-oriented encounter between two or more people. They occur in every corporation everyday innumerable times, and they are responsible for a large measure of the work that gets done.[21]

This is similar to the method of Ed Carlson of United Airlines, which he called management by walking about (MBWA),[22] a term adopted by William Ouchi in *Theory Z*. The informal meetings in the course of a day's work are more important than most American managers realize.

On a trip to New Jersey some years ago, I met the president of Scripto, Inc., who said he made his reputation and based his success on a philosophy that closely resembles MBWA:

I tell my managers that we are going to do all of the sensible things our accountants tell us to do like reducing overhead. But above that, I tell them to get out into the plant and talk to the employees. And I don't mean a nod in passing. I mean call them by name and ask them about the family. Get to know some of the things that interest them. And ask them about the job. That turns things around.

That's upward communication at its best. And it is downward communication, too, of course.

MANAGER'S MEAL

Closely allied to the general meeting is the sharing of a meal by managers and their employees. Connecticut Mutual Life Insurance Company provides free breakfasts to employees who sign up to sit at an executive's table in the cafeteria to participate in discussion in which no question is disallowed.[23]

Lack of communication between employees and senior managers at GTE Lenkurt, Inc., inspired breakfast meetings for both groups. Topics discussed include GTE's future plans in the radio industry and the company's economic stability. One employee said that the breakfast meetings "feel like it's an introduction to solving the communication problem. We've got to keep the momentum going though."[24]

Sonoco Products Company President Charles W. Coker, Jr., does the same thing but with luncheon meetings. Employees are selected randomly for the luncheons.[25]

Bailey Controls Company began in 1974 using breakfast meetings for communication with both salaried and hourly employees. Employees who express interest in attending are invited by the president and encouraged to ask questions and participate in discussions. The host—the president or a department head—offers an update on company activities and answers questions submitted by employees prior to the meeting. Further discussion follows. So successful has the program been that the company expanded it in 1981 to include monthly meetings with members of the community.[26]

PLANT PANEL

The plant panel is a group of employees who are asked an opinion on a controversial question which, with pictures, is published in the company newspaper. Usually four opinions are included together with an editorial on the subject in that issue.

The idea may be implemented in other ways. Often called an employee council, it is a form of upward communication that is close in form to the Japanese quality circle. It is comprised of employee representatives from throughout the plant who meet periodically with management to discuss problems they are having in the plant. The value of it is that they know they are speaking for the group in the plant and not just themselves and feel freer to discuss sensitive issues.

At Taylor Instruments Company, a "management forum," a panel composed of individuals from the various functions of the business and from various levels, meets regularly. Several such panels are operating at any one time. Questions discussed are those selected by top management, which reviews the results. In addition to a better understanding by each participant of the functions of other employees, much upward communication takes place among the participants and top management when it reviews the panel reports[27]

A similar technique, known as the syndicate method, has been used by Johnson & Johnson. A syndicate or committee is established to investigate a broad aspect of the business. "The syndicate makes an intensive study, devoting several weeks of full-time investigation to the problem, reviewing the literature, calling in experts to testify, and visiting business and industry to observe their practices."[28] A report of the findings is then presented to top management in the form of a written report and an open forum.

McCormick & Company makes use of the multiple management system, designed to improve upward communication and discover management talent among junior executives. A junior board of executives of seventeen men was selected to operate independently of the senior board of directors. They elected a chairman and secretary, set up their own schedule of meetings, and drew up their own bylaws. They had the right to discuss anything in the business and were assured that top management would not look over their shoulder. Every recommendation from this board had to be unanimous. Each recommendation then had to be approved by the president or senior board. In the first five years of operation, the junior board sent 2,019 recommendations to the senior board, and only 6 were rejected.[29]

Another variation of the plant panel is the unique program called "CUE" at General Electric's Bridgeport, Connecticut, plant. It formalizes and makes more reliable upward communication of employee reactions to management decisions, current developments, and issues to ensure more accuracy and less waste in downward communication. The procedure takes place in five steps:

1. The department general manager, communicator, and employee relations manager meet to determine what they need to know, in terms either of operating the business or of employee reactions to a company policy or practice.
2. When the question is determined, special CUE cards are printed and distributed down the organization.
3. Each supervisor studies the question and, as a result of his regular contacts with the people reporting to him, gives his best judgment of employee thinking on the question.
4. The cards are passed up the organization, with each supervisor seeing the cards but having no editorial prerogatives. This upward communication takes place at all levels.
5. The CUE card results are consolidated and evaluated. The results are weighed against what employees are saying in other data collection vehicles.

The CUE system encourages supervisors to stimulate upward communication and provides a fast feedback system on a specific question.[30]

TELEPHONE HOTLINE

We saw in Chapter 9 that telephones are used by some companies for downward communication purposes. Not surprisingly, they are also used for communicating messages up the line.

Long Island Lighting Company in 1965 introduced the "Dial Information Please 444" system for its 5,500 employees scattered all over the island. By dialing Hicksville Extension 444, employees can place any question into a clearinghouse, which gets the answer for them. The operator personally greets the caller, asks his identification, tells him to state his question, and assures him that he can expect a call in reply.[31]

At Exxon, a recording device takes telephone questions from employees, and answers are posted on bulletin boards the next day. This company has also had considerable success with the quickie survey, a poll of employees on a single topic or just a few related questions to get a fast sampling of employee thinking. If anonymity is unnecessary, it can be conducted orally by supervisors or opinion samplers.[32]

Burlington Northern has a "Dial the Boss" internal telephone system, which records and passes employee queries on to the chairman or vice-chairman of the board. Answers are mailed to the questions.[33]

Employees at Republic Steel wanting to know what time it is call the employee hotline. A recording gives them the time, temperature, and weather; callers then hear a message—tips on safety, for example, or an update on a crisis. These messages last ten seconds to one minute, addressing topics such as a new company dental plan, an employee insurance program, or Red Cross drives. The systems can be designed to allow an employee to ask questions on the recorder.[34] Thus this predominantly downward communication method is a means of upward communicating.

The same is true of a program at Weyerhaeuser Company, Tacoma, Washington. That company operates six hotlines at lumber plants in Washington, Oregon and Oklahoma. Three-minute recorded messages announce major changes in company operations, recognize outstanding work performance of individuals and groups, and provide information of an employee-relations nature such as facts about fund-raising campaigns or sources of free firewood for employees. Callers may ask questions or make comments following a recording. Questions or comments of wide interest are published, with management responses, in a hotline bulletin or the employee newsletter. Operating 24 hours a day, the hotline may be reached from outside for employees without access to a phone during working hours.[35]

Atlantic Richfield has a hotline called OFFER, Open Forum for Employee Response. It is limited to employee questions and complaints.

Questions are channeled to the appropriate department; both question and answer are posted on bulletin boards within two weeks so that employees who have the same question will also benefit. "A hotline is such an inexpensive thing to maintain, but it's important for employees to know they have this outlet," David Orman, manager of employee communication, said. "It is not a substitute for employee–supervisor communication, but there are certain policy questions that supervisors are not equipped to answer."[36]

OTHER METHODS

Among other methods of personal upward communication are interviews, the open-door policy, grievance procedures, the employee counselor, and the rumor clinic.

Interview

Interviews of all kinds are forms of upward communication. Questions are asked and the interviewee answers, but he asks questions and makes comments too and thus upward communication takes place. Exit and transfer interviews are a form of attitude survey. Most of them, however, tend to be biased; employees disguise their true feelings to leave the company on a positive note or get off on the right foot in a new assignment. As with the attitude survey, these are a waste of time and money unless the results are put to constructive use.

Open-Door Policy

In the open-door policy, the "door of every manager from the first-line manager to the president himself should always be open to any employee," says Saul Gellerman.[37] Some companies use this policy for grievances, primarily; others use it mainly for suggestions; still others use it for all communications.

Pascale and Athos report that Larry T. Kemper, regional manager of United Airlines, who oversees 20,000 employees in the western United States, sought to affirm the company's use of the open-door policy— "The company's committed to having all levels of management open to communication from below."[38]

Use of the open-door policy can be risky, of course, depending on the company. If you make a proposal related to your job, for example, that your own boss has rejected, you can take the idea over his head to his boss. If you are right, you stand to gain a great deal. If you are wrong, however, you may lose a great deal more.

Digital Equipment Corporation of Maynard, Massachusetts, is one company that follows the open-door policy, as reported in *Personnel World News*, the quarterly employee newsletter. The article stated that the policy reinforces the company's support of the individual employee and forms the backbone of the company's employee relations effort. "If employees feel an aspect of work life can improve, they should feel free to discuss it with their supervisor or manager. If a resolution is not reached, employees should feel free to go to the next level of management. An effective open-door policy is when supervisors, managers, and employees are committed to addressing problems, even if it means the involvement of others in the corporation."[39]

Grievance Procedure

A grievance procedure stipulates that employees with grievances or problems have the right to have the problems considered at successively higher levels until they reach the general manager's office. Steps followed are discussions of the problem between the employee and his foreman, the employee relations counselor, the employee relations manager, and the general manager. The grievance procedure is seldom used, however, because most employees are afraid to break the chain of command.

At Sandoz Corporation, the Personnel Department handles grievances. That department investigates the problem and recommends a course of action to the employee. Because the company wants all employees to understand the procedure, details are published in both the company policy manual and the employee handbook.

Employee Counselor

Some companies use an employee counselor to deal with employee problems before they grow in size or number. This has been found to be particularly effective where there is a large number of female employees. The counselor tours the plant to talk to employees, attends employee social activities, visits employees' homes, and sees individuals by appointment to discuss problems that arise on the job.

The counselor must seem to be on the employees' side at all times. Often a plant doctor or nurse serve in the capacity of counselor, too. Some companies appoint the shop reporter counselor, who functions as both as he circulates in the plant searching for news. He must thus get to know the employees to learn what they are thinking. A danger of this and other techniques is that they seem devious to the employee, seem to bypass the foreman, and appear to undermine and threaten his authority.

The management of Sandoz considers supervisors as employee counselors because they are usually available to the employee. Personnel

Department feels this a natural and unplanned form of upward communication that enhances employee–supervisor relationships. Supervisors attend regular employee meetings and attend management development programs to develop counseling skills. The personnel manager is also available as a counselor, as are the nurse and physician.

Rumor Clinic

In a rumor clinic, employees are invited by the plant manager to write him concerning rumors that have come to their attention. Those who write receive a straightforward reply in writing. Rumors which seem to be of greatest importance are included in the company newspaper. This informs management of the types of anxieties and problems employees are having. It is the best method developed to quash rumors which otherwise could sweep through an organization with very unsettling results.

NOTES

1. Dunsing, "You and I Have Simply Got to Stop Meeting This Way," p. 5.
2. Roberts, "Face-to-Face: Eliminating Bias from Meetings," in *Without Bias*, ed. Pickins, p. 115.
3. Pascale and Athos, *The Art of Japanese Management*, p. 70.
4. Scholz, *Communication in the Business Organization*, p. 67.
5. This list was compiled from several sources, including Feinberg and Thompson, *Applied Business Communication*, pp. 314–15.
6. Dunsing, "You and I Have Simply Got to Stop Meeting This Way," pp. 5–6. Reprinted by permission of the publisher © 1976 by AMACOM, a division of American Management Associations, New York. All rights reserved.
7. "How to Conduct Productive Meetings," p. 10.
8. Ibid.
9. Ibid.
10. "Meetings Offer CEO Communication Impact," pp. 1, 7.
11. Ibid.
12. Ibid.
13. Ibid.
14. "Face-to-Face Meetings Keep Channels Open," pp. 1, 2.
15. "Communication Meetings Reach Over 1,500 Employees," pp. 1, 2.
16. "Foreman's Development Program Launched This Month," pp. 4, 6.
17. "Top Management Discusses Issues at Employee Meetings," p. 4.
18. "Some Answers on Company Finance, Rate Publicity, Interconnection," p. 2.
19. "SDG&E Summer Power Reserves Good, Employees Told," p. 4.
20. Emig, "Matching Media with Audience and Message," in *Inside Organizational Communication*, ed. Reuss and Silvis, p. 101.
21. Foltz, "Communication in Contemporary Organizations," in *Inside Orga-*

nizational Communication, ed. Reuss and Silvis, p. 14.

22. Pascale and Athos, *The Art of Japanese Management*, p. 160.

23. Farinelli, "Fine Tuning Employee Communication," p. 23.

24. "Elsewhere," *Communication World*, June 1982, p. 22.

25. "President's Communication Luncheon," p. 4.

26. "Breakfast Meetings Work at Bailey Controls," p. 6.

27. Scholz, *Communication in the Business Organization*, pp. 68–69.

28. Planty and Machaver, "Upward Communication: A Project in Executive Development," in *Business and Industrial Communications*, ed. Redding and Sanborn, p. 352.

29. Heyal, *How to Communicate Better with Workers*, p. 283.

30. Scholz, *Communication in the Business Organization*, p. 71.

31. Heyal, *How to Communicate Better with Workers*, p. 378.

32. Scholz, *Communication in the Business Organization*, pp. 63, 65.

33. Farinelli, "Fine Tuning Employee Communication," p. 23.

34. "Hotlines Make Communication a Call Away," p. 6.

35. Ibid.

36. Ibid.

37. Gellerman, *The Management of Human Relations*, p. 77.

38. Pascale and Athos, *The Art of Japanese Management*, p. 88.

39. "Elsewhere," *Communication World*, September 1982, p. 18.

13

Quality Circles in America

The part of Japanese management that is receiving the most attention worldwide is the quality circle. As we saw in Chapter 5, quality circles began in Japan as a result of the work of two Americans, W. Edwards Deming and Dr. Joseph M. Juran, both of whom lectured extensively on the use of statistics in quality control, and a Japanese professor, Dr. Kaoru Ishikawa, who applied the Americans' ideas in a uniquely Japanese way to create the quality control circle. Many years later, ironically, that approach was brought to America by the Japanese. In this chapter we examine briefly the background of quality circles in America and then review in the form of short case studies, most of them taken from the companies' own publications, experiences of American corporations in using quality circles.

BACKGROUND

The adoption of the quality circle in America has been a matter more of necessity than choice. For twenty years beginning in 1947, American productivity grew at an average annual rate of 3.1 percent. From 1966 to 1976, the United States attained a productivity growth lower than that of any of the eleven top Western industrial nations. During the 1970s, productivity growth fell to 1.6 percent a year, and in 1979 and 1980 there was a decline in the productivity rate.

It's not surprising, then, that American management is very concerned about productivity and that corporate communications are covering the subject extensively (see Figure 10). In the 1980 Annual Report of Cincinnati Milcron Inc. is this: "Productivity is the most vital sign of a nation's

PRODUCTIVITY
BENEFITS/CONSEQUENCES

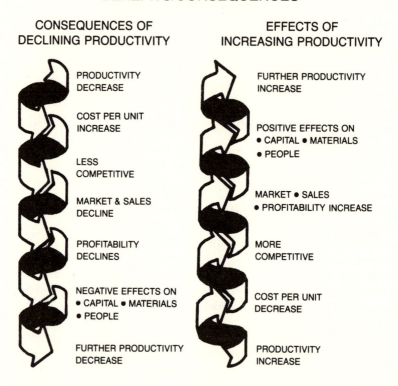

CONSEQUENCES OF
DECLINING PRODUCTIVITY

EFFECTS OF
INCREASING PRODUCTIVITY

PRODUCTIVITY
DECREASE

COST PER UNIT
INCREASE

LESS
COMPETITIVE

MARKET & SALES
DECLINE

PROFITABILITY
DECLINES

NEGATIVE EFFECTS ON
• CAPITAL • MATERIALS
• PEOPLE

FURTHER PRODUCTIVITY
DECREASE

FURTHER PRODUCTIVITY
INCREASE

POSITIVE EFFECTS ON
• CAPITAL • MATERIALS
• PEOPLE

MARKET • SALES
• PROFITABILITY INCREASE

MORE
COMPETITIVE

COST PER UNIT
DECREASE

PRODUCTIVITY
INCREASE

Figure 10. The effects of declining productivity and increasing productivity.

economic health. A rise in productivity means more goods and services at lower costs. It makes for more jobs and higher wages. It raises the standard of living and creates opportunities for further growth."[1] *The Consolidated Aluminum Quarterly* included this in its third quarter 1982 issue: "Productivity is one of the most powerful ideas in the world today. And the idea of a productivity increase is one of the most compelling promises we can make for a better life in the future."[2]

The mass media also have begun to give considerable coverage to

America's falling productivity. The NBC White Paper, "If Japan Can, Why Can't We?" included this ominous observation: "Unless we solve the problems of productivity, our children will be the first generation in the history of the United States to live *worse* than their parents."[3] Toward preventing that, American industry is trying several remedies in an organized fashion. One of them is the quality circle.

America has two organizations which are trying to do something about improving productivity: the Quality Circle Institute, Red Bluff, California; and the American Productivity Center, Houston, Texas.

The Quality Circle Institute, founded in 1979, calls itself the most active organization outside of Japan in quality circle work. It concentrates on implementing quality circles and publishing educational and training material. Founder Donald Dewar has been involved with quality circles since the work captivated his imagination in 1973 during a trip to Japan. He was a charter member and founder of the International Association of Quality Circles, which has a headquarters in Midwest City, Oklahoma. This organization publishes a quarterly journal and conducts seminars and conferences. It also publishes educational materials, as needed.

The American Productivity Center was started in 1977 by Dr. C. Jackson Grayson, Jr., with support of $10 million pledged by 75 national corporations and foundations. That support base has grown to 300 organizations. Today, with a staff of 90 professionals in its new Houston headquarters, the center works toward improving productivity and the quality of work life in the United States. It seeks to accomplish that through publications, educational and training programs, individualized services, and visits to the center.

In the federal government, a part of the Commerce Department is working on productivity problems. The Office of Productivity, Technology and Innovation was created in February 1980 to work with industry in establishing industrywide "best practices" programs. Through them, everyone will exchange ideas on how to produce efficiently.[4]

Americans are gradually accepting the quality circle, diagrammed on Figure 11, as one solution to lagging productivity. It is part of the desperate search for solutions.

The American Productivity Center has said that 1986 is the year when the United States will lose its productivity preeminence among nations. France will surpass America first, followed soon thereafter by West Germany, Canada, and Japan. "By 1992, the United States will have fallen to fifth place unless we make sharp changes in our economic policies and established managerial habits," predicts "Productivity: The Problem That's Made in America" in the spring–summer 1982 issue of *Grace Digest*, house magazine of W. R. Grace & Company.[5] The sharp changes are possible because, in a national survey by Louis Harris and Associates, it was determined that nearly 80 percent of the American people now

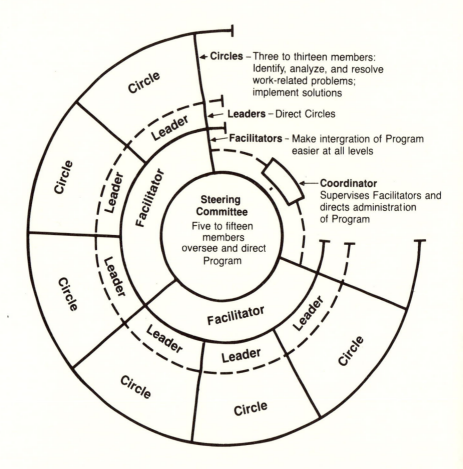

Figure 11. Coordination of the work of quality circles is by the Steering Committee and the Facilitators. (Source: "Our experience with quality circles," by J. Hanley, *Quality Progress,* February 1980, pp. 22-4. Copyright 1980 by the American Society for Quality Control. Permission to reprint granted.)

regard productivity as a serious problem requiring urgent action.[6] That's a start in finding a solution.

Another step is making sure every American worker understands what productivity is and knows how to improve it on the job. Company communications are helping in that regard. The *Grace Digest* article mentioned above includes this definition: "Productivity is the amount of output you get for a given amount of input. The inputs are labor, capital (factory buildings and equipment), land, and natural resources."[7]

The first American firm to begin using quality circles was Lockheed Missile and Space Division in 1974. By the end of 1975, that company had fifteen circles operating and two years later double that number, with an estimated saving of $3 million and savings-to-costs ratio of six to one.[8] That is the same ratio that the Quality Circle Institute predicts any quality circle in any company will achieve.

Other companies which adopted quality circles in the beginning were Smith Kline Instruments, Inc., and the United States Envelope Company. They were joined later by AMF Harley Davidson, American Airlines, Babcock and Wilcox, General Motors, Honeywell, Hughes Aircraft, 3M, and Westinghouse. By 1978, only about 25 companies were using quality circle techniques, but interest was increasing rapidly.[9]

Weyerhaeuser Corporation began a quality circle program in its Olympia, Washington, plant in June 1981. Employees, including one who has since been laid off, meet during working hours. "We'd been hollerin' about little things over the past twenty years," said one employee, "and no one listened. Now that our supervisor meets in our circle with us, he understands what we've been hollerin' about. He gets more involved in our job—and I guess we understand his job better too. We really have a say in how our department works. Yeah, I'd say this program works."[10] In one year, the number of circles at Weyerhaeuser has grown from two to eight, involving about 45 employees.

Honeywell Inc. has had quality circles since 1974 and has applied them in areas as remote from the factory as marketing communication. The corporate quality circle coordinator remarked that the meetings, on company time, "are the fastest way of bridging the information gap between hourly workers, supervisors, engineers, and management." In two large Honeywell plants, machine use increased from 50 percent to from 85 to 95 percent. In another plant, productivity increased 28 percent, from 70 percent to 98 percent.[11]

At Northrop Corporation's Aircraft Division near Los Angeles, quality circles have brought savings nearly as huge as the 747s they produce. The 55 circles are of employees in operations making parts for that airplane. "During the two years that we've emphasized that it is us rather than them and me, the cost of the 747 unit we're delivering to Boeing went down 50 percent," said the division's vice-president for commercial operations. During the period of the savings, the work force was quadrupled due to expanded business, and many of the new employees had to be trained.[12]

CASE STUDIES

The pattern of adoption of the quality circle in American companies has been fairly uniform. Usually the need to improve productivity prompts a search for practical methods. Someone in the company hears about quality circles and the part they have played in Japan's success, after which that person consults with top management to discuss the feasibility of the technique for their business. Then one or more parties attend a seminar on the method and visit companies, maybe some in Japan, that use quality circles. Shortly thereafter, the process of introducing the program begins.

Some companies call quality circles by other names, but for the most part the procedure remains the same. If there is an Americanization, it is that the focus is less on statistics and more on human relations and communication.[13]

At Hoover Company, quality circles are called the Circles of Opportunity Program (CO-OP). The program was begun in late 1981 with four pilot groups. Four new groups in the second phase started five months later.[14]

Quality circles at Hewlett-Packard are called quality teams; there are hundreds operating today. According to the company magazine, *Measure*, this is the background of the quality teams:

1. Hewlett-Packard's joint venture company in Japan, Yokogawa-Hewlett-Packard, has continued to expand its quality circle activity, which began at the factory in 1973. YHP now has 214 circles, more than 60 percent of them in sales and customer service.

2. Pioneer efforts by four U.S. divisions—Manufacturing, Colorado Springs, Loveland Instrument, and Desktop Computer—and HP Malaysia in starting their own quality circle activity in late 1978 and early 1979 led directly to development of a companywide training course introduced in 1980. HP uses its own term, Quality Teams, drawing upon the concepts of quality control circles, quality of work life, and the HP Way (some divisions prefer other terms for their activity).

3. In 1979 eleven HP manufacturing, product assurance, and materials managers led by Vice-President of Manufacturing Services Ray Deméré visited Japan to look over successful manufacturing techniques. One of the messages they brought back was that quality circles of production workers played an important role in the quality of Japanese workmanship.

4. The NBC-TV documentary, "If Japan Can, Why Can't We?" on Japanese accomplishments in improving quality received wide interest in March. W. Edwards Deming, one of the stars of that show, gave a two-day seminar for HP management on the importance of statistical control.

5. The latest count showed 43 HP entities in various stages of training or developing quality teams, with a number of others interested in getting started.[15]

In addition to the value to the company in improved productivity is the benefit to the individual, according to Maggie Johnson of Hewlett-

Packard's Corporate Training Center, who works full time on quality team assignments:

One of the fringe benefits of quality teams that I've seen is individual, personal growth. Employees who were very, very quiet people have been willing to make phone calls to support the group and to talk to engineers. They've all learned how to collect data, write minutes, and do public speaking—everyone on the team had a part in our first presentation.

Amazing things happened in our group, I just can't believe the growth that people experience through quality teams.[16]

At some Burlington Industries Inc. locations, teams are called quality circles and at others they are called work effectiveness teams. One difference between the two is that participation in quality circles is voluntary, but everyone in a work group participates in work effectiveness teams.

Development of quality circles at Burlington parallels that in other companies.

At Burlington, many people had an interest in programs designed to encourage more employee participation. In 1979, Gib Bernhardt, plant manager of the Raeford Dyeing plant, was the first to become involved, with a pilot project at the Menswear Dyeing plant in Raeford, North Carolina.

Then, in mid-1980, Graham Pope, group manager of the Industrial Division, started using the quality circle concept at the Kernersville Finishing Plant and the Greensboro Finishing Plant. Both plants were using the circles on a limited, pilot basis while the effectiveness of the program is being evaluated.

"This isn't something that we can rush," Marvin Pinson, manufacturing group vice-president, said. "All of these plants are pioneering some new concepts for their operations, and we know we can't implement them overnight. But we're already seeing results at the Raeford plant. Quality is better and attitudes and morale are good. People are concerned and interested in making these ideas work."

And involvement at Burlington is spreading. Already the Lees Carpets Division is starting quality circles training at each of its plants as part of a pilot project, while the Domestics, Burlington House Decorative Fabrics and Hosiery and Socks Divisions are looking seriously at the program. At the corporate offices in Greensboro, quality circles are also being considered.[17]

The company makes sure that participants have a good idea of what a quality circle can do. It has specified the following objectives for a quality circle:

- To reduce errors and improve quality.
- To promote job involvement.

- To promote creative problem-solving activity.
- To inspire more effective teamwork.
- To improve communications.
- To build an attitude of "problem prevention."
- To promote personal and leadership development.
- To promote cost reduction.[18]

At Ethyl Corporation's William L. Bonnell plant in Carthage, Tennessee, quality circles, called Bonnell Action Teams (BAT), have been in use for four years. "BAT calls for involvement of its 400 employees in problem solving, goal setting, and goal attainment."[19]

With the approval and support of E. Malcolm Harvey, Ethyl's Vice-President–Aluminum, the BAT program was born at Carthage in 1977 as Mr. [Shelby] Lowe [Carthage plant manager] and members of the plant's administrative staff mulled over methods of improving quality in the plant's extruded aluminum products.

Mr. Lowe said that he had been reading about the successes of Japanese industry in improvement of productivity by allowing ideas of employees to help shape plant operations. Quality was the immediate goal of the Japanese circle programs. But, Mr. Lowe said, Japanese industrialists soon learned that their quality programs also yielded more satisfied employees and higher levels of productivity.... While improving productivity has been a top priority within Ethyl's operating division for some time, Ethyl formalized its corporate commitment in May, when Dr. Miller was named to the productivity position in the Corporate Budget Department in Richmond. What can be done to improve Ethyl's productivity? "All employees can have a significant impact on productivity," Dr. Miller noted. "By avoiding waste of time and materials, by becoming more involved in our jobs, each of us can help our divisions and departments get more output out of less input—the name of the productivity game."

One specific method of improving performance, quality control circles, has been implemented successfully at Ethyl's William L. Bonnell Company plant in Carthage, Tennessee. The program has been extended to Bonnell's Newnan, Georgia, operation as well as several other Ethyl divisions. Through participation in decision making and problem solving, quality circles provide employees direct opportunities to improve their "quality of work life" and enhance productivity.

In addition to the group meetings, the doors of management offices were opened to all personnel in an attempt to tear down the wall between management and labor.

It worked. Employees with problems or suggestions now feel free to approach Mr. Lowe in his office with suggestions or problems relating to plant operations.

Mr. Lowe noted that the key to the quality circle and BAT programs' successes are the working men and women involved. The morale and general work attitude of a company's work force is critical to the success of such a program. Bonnell's first priority in instituting the BAT program was to gain the confidence of the entire work force.

The basic question Bonnell management asked its workers was, "How can we help you do your job better?"

He and his staff were unprepared for the mass of information employees sent into the office initially. Five hundred problems kept management busy for eight months responding to inquiries, Mr. Lowe said.

This is another critical factor in the BAT program. Every employee suggestion or grievance receives a written response, either to explain why management action is impossible or detail what action will be taken.[20]

Since 1977, the company notes, there has been a 20 percent reduction in customer returns. Management has noticed other improvements.

"When the employees know their comments are being honored, they feel more a part of the company, have better morale, and feel free to express themselves to management at any time," Mr. Lowe said.

For Bonnell, the program has resulted in higher productivity and increased customer satisfaction with the plant's products.... Employee turnover has dropped from 5.1 percent per month average for the 1970–77 period to 0.5 percent for 1980, an indication that Bonnell employees are satisfied with their jobs.

Absenteeism has been reduced drastically, and the company's safety record has shown equally impressive improvement. There has been a 57 percent improvement in attendance and a 100 percent improvement in safety from 1977.

In addition, the BAT program has served as a catalyst and model for the implementation of several quality circle–type programs at other Ethyl locations.[21]

Anchor Hocking quality circles each have a different name: Employees for Better Productivity, People for Progress, People Who Care, and Action Group.

In November 1980, Plastics Inc., an Anchor Hocking subsidiary, initiated quality circles in its Coon Rapids Plant with the formation of Employees for Better Productivity. By doing so, it joined the ranks of a very elite group. By the end of last year, there were only 150 companies in the United States with a quality circle program. Today, there are over 1,000 companies with active circles.... When Plastics Inc. embarked on its program, the quality circle concept was explained to all plant employees during a series of shift meetings. It was explained that quality circles are small groups of people who share their ideas and opinions with management and together attempt to solve job-related problems. Since quality circles are solely based on volunteers, volunteers were solicited. The response was "fantastic," says Dale A. Thompson, special projects manager and program coordinator. Plans were then set to start one circle and later expand to more.

During the first two meetings, the technique of brainstorming is taught and utilized to pick a name for the group and to identify which problems are to be "attacked." "During brainstorming," explains Thompson, "any criticism or wild enthusiasm is not tolerated because if the problem is good or bad or real or important will be decided by group consensus rather than individual shouting and chest-beating." The groups, by a method of voting, elect which problems are to be worked on. The circle members decide on areas of concern. Although management may recommend a specific problem to be solved, the decision rests with the group.[22]

Progress in improved productivity, product quality, processes, and working conditions has already been noted. Other improvements include these:

Plant communication has been improved through better electronic speaker maintenance and by development of communication links from packers, lead people, lead maintenance, general maintenance, and plant supervision. "People are working together and are responding to each others' needs," Thompson notes, "therefore making everybody's job easier.... Our objective with quality circles has been to increase communication with all plant employees and thereby, through quality use of everyone's skills and talents, make Plastics Inc. more productive, more competitive, and a better place to work."[23]

Ford Motor Company is embracing quality consciousness in a serious way. The company has hired as a consultant the same W. Edwards Deming who introduced the concept of quality control through statistics to Japan. Deming's message to Ford management is simple, as described in the April 1982 issue of *Ford World*:

The system, not the workers, is to blame for most quality problems. And that system is the responsibility of management.

Deming feels so strongly about this point that he refuses to consult for companies that lack top management commitment to quality control. "If the president doesn't have time, neither do I," he says. Ford President Donald Petersen has made it abundantly clear that he has the time as well as the commitment. In introducing Deming at the recent seminar Petersen said: "I am absolutely committed to the use of statistical approaches to prevent quality defects. All Ford employees, I believe, by and large report to me. That should mean they would feel as committed as I do."

Having received the support from the top, Deming went on to explain his quality message, a message that has been part of the accepted wisdom for decades in Japan. In essence it calls for using a few relatively simple techniques to monitor and analyze information about a process, then determining what if any corrective actions need to be taken, and, finally, assessing the results.

Quality problems are caused by a particular tool or worker only a small percentage of the time, Deming says. Most defects, however, can be traced to causes such as a faulty production system. Therefore, Deming emphasizes that quality control is not governed by either lazy or motivated workers. In fact, in a properly designed system, workers will be motivated, Deming says.[24]

Herbert E. Striner, Dean of the College of Business at American University, agreed with Deming on the NBC program, "If Japan Can, Why Can't We?" when he said:

There are over 200 Japanese companies operating in the United States today, using American workers, and apparently, based on the product they're turning out, the product is fine, they're doing well, and it's not the American worker, as far as I can determine, that's a major part of the problem of productivity.[25]

Ford Motor Company's study of the Japanese approach has included a trip to Japan by several executives of the company with officials of the United Auto Workers Union in mid-1981 to examine firsthand Japanese industrial methods. The trip is described in two special supplements to Ford's company newspaper, *Ford World*, in the August and September 1981 issues.

Control Data is another company which asked Dr. Deming to teach employees his methods. The July–August 1981 issue of *Contact*, the company magazine, reported that nearly 400 employees attended a four-day seminar carrying a "thick, blue book with the formidable title: 'Management of Statistical Techniques for Quality and Productivity.' " Asked during the seminar why the Japanese were so receptive to ideas, Dr. Deming responded: "Maybe they're smarter. No Japanese is ever too old or too successful to wish to learn. They're great respecters of knowledge."[26]

In Japan, major corporations compete for the Deming Prize, a silver medal. "The prize is considered more important than the Nobel Peace Prize in Japan, where the Deming award ceremonies are nationally televised."[27]

Sheller-Globe circles are known as GREAT—Grabill Responsible Employee Action Teams.

For more than two years, a number of individuals at Sheller-Globe have been investigating ways to improve quality, productivity, and operating efficiency. Their investigation has included visits to several other companies to study and evaluate quality circle programs already established by those firms.

A series of comprehensive guidelines have been established, and a corporate commitment has been made to initiate a pilot circles program at Sheller-Globe's Grabill Plant, Grabill, Indiana, a manufacturer of thermoplastic steering wheels for cars, trucks, and industrial equipment.

Known as the GREAT program—Grabill Responsible Employee Action Teams—the quality circle program will be tailored specifically to meet the requirements of the people, products, and industrial climate of the Grabill Plant, according to David C. McCrary, corporate director of product reliability.

"Although the quality and productivity circles won't solve all problems," McCrary says, "the program will further utilize the intelligence, creativity, skills, and experience of the people at Grabill."[28]

George Sederberg reported in a talk to the 1981 Japan–America Business Conference in Lincoln, Nebraska, that his company, Cincinnati-

Milacron, has introduced 53 quality circles, "not only in marketing but also in engineering. We have circles of secretaries, laboratory technicians. We are looking now to put circles in purchasing areas and our service part areas also." He reported this experience in pre–quality circle days:

I won't forget the one experience I had with the gentleman on the circular grinder that I asked if there was a way that he thought his job could be done more efficiently, and he immediately went to his tool box and came out with a sketch of a new type of fixture which he thought could be put on the machine that would improve the productivity of the machine twofold. It was a very clever suggestion, and I said, "Charlie, why don't you tell your foreman about that?" He said, "He never asked!" A lot of people that we talked to had suggestions about improving their work functions, but they had no incentive at all to go to their foremen and tell them about it.[29]

Sederberg had been assigned the responsibility for improving his company's productivity, and this incident occurred during the planning stages of his work.

Schering-Plough Corporation's circles are called work quality circles. The program was described in *Schering-Plough World*, the company newspaper:

What started as a test pilot of eight circles in pharmaceutical operations only a year and a half ago has mushroomed into a permanent activity that currently boasts some 30 teams in Pharmaceutical and U.S. Home Products divisions. Involving more than 240 employees, the concept is expected to expand to some 46 teams by year-end, including eight in consumer operations in Memphis and Dayton and several in Canada and Belgium. . . .

"Work Quality Circles fit in with our corporate philosophy that calls for a meaningful response to employee aspirations to achieve their full potential," notes Chairman Richard J. Bennett, who championed the development of the circles at Schering-Plough. "And equally important, the concept offers significant long-term opportunities for improving operating efficiencies, and hence raising productivity in many areas of the company."

Since their inception, the circles seem to have done just that. Projects have improved product quality, raised productivity, lowered operating costs, and generated significant improvements in the work environment. Yet circle members in pharmaceutical operations, which have the oldest circles, say that the biggest benefit is the chance to improve their work environment.[30]

3M Corporation organized its first quality circle in 1978:

Harold J. Meyer, quality assurance manager for Data Recording Products plant in Weatherford, went to Japan in 1978 to study quality circles. He was impressed by what he saw.

"In Japan, the entire nation is what you might call a family business, where employees are an integral part of companies. It's a Japanese tradition that employers make a lifetime commitment to their employees.

"As many as 60 to 70 percent of Japanese are simultaneously involved in quality circles in their companies," he said, "working as mini-engineers and thinkers and planners in addition to their regular job assignments. Overall, up to 98 percent of a plant's work force will participate in circles."

Following Meyer's trip, Data Recording Products implemented quality circles first in Weatherford and later in Camarillo. Setting one up is fairly simple. You need a leader, some volunteers, and something to improve.[31]

Although quality circles are also used at 3M for white collar workers, such groups are called business development units (BDU).

Generally a BDU consists of six to seven middle managers, each from a discipline in the division, who design a business strategy for a product or market. . . . Groups are used for identifying future business opportunities, managing current business situations, developing and improving products, developing new markets, improving profitability and long- and short-term planning. . . . The BDU meets monthly; the Management Committee reviews BDU proposals quarterly. This reporting schedule coincides with . . . [the] requirement that "the line of communication between the BDU and the operating committee be short."

Like the quality circle for factory workers, the BDU is valued for involving middle managers more in the decision-making process.[32]

Dresser Industries, Inc., has four quality circles in its Galion Manufacturing Division. They "have developed eight cost-cutting suggestions that should be able to reduce the division's projected annual expenses related to manufacturing by more than $46,000," according to *Dresser News*.[33] A member of one of the quality circles recalled how they came up with one of these improvements:

During one of our weekly circle meetings, we decided to try to correct some trouble we were having with broken pressure seals on one of our cylinder assemblies. Sometimes the seals were accidentally damaged by machine work we were performing on the cylinders. In 1980, 134 cylinders had failed inspection because of leaking seals. At that rate, the problem was costing Galion just about $934 a year.

"Our circle brainstormed the situation and came up with some ways around the problem. We passed our best idea over to the Inspection and Manufacturing Engineering Departments, which decided to test our recommendation." Smiling, [Bob] Pauley [a machine operator and member of Galion Plant No. 5 quality control circle] said, "None of the seals on test cylinders coming out of our work area failed inspection."[34]

The Firestone Tire and Rubber Company has been "actively involved in the concept [of quality circles] for three years in the United States and is now expanding the program into international operations," said an article in *Firestone nonskid*. In April 1982, fifteen facilitators of Firestone quality circles met in Akron for three days for the first time to share ideas and experiences on the quality concept.[35]

W. R. Grace & Company uses quality circles in its TEC Systems of Polyfibron Division. The program began in 1980 with TEC's general manager reading about Japan's successes. After a thorough investigation, circles were formed in the electrical, assembly, fabrication, shipping, accounting, bench welding, engineering, maintenance, machine, and material control departments. Participants received eight weeks of training. Benefits to the company have been improved communication between workers and management, better attendance, fewer grievances, lower turnover, and, in the end, better productivity.[36]

Amhoist Hoist and Derrick Company of St. Paul initiated action teams in its Crosby Group in 1982. To start, fifteen facilitators received training in brainstorming, encouraging member participation, conflict resolution, cause-and-effect analysis, presentation skills, group dynamics, and management presentations. The company's expectation was to have pilot action teams in operation by midyear. [37]

Amhoist supplements its action teams program with another called Ideas for Improvement.

In addition to their participation in action teams, eligible employees can communicate their productivity ideas to management by submitting written recommendations through the Ideas for Improvement program, which is currently being implemented for all hourly employees at most Amhoist facilities. Details regarding the program are provided on bulletin boards and through a Partners in Progress training module.[38]

Some companies are rewarding quality circles monetarily for their ideas and suggestions, just as suggestions submitted by individuals are rewarded, as discussed in Chapter 13. Northrop Corporation, for example, presented one such circle $5,000 for a suggestion.[39]

By no means are all attempts to apply quality circles successful. "Recent research shows that as many as 75 percent of initially successful programs were no longer in operation within a few years."[40]

Lockheed, for example, has gradually discontinued its quality circles, supposedly because the employees most instrumental in bringing the technique to the company left and, as a result, interest in the method declined. Even in Japan, about a third of attempts to apply quality circles are unsuccessful. Others continue to operate with only moderate success.

Problems have included poor relationships of managers and employees, incompetent middle managers who feel threatened by the process, resistance of unions, lack of education in quality practices, and management's philosophy toward such programs.

At one GM plant, the staff person [facilitator] in charge of QC circles was astonished to find suddenly that his best circle leader had been transferred into a new department. The facilitator had lost his best leader and gained nothing.... In another company the circles and facilitator were instructed to make reports to the manufacturing manager. Middle management felt that the reports made them look as though they weren't doing their jobs; that they were a way of checking on them. They responded by refusing to cooperate with the facilitator.... At Lockheed Missile and Space Company the workers had gone out on strike for higher wages, and when they returned, management found a distinctly cooler attitude toward the circles by the formerly enthusiastic participants. Since they had not gotten the higher wages they felt that they had coming to them, the workers responded by withholding their cooperation. They were saying in effect, "If you won't give us a fair wage, then we won't participate in your circles." Management failed here in that the workers saw the circles as something that served management's interests exclusively. Since they saw themselves as doing a favor for management by participating, they could also choose to withhold this favor if they were not treated in the way they had expected.[41]

This illustrates a difference between Japanese and American quality circle programs: in Japan, quality circles are run entirely by the workers; in the United States, quality circle programs are under the direction of management, which controls worker activity.

More and more management theorists are saying that the focus of productivity in the United States should be on management, however. "Of the estimated $600 billion paid to office employees each year, $465 billion, or nearly four-fifths, goes to managers and professionals," reports an article in *Long Lines*, publication of the AT&T subsidiary of the same name.[42]

Akio Morita, chairman of Sony Corporation, says: "The problem in the United States is management." Sony's experience in the United States shows that American workers are equal to Japanese workers when they are dealt with fairly.[43]

Companies should not attempt to apply quality circles if they are unwilling to comply thoroughly with the guidelines presented for their use.

"Quality circle programs are doomed to failure in the United States unless the value of the person is put before the value of the machine," said labor relations consultant Wayne Alderson, Pittsburgh, Pa.

According to Alderson, the quality circle concept works in Japan because the Japanese ability "to capture the minds of the people by making people a priority." He claims that many similar programs are failing in the United States because the American worker sees them as just another management gimmick.

"Increasing worker involvement and responsibility with the object of increasing productivity is the wrong approach," he said. "The first step is treating workers with dignity and respect. That, in turn, will produce a 'by-product' of increased productivity that would be unsurpassed in our history."[44]

To coerce employees to participate, for example, is a way to weaken the circle. To fail to provide rapid feedback on ideas is another. Weakness in leadership is a third.

Problems with the company at large will doom quality circles to failure. A company experiencing turmoil should not try to improve the situation with quality control circles. That is not their intent. They were meant to be used to improve a company that already functions well.

"Ironically, quality circles are based on a management philosophy that depends on communication excellence for effectiveness," said Myron Emanuel, director of business communication programs for Towers, Perrin, Forster & Crosby, Inc., a public relations firm. "The communication department has the job of explaining quality circles to employees, and convincing them that they are not a threat." Where management misses the boat is by not including the organization's senior communication officers in initial planning stages. "Otherwise, quality circles turn entirely into productivity-oriented programs, ignoring the employee's great need for information."[45]

A company which is unwilling to introduce broad changes as a result of quality control activity should not begin the program. Changes in both management style and structure of the organization are often called for, and if they are not possible, the quality control program will be stymied.

Finally, a company must be willing to provide sustained support for the program. When it is new, interest is high and success assured. In time, however, interest fades and so does success.

Honeywell, Inc., has had considerable success with quality control. In 1979, it had 40 circles; in 1980, 103; in 1981, about 300. "The superior doesn't have any monopoly on brains," a Honeywell executive says. "The modern worker is smart, smarter than many management people suspect."[46]

By participating in quality circles, employees gain a feeling of involvement in the company, sometimes for the first time. Recognition of their efforts is another reward, again sometimes for the first time. Finally, some companies have made it a practice to reward suggestions accepted from quality circles, as discussed previously.[47]

It is important to keep in mind that the use of quality circles is just one of several reasons for Japan's strong record of productivity. Others are the activities of the Japan Productivity Center, described earlier; an export control law passed in 1936 with labor's backing which requires that all goods for export pass rigid tests; and automation, particularly the use of robots, in which Japan leads the world.

Another reason for Japan's success must surely be the country's highly disciplined work force, which is treated in ways that bring out its highest potential for high quality work—for the good of the company and the country. Although America can adopt the use of the quality circle easily enough, it will take a while longer to apply some of these more important qualities of Japanese management style.

NOTES

1. "The Crisis," p. 10.

2. "Productivity ... What It Is, Why It Matters," p. 10.

3. "If Japan Can, Why Can't We?" transcript, part 5, p. 4.

4. Ibid., part 1, p. 4, and part 5, p. 2.

5. "Productivity: The Problem That's Made in America," p. 23.

6. Ibid.

7. Ibid., p. 24.

8. Blair and Hurwitz, "Quality Circles for American Firms? Some Unanswered Questions and Their Implications for Managers," p. 3.

9. Gryna, *Quality Circles*, p. 15.

10. "Ideas at Work," p. 4.

11. Waller, "Yanks Borrow Japanese Keys to Quality," pp. 96–97.

12. "What Happens When Workers Manage Themselves?" p. 64.

13. "Teamwork Takes Off," p. 8.

14. "New Circles Chosen," p. 4.

15. "Teamwork Takes Off," p. 8.

16. Ibid., pp. 4–5.

17. "Teamwork Is Basis of New Management Style," p. 4.

18. Ibid.

19. "Japanese Formula for Success Proves Healthy for Bonnell's Carthage Plant," p. 4.

20. Ibid.

21. Ibid.

22. "Quality Circles Work at Plastics Inc." pp. 10–11.

23. Ibid.

24. "Deming Pitches Quality, Productivity," p. 3.

25. "If Japan Can, Why Can't We?" part 1, p. 11.

26. Dineen, "The Force Behind Quality Consciousness in Japan Speaks to Control Data," p. 8.

27. Ibid.

28. "Grabill's GREAT Program Gets People Involved," p. 3.

29. Sederberg, comments in panel discussion.

30. "Quality Circles Activities Boom," pp. 1, 6.

31. "Quality Circles: Putting Better Ideas Into Production," pp. 1–2.

32. Ibid.

33. "Quality Circle Employees Become Problem Solvers," p. 4.

34. Ibid.

35. "Quality Circles ... Sharing Ideas Voluntarily," p. 1.

36. "Workers Give TEC Ideas," p. 3.

37. "Crosby's Seven Manufacturing Plants Represented at Action Teams Training," pp. 4, 8.

38. "No Substitute for People's Efforts in Productivity Equation," p. 9.

39. "Quality Circles Group Given $5000 Award," p. 8.

40. Goodman, "Quality of Work Projects in the 1980s," as cited in Blair and Hurwitz, "Quality Circles for American Firm?", p. 7.

41. "Why Some Won't Circle," p. 77.

42. Donnelly, "Productivity at the Top," p. 2.

43. Waller, "Yanks Borrow Japanese Keys to Quality," p. 100.

44. "Productivity Called By-Product of Respect," p. 9.

45. "Quality Circle Programs Bypass Information," p. 7.

46. Widfeldt, "Jumping on the Quality Control Bandwagon," p. 32.

47. Pauly, Contreras, and Marbach, "How to Do It Better," p. 59.

PART III

COMPARISON AND CONCLUSION

14

Comparison

Comparing corporate life in Japan and the United States necessarily begins with the broad areas of contrast in the countries themselves. Many of these differences involve complete opposites. The comparison continues with a description of those characteristics in which the respective national approaches are merely different.

Such differences in countries and cultures lead naturally to a discussion of contrasts in their respective business organizations. Finally, both the differences in the countries and cultures and in the corporations have meant that communication techniques in the organizations differ. This chapter compares those aspects of these two countries in that order.

THE COUNTRIES

The Introduction includes some contrasts between American and Japanese cultures. A broader look at the countries reveals areas of even starker differences (see Table 7).

Japan is surely the most homogeneous country in the world and America the most heterogeneous. America was settled by Caucasians, mostly, who displaced the Indians, members of the Mongolian race. Invaders of the islands now known as Japan were Mongolians who displaced the native Ainu, members of the Caucasian race.

Settlement of Japan was a centuries-long, step-by-step process; and Japanese cultural patterns are derived from China. America was created as a sudden act of rebellion from England from which its culture developed in the pattern of early Mediterranean cultures.

Japanese culture today emphasizes group activity, hierarchy, harmony

Table 7
Comparison of Culture in Japan and America

Japan	America
Mongoloid race	Caucasian race, primarily
Displaced the Ainu, who are Caucasian	Displaced the Indians, who are Mongoloid
Culture derived from China, primarily	Culture derived from England, primarily, and influenced by Mediterranean cultures
Populace nearly totally homogeneous	Populace extremely heterogeneous
Emphasizes group activity, hierarchy, harmony, and indirect language	Emphasizes individualism, equality, confrontation, and direct language
People reserved and formal	People assertive and informal

and indirect language; American culture stresses individualism, equality, confrontation and direct language. Japanese people tend to be reserved and formal; Americans are assertive and informal.

The differences between the Japanese and American cultures are often best expressed by those with experience in both. Takashi Fujioka, production manager of Moralco Ltd., an Alcoa subsidiary that produces tabular alumina near his hometown in Kyushu, Japan, received a master's degree and doctorate from Carnegie Mellon University in Pittsburgh. There he met and married an American girl. His return to Japan was more difficult than he expected.

While I was in America, I got used to the more casual American way of life. Japanese society is much more structured. When I sometimes do or say things the way an American would, the Japanese think I'm "uncultured." For example, in Japan, if someone offers you a cup of tea, you should first say "no," even if you want it. Then they ask you again and you can say "yes." I find myself saying "yes" the first time! I'm sure they think I'm a barbarian. But those little things mean a lot to the Japanese.[1]

Here is an experience of Takeo Doi, a psychiatrist and the author of *The Anatomy of Dependence*:

Not long after my arrival in America I visited the house of someone to whom I had been introduced by a Japanese acquaintance, and was talking to him when he asked me, "Are you hungry? We have some ice cream if you'd like it." As I remember, I was rather hungry, but finding myself asked point-blank if I was hungry by someone whom I was visiting for the first time, I could not bring myself to admit it, and ended by denying the suggestion. I probably cherished a mild hope that he would press me again; but my host, disappointingly, said "I see" with no further ado, leaving me regretting that I had not replied more honestly. And I found myself thinking that a Japanese would almost never ask a stranger unceremoniously if he was hungry, but would produce something to give him without asking.[2]

On another occasion, Doi observed this about an American custom:

The "please help yourself" that Americans use so often had a rather unpleasant ring in my ears before I became used to English conversation. The meaning, of course, is simply "please take what you want without hesitation," but literally translated it has somehow a flavor of "nobody else will help you," and I could not see how it came to be an expression of good will. The Japanese sensibility would demand that, in entertaining, a host should show sensitivity in detecting what was required and should himself "help" his guests. To leave a guest un-familiar with the house to "help himself" would seem excessively lacking in consideration. This increased still further my feeling that Americans were a people who did not show the same consideration and sensitivity towards others as the Japanese.[3]

When differences like these exist in their lives, it is easy to imagine that there are differences within the organizations in general in the two countries and in the communication practices of those organizations.

THE COMPANIES

So numerous are the differences between Japanese and American corporations that they will be discussed in relation to business in general, to management of the business, and to the employees of the business.

Business

Overall conduct of the business in America and Japan differs consid-erably, as shown in Table 8. For one thing, the relationship between a corporation and the government is cooperative in Japan and adversarial in America. Gibney explains:

Where the American tradition holds government and business to be perennial adversaries, in Japan they have always been closely related. The American out-look on government–business collaboration has, of course, changed with the times; but it is always an uneasy relationship. If not the extreme of determined free enterprisers denouncing government interference, we present the more distressing spectacle of cost-plus contractors cozying up to government agencies or corporations readily intimidated into mailing extravagent party campaign contributions. The Japanese have more open connections. Because their heavy

Table 8
Comparison of Business in Japan and America

Japan	America
Government and business are allies	Government and business are adversaries
Ownership of company by employees	Ownership of company by stockholders
Debt financing of company	Equity financing of company
Business target is market share at home and abroad	Business target is quarterly and annual profit
Businesses strive for permanance	Businesses strive for efficiency
Based on military metaphor	Based on success strategy
Organization chart a formality	Organization chart shows responsibility and authority relationships
No job descriptions	Job descriptions important
Informal organization dominant	Formal organization dominant
Long-term focus	Short-term focus
Companies dependent on subcontractors	Companies more self-sufficient

industry has been largely created by the government, it has always seemed natural to accept the administrative guidance of the Ministry of International Trade and Industry, or its prewar predecessors, as a complement to doing business, rather than an impediment. Government bureaucrats continue to accept senior posts in business (largely sinecures) after their early retirements at fifty-five, a practice cynically called "descents from heaven" (*amakudari*) by hostile newspaper commentators (who only rarely receive directorships when *they* retire).[4]

Striner said in the NBC documentary, "If Japan Can, Why Can't We?":

Part of what happens in Japan is that the government will sit down with the manufacturers and determine what we can do to help you, what can we do to cooperate for the benefit of the entire economy. While here we have this adversarial relationship, this clean, clear demarcation that we so love between government and industry.[5]

In a later NBC program, "Japan vs. USA: The Hi-Tech Shoot-Out," broadcast August 14, 1982, W. J. Saunders III of Advanced Micro Dynamics Corporation observed: "It is virtually impossible for any company to compete with a sovereign nation."[6] That's how most outsiders view the competitive struggle with Japan. In an article in the *Pacific Basin Quarterly*, Tsurumi states well the Japanese viewpoint:

The Japanese government's role is to develop, through consultations with business, labor, and academic circles, broad national goals for industrial growth. This is why economic planning in Japan is called indicative economic planning. Economic plans formulated by the government merely "indicate" the desirable directions of the Japanese economy. Actual implementation of the plans is accomplished through competition for the survival of the fittest among the private firms. Once private firms are in accord with the economic policies of the government, you will find that there is less uncertainty regarding the specific objectives in the long-range planning of each firm.[7]

The branch of government that works with business is the Ministry of International Trade and Industry, which sets goals for Japanese industry every ten years.

The American adversarial system between companies and suppliers, companies and consumers, and companies and the government stems from a number of qualities of American life: the individualism that created the country, the Bill of Rights, the pioneering spirit, and economic Darwinism, whereby only the strong survive. The system could not be changed without changing the entire free enterprise system as it exists in America.

Another basic difference between Japanese and American companies is their system of financing. America's debt-to-equity ratio is 20:80, meaning that 80 percent of its financing comes from shareholders. Japan's is reversed, with 80 percent coming from banks.

This difference creates opposing philosophies for operating the organizations. In the United States, the approach is: "The firm belongs to the stockholders. We need to make profits for them." The Japanese say: "Legally, the firm belongs to the stockholders. But more important, morally speaking, the firm is the collective property of all the members, from the president down to the rank and file."[8] Indirectly those employees have a lot to do with their company's financial backing.

Personal income savings in Japan averages 22 percent of disposable income, higher than West Germany's 15 percent and America's 5 percent. The Japanese deposit these funds in city and commercial banks, which use them for investment loans to businesses. Japanese industry, particularly heavy chemicals and durable goods, is said to generate half of its growth from such funds.[9]

American companies must show results to shareholders in quarterly and annual profits. Management is pressured to achieve such short-term results, even at the expense of longer-term gains. Japanese managers carefully cultivate relationships with bankers, to whom they turn for help. They are freed from having to show short-term progress at the expense of planning long range.

Thus the Japanese company is better able to see opportunities in worldwide markets than are American managers, who concentrate on the domestic market for the required profits. Also, Japanese efforts are toward permanency, while American companies concentrate on achieving the greatest efficiency.

Businesses in the two countries plan their work according to very different strategies. Japanese managers function in a military metaphor. The Americans work in a success strategy.

Organization charts are very general, almost useless, and job descriptions are not used in Japanese companies. Both are important parts of American business life.

Cost of labor is also quite different. Citibank of New York reported these figures for hourly compensation in manufacturing for 1982, stated in dollars: "United States, $12.61; Sweden, $11.17; Netherlands, $10.91; Belgium, $10.11; West Germany, $10.06; Canada $9.36; Denmark, $8.10; France, $7.57; Britain, $7.35; Italy $6.97; and Japan, $5.72." Japan's wage rate is half that of the United States, allowing the Japanese to sell cars in America for $1,500 to $2,000 less than American car companies can.[10]

In addition to these broad differences, there are differences in the lives of both managers and employees in the two countries.

Managers

Beginning with their boards of directors, companies in Japan and America give different experiences to managers (see Table 9). There are more board members in Japan, and the composition of the boards is very different. In Japan, the board of directors is comprised mainly of employees, including former union leaders; in America, board members are mostly outsiders, with only a few of the top officers also serving as members.

There is also variation to a member's duties. An American member is usually knowledgeable about the company's business. Not so in Japan, according to Nakane:

Some American executives visiting Japan have expressed surprise that so many Japanese directors are unable to explain the details of their own enterprise. They rely cheerfully on their beloved and trusted subordinates to run the business; of much greater concern to them is the maintenance of happy relations among the men, for in this they believe lies the key to business success.[11]

Because employees in Japan tend to progress through the ranks at a predetermined rate, top executives tend to be uniformly in their sixties.

Table 9
Comparison of Management in Japan and America

Japan	America
Board of directors has average of 14 members	Board of directors has average of 8 members
Board of directors comprised mostly of employees	Board of directors comprised mostly of outsiders
Age of top executive in sixties	Age of top executive in fifties
Chief executive not involved in day-to-day operations	Leaders expected to have impact on company affairs
Authority and responsibility diffuse	Authority and responsibility specific
No major distinction between managers and workers	Sharp distinction between managers and workers
Passive management style	Aggressive management style
Vertical relationships predominate	Horizontal relationships predominate
Management by human relations	Management by objectives
Resists change	Fosters change
Avoids conflict	Invites conflict
Unified decision making	Individual decision making
Decisions flow upward	Decisions flow downward
Average length of service in job of president is 13.4 years	Average length of service in job of president is 5.7 years

In America, there is much more flexibility, so top executives are usually in their fifties.

The style of managing the two companies is considerably different, too. In Japan, management focuses on human relations and in doing so attempts to avoid conflict and to create a stable business life. This style resists change.

American managers' aggressive style follows a management by objectives approach, which fosters change and invites conflict. Here, horizontal relationships predominate, unlike in Japanese firms in which important relationships are vertical. In these vertical associations, decisions flow upward in Japanese companies, opposite to those in the American business.

Much of this affects employees as well as managers. However, there are qualities concerning employees alone that are different in the two countries.

Table 10
Comparison of Employees in Japan and America

Japan	America
Lifetime employment	Mercenary employment
Slow promotion	Rapid promotion
Enterprise union	Trade union
Selection of new employees from elite	Selection of new employees from wide spectrum of populace
Company recruits people of particular education and age to fill general vacancies	Company recruits people with particular skill and experience to fill specific jobs
Selection of employees based on total personality	Selection of employees based on expertise
Nonspecialized career path	Specialized career path
Seniority basis for promotion and raise in pay	Merit basis for promotion and raise in pay
Promotion from within	Hiring from outside
No job changes between companies	Frequent job changes between companies
Group activity	Individual responsibility
Mandatory retirement age is 55 for most employees	Mandatory retirement age is 65
Retirement benefits are 3 to 5 years worth of bonuses	Retirement benefits are high percentage of salary for rest of life
High turnover at end of career with loss of valuable sources	High turnover at all levels

Employees

As discussed earlier, employees of Japanese corporations have an experience very unlike that of American employees (see Table 10). The Japanese company hires recent college graduates, primarily from elite colleges. The new employees are expected to be generalists in the organization for which they will work for their entire careers. They will be promoted according to age and length of service instead of merit, and at age 55 they will retire.

Japanese companies have six times more people involved in solving operational problems than do U.S. companies. They employ twice the number of middle managers and supervisors, on the average. Americans ask how many people a manager can supervise to employ the smallest number of managers. In Japan, they ask how many managers are needed to provide the best supervision and to improve the quality of production.[12]

Employees of American firms, on the other hand, are hired for specific jobs, perhaps after having worked for one or more other companies. Promotions for them are based on merit, for the most part, and retirement is at age 65 or sooner, if desired.

There is a difference in attitude toward employees by managers in American and Japanese companies. When there's a problem in the Japanese firm, management takes the blame. In America, it's the worker who is considered responsible for problems that arise. The result is demoralized workers and inevitable inefficiency, disinterest in the job, and absenteeism.

Attitude of workers toward their jobs is also different. The Japanese worker makes a total commitment to the job; the American worker segments his life between his work and other important parts of life, primarily his family.

The Japanese corporation, Nakane says, buys future labor, whereas the American company buys immediate labor.[13] For the worker, that means job security in Japan and job insecurity in America.[14] As a result, turnover rate is 25 percent in America and only 6 percent in Japan.[15]

At the end of a career, the situation is reversed: retirement insecurity in Japan, where no lifetime pensions are provided; and retirement security in America, where pensions are provided.

The way in which a worker functions on the job is also considerably different in the two countries. In America, as previously discussed, the functioning unit is the individual; in Japan, it is the group. The satisfactions that workers derive from the jobs are correspondingly different. Bairy explains:

For instance, a recent researcher among middle management personnel in the United States and in Japan purported to discover that self-actualization was the principal motivation of parallel groups in both countries—in other words, that the focus of motivation in the United States is, for all practical purposes, the same as that in Japan. But alas! self-actualization in the United States and self-actualization in Japan have very different meanings. In the States it is tantamount to the enhancement of the individual, whereas in Japan it is tantamount to the enhancement of the group.[16]

In the United States, there is separation between the departments. If you work in production, you are not expected necessarily to talk to those in engineering. In Japan, the traditional egalitarianism breaks down such barriers. Everyone parks in the same lot, eats in the same cafeteria, wears the same uniform, and talks to everyone else, regardless of department.

On the other hand, regimentation on the job is developed in Japan to a degree that would be objectionable to the American worker. A recent UPI article, "Honda's U.S. Plant Not Likely to Follow Japanese Pattern," said this about the work routine in Japan:

The 220-acre Suzuka plant, like other Japanese auto plants, operates two shifts a day, five days a week.

Early-shift workers start drifting in at 6:30 A.M., in time for the 6:50 whistle. They don uniforms.

The company says the uniform—white overalls and a dark green cap printed with the Honda logo—is worn by everyone from plant manager to janitors.

At 7 A.M. sharp, the machines rumble to life.

At 9 A.M., another whistle. The machines stop for seven minutes, allowing workers to stretch and go to restrooms.

"Basically, workers are not allowed to take time off for toilet when the line is moving," explained Toshio Nishimura, a 36-year-old line foreman.

"In case anyone needs it, he would have to ask leave, and I myself or my deputy would have to take his place at the line," he said. "But most of our people follow rules. We are professionals."

To become a Honda "professional" typically demands an education background above senior high school level. Once employees, the man becomes a Honda *shain* (pronounced shah-in), or company member, and that applies to those in the management as well as the rank and file—an equality of identity, and perhaps rapport, that is typically shown at lunch time.

At lunch time, between 11:30 and 12:15, managers and employees at Suzuka share the same fast-food cafeteria. All eat a company-subsidized meal at 155 yen (75 cents) each.

According to a U.S. Transportation Department–sponsored study released late last year, unauthorized absences average 8 percent in the United States, 2 percent in Japan.

At the Suzuka plant, Miyazake said, "Absenteeism is nearly zero."

During the lunch break, a young assemblyman was asked if he had ever taken a working day off.

"No, I have never gone AWOL" is the way Sakuno Sano replied. Sano, in his early twenties, said he has been with Honda four years.

"Late?" he answered, as if another question were a joke. "No."

Then, the 45-minute lunch time was up. Sano and fellow workers trooped back to their shop for the rest of the day's shift, for which they get paid an average salary of 3.2 to 3.3 million yen ($13,900 to $14,350) a year.[17]

Needless to say, the experience of the American worker scarcely corresponds to that at all.

COMMUNICATION IN THE CORPORATIONS

Communicators like to say that communication used to be a chapter in the management textbook but now it is the whole book. While that is

Table 11
Comparison of Internal Communication in Japanese and American Corporations

Japan	America
Purpose of communication to transmit information and provide emotional massage	Purpose of communication to transmit information
Strong system of informal communication	Strong system of formal communication
Strong upward communication	Strong downward communication
Strong horizontal communication	Weak horizontal communication
Nonverbal communication an important part of message	Nonverbal communication almost totally ignored
Prefer indirect communication	Prefer dirct communication
Strong group-nurturing system of decision making by consensus	Nurturing of individuals
Meetings frequent and long	Fewer and shorter meetings
Prefer compromise and conciliation at meetings	Invite confrontation at meetings
Communication shorthand established by long-term associations	High mobility of employees eliminates communication shorthand
Communication by personal contact	Communication by paper work

certainly not true of American corporations, it is useful as a comparison of the communication systems in American and Japanese corporations: communication in the American corporation is a chapter in the management text; in the Japanese company, it is the whole book! (See Table 11.)

If we look at the communication system on their respective management charts, we would see great differences between the Japanese and American systems. In the American system, downward communication predominates and horizontal communication is a distant third. In the Japanese company, upward communication is dominant, followed closely by horizontal communication. Also, because the informal system in Japan (the *habatsu*) is semi-organized and extremely influential in the Japanese organization, it is included on a formal chart of the Japanese system. On the American chart of the formal communication, the informal system—the grapevine—is omitted because it functions separately and totally randomly.

Koichi Hamada has described the difference between Japanese communication methods and those in American corporations as that between the "logic of adaptation" and the "logic of choice." The Western pattern is to specify the possible alternatives for choice and then to choose one strategy. "The Japanese pattern of communication or negotiation is to adapt its attitude depending on the attitude of other parties."[18] The system of *ringisho* illustrates well the Japanese approach. Kunihiro Masao agrees:

I believe that communication between cultures is, more than anything else, communication between different systems of logic. As stated by E. S. Glenn, the well-known American interpreter for several presidents, if one deals with interpreting only on the linguistic level, and assumes that if the proper interpreters and translators are put to work everything will fall into place, the bridge-building effort is doomed to failure. The biggest hurdles are on a different level, that of logic and thought.[19]

In Japanese society in general, communication flows far less freely than it does in America. However, though they say less and say it less directly, the Japanese are constantly sending and receiving nonverbal messages. Americans tend to overlook that part of the communication process.

A great deal of pressure is placed on the Japanese because of this need to be continually attuned to others' messages. Barnlund reported one individual's view: "One Japanese described his communication as a three-act play: 'Premeditation,' 'Rehearsal,' and 'Performance.' Each encounter is planned in advance, messages rehearsed, and remarks offered according to plan. The aim is to anticipate disagreements and avoid any challenges that could embarrass or harm others."[20] No outsider could really understand the burden of such a system.

In the Japanese corporation, communicating is not delegated to an individual or a department as it is in American companies. In Japan, responsibility for communication is given to the personnel department; however, in this system which emphasizes human relations, that responsibility is easily relayed to each employee. Ask a Japanese which department he considers most important in his company and he will invariably specify the personnel department, an answer that almost certainly would not be offered by an American employee.

Even more important than the pervasiveness of communication in the Japanese corporation is the type of communicating that takes place. The Japanese recognize the importance of communication in general and of upward communication in particular. Louis Williams, senior vice-president of Hill and Knowlton, Inc., said in a speech entitled "Communications for Profit, the New CEO Role," "The Japanese do not communicate because they believe it is the right thing to do to build a better system or procedure. They communicate because they know that by doing so they will improve productivity, and that if productivity is improved, the individual worker's lot in life will be improved."[21]

In the NBC program, "Japan vs. USA, the Hi-Tech Shoot-Out," Keiske Yawata of NEC Electronics, USA, said, "Japanese have learned that communication, particularly competitive analysis, is vital to the success of business."[22] Later in that program, the narrator said, "Information is a key element in the Japanese management system of consensus, under which top corporate executives agree on the wisest course. They need information to do that, and it is gathered for them from around the world. The system works."[23] If American managers could learn that lesson—the importance of communication, particularly upward communication, to an organization—I believe, many of their problems with productivity would disappear.

NOTES

1. "Mandarin Oranges and Origami," p. 10.
2. Doi, *The Anatomy of Dependence*, p. 11.
3. Ibid., p. 13.
4. Gibney, *Japan*, p. 174.
5. "If Japan Can, Why Can't We?" transcript, part 1, p. 6.
6. "Japan vs. USA, the Hi-Tech Shoot-Out," transcript, p. 3.
7. Tsurumi, "Productivity: the Japanese Approach," p. 10.
8. Tsurumi, *The Japanese Are Coming*, p. 225.
9. Baranson, *The Japanese Challenge to U.S. Industry*, p. 10.
10. Bauder, "U.S. Productivity West's Lowest," pp. H11, H18.
11. Nakane, *Japanese Society*, p. 69.
12. "Business Hotline," p. 6.
13. Ibid., p. 19.
14. Cleaver, *Japanese and Americans*, pp. 99–100.
15. Harding, "Needed a String to Pull," p. 4.
16. Bairy, "Motivational Forces in Japanese Life," in *The Japanese Employee*, ed. Ballon, p. 55.
17. "Honda's U.S. Plant Not Likely to Follow Japanese Pattern," p. 11.
18. Hamada, "Japan's Role in the World Economy," in *Japan, America and the Future World Order*, ed. Kaplan and Mushakoji, p. 194.
19. Masao, "The Japanese Language and Intercultural Communication," in *The Silent Power*, ed., Japan Center for International Exchange, p. 67.
20. Barnlund, *Public and Private Self in Japan and the United States*, p. 131.
21. Williams, "Communications for Profit, The New CEO Role," p. 10.
22. "Japan vs. USA, the Hi-Tech Shoot-Out," p. 23.
23. Ibid., p. 28.

15

Conclusion

Beyond the comparisons in the previous chapter, there are certain broad statements that can be made about communication in Japanese and American firms and about those corporations in general:

1. Japanese business successes are attributable in large measure to their excellent communication programs, which make every employee a communicator.
2. As we move into the Information Age, this communicating ability will give the Japanese company a distinct competitive edge over corporations in other countries.
3. American business persons can copy Japanese techniques only to a limited extent. A primary need in the American corporation, for example, is improved upward communication, provided in part by the rapid adoption of quality circles.
4. Beyond that, however, Japanese managerial techniques are part of an economic system that is neither totally capitalistic nor communistic. Instead, it is a brand new hybrid that could not be copied satisfactorily anywhere else.

This chapter describes these conclusions in greater detail and looks at the future of the corporation and its communication program in both countries.

COMMUNICATION PROGRAMS

The Japanese communicate better than the Americans. Their culture requires it; their training includes it. Because of their language, they are able to communicate more by saying less than Americans do, and they extend the information interchange to nonverbal signals.

To their great benefit, the Japanese use their communication skills in their business affairs; indeed, it would be impossible for them not to. Everyone in Japan communicates constantly. In the corporation, communication flows in every direction with particular emphasis on upward messages, which has been of inestimable value to the company.

"On the average," Vogel says, "Japanese companies collect and process information more thoroughly than their foreign counterparts."[1] Tony Hain of the General Motors Institute, speaking at the Japan-America Business Conference held at the University of Nebraska, Lincoln, in October 1981, said:

Another hallmark of the Japanese firm is higher information density. Important information. If you work in Japanese firms, you'll see strategic information being pushed down. They'll have quarterly management briefings that workers come to as well. They'll review the state of the business—those factors that take place in the environment that'll shape the industry and shape the plant.

Hain sees the average workers receiving the same data base as the general supervisor of manufacturing at General Motors: "That leads to a lot of significant things. Employees of Japanese companies in the United States turn in a lot of suggestions, good quality suggestions. Decentralization of communication and the tremendous amount of managerial information that goes to the worker is very, very important."[2]

INFORMATION AGE

The Information Age is the third great transformation in our planetary pattern of living.* Alvin Toffler calls it the Third Wave, in a book by that title. After surviving for millions of years as hunters, humans learned to grow their food. Beginning about 8000 B.C., the Agricultural Age evolved to its present state, in which only 3 percent of all workers are in agriculture. The Industrial Age began in England in the late seventeenth century with the invention of the steam engine. That era swept across Europe and the rest of the world, and it is now on the downturn of its 300-year cycle. It is predicted that by the end of that cycle, only 3 percent of all workers will be engaged in the manufacture of products. The Information Age began nearly 30 years ago in America,

---

*The material in this part was first presented in a talk, "Japan and America in the Information Age: Who Has the Competitive Edge?" at the Second Japan–United States Business Conference, Tokyo, Japan, April 4–6, 1983.

when white collar workers outnumbered blue collar workers in 1956 for the first time. More workers were then dealing with information than were producing goods.[3] In the following year, Russia launched Sputnik, starting what John Naisbitt in *Megatrends* calls the "globalization of the information revolution."[4] The shift from an agricultural society to an industrial one took a century; the shift to an information society took only two decades.[5]

Life in the Information Age will be almost totally different. "We're heading into a period where change is the norm," said one American manager.[6] The rate of change is increasing, as is the magnitude of those changes. One change will be increased population. When the Information Age was beginning in the mid-1950s, I remember being told as a high school student that the population of the world was 2.5 billion. Today it is a billion and a half larger at 4 billion. By the end of this century, it is expected to be 6 billion—a gain of 2 billion in less than two decades. About 90 percent of the increase will be in developing countries.[7] Another change will be accelerated accumulation of knowledge. Human knowledge doubled every ten years to 1950 and every five years to 1970.[8] By 1995, futurists predict, knowledge will double every year.[9] Robert Hilliard of the Federal Communications Commission described the knowledge revolution this way:

At the rate at which knowledge is growing, by the time the child born today graduates from college, the amount of knowledge in the world will be four times as great. By the time that same child is 50 years old, it will be 32 times as great, and 97 percent of everything known in the world will have been learned since the time the child was born.[10]

In the five centuries from the time of Gutenberg in 1450 to 1950, some 30 million printed books were published worldwide. In the next quarter century, an equal number appeared.[11] By the year 2040, there will be an estimated 200 million *different* books. A library will require 5,000 miles of shelving to store just one copy of each book; a card catalog will require 750,000 drawers. At the same time, the world will be producing several thousand hours per day of new television programming, compared with the several hundred hours per day produced now.[12] This volume of information will be manageable by new methods of information storage and retrieval.

Although information has always represented power, in the Information Age it will be the source of wealth as well. Some will be information rich; others will be information poor.

Information is an economic entity because producing it costs something and people are willing to pay for it.[13] Of considerable benefit in this trend is the fact that the resources required will be renewable, replacing today's exhaustible resources.[14]

In such a society, value is increased by knowledge instead of labor.[15] "The systematic and purposeful acquisition of information and its systematic application," says Peter Drucker, "rather than 'science' or 'technology,' are emerging as the new foundation for work."[16] Some scholars believe that the university will replace the factory as the central institution of society.[17]

Access to information will allow better control of the future. In acquiring information, people will be interacting with one another more than with machines and products. The result will be a geometric increase in all forms of communication—personal, print, and electronic.[18]

By the end of this decade, for example, there will be some 1 billion telephones worldwide, almost all capable of dialing direct any of the others.[19] In addition, portable telephones, cigarette-pack size, will be used to call anyone anytime.[20] These are being tested now in New York and Chicago.

Such telecommunications are made possible by an elaborate satellite system. In 1965, the American company Comsat launched a satellite called Early Bird, which handled 240 telephone calls at a time and one television channel. Since then, 30 additional satellites have been launched. Today 106 countries belong to a satellite network developed by INTELSAT, an international joint venture. Each satellite launched today can handle 13,000 telephone calls and two television channels at a time. Plans include satellites in three or four years that can handle 40,000 telephone calls and three television channels.

The result is an international communication network to which any country can connect by constructing an antenna to access the satellites. This is becoming more and more affordable. To lease a single telephone circuit cost $5,500 a month in 1965. Today it costs $800 a month.[21] Soon a receiver "dish" no larger than a rooftop television antenna will replace today's $20 million earth receiving station.[22] The last barrier to universal use of satellites will vanish.

The other technological development that brought on the Information Age is the computer. The basis for the knowledge economy is computerization instead of mechanization. The transistor first and then the integrated circuit made it possible to store a great deal of information and to transfer large volumes of information from one place to another rapidly. Both this ability to extend our brain power electronically and the communication capabilities worldwide from satellite systems have made possible an Information Age. Austrian Chancellor Bruno Kreisky has said that what networks of railroads, highways, and canals were in the past, networks of telecommunications, information, and computerization are now and will be in the future.[23]

Everyone in the Information Age will be computer-literate. Some 75 percent of all jobs as early as 1985 will involve computers in some way.[24]

Table 12
Contrasting the Industrial and Information Ages

Industrial Age	Information Age
Total of human knowledge doubles every ten years	Total of human knowledge doubles every year
Shift from Agricultural Age took a century	Shift from Industrial Age took two decades
Based on mechanization	Based on computerization
Growth measured by GNP	Growth selective and purposeful
Separate national economic structures	Unified worldwide economic structure
Developing countries play only marginal role in worldwide economic activity	Developing countries participate in worldwide economic structure by taking over basic industries
Data bases numerous and scattered	Worldwide data base provides best, most current information available
Information shared worldwide by delayed transmission	Instantaneously shared information worldwide made possible by satellites

By 1995, sophisticated computers are expected to be connected to a worldwide data base, providing the best, most current knowledge.[25] There will then be some 80 million personal computers in the United States alone.[26]

These characteristics of the Information Age and others are contrasted on Table 12 to parallel qualities of the Industrial Age. One of them is that, for the first time, the Information Age will bring an interdependence of all the world's countries.

When the world fully recovers from the present recession, futurists predict, the economic structure will be different. Certain industries will never attain their former vitality in America and Europe because populous developing countries will take over industries that are labor-intensive and have low technology content. The center of production of industries such as steel, automobiles, railroad equipment, appliances, textiles, shoes, and apparel will have shifted to other parts of the world, such as Southeast Asia.

The old industrialized countries will be unable to compete in those industries, and they will be busy serving the demand for products and services that are more sophisticated and require an advanced technology.[27] By the end of this century, 85 to 90 percent of the world's population will be engaged in this activity, which Princeton economist Fritz Machlup has termed "knowledge industries."[28] In these industries, present production processes will be obsolete.[29] Toffler has suggested that the new industries will be electronics and computers, space technology, sea exploration, and biological developments.[30]

Although business organizations began much earlier, the corporation as we know it dates back only 80 years and has evolved to accommodate increased size and expanding technology. (Factories existed in the City-states of Sumer [Ur and Sippar] in 3000 B.C. They were "private, royal and temple factories set up to produce goods for local consumption and for export.")[31] The future will bring further changes to corporate structure, management styles, and goals, some of them shown in Table 13. Toffler predicts a "thoroughgoing reconceptualization of the meaning of production and of the institution that, until now, has been charged with organizing it."[32]

It will have to be what David Mitchell, vice-president of Business International, Ltd., of England, calls an "adaptable company."

There are a number of characteristics inherent in an adaptable company: It has a shallow hierarchy—you can never get action out of these multi-layer companies; there's a global-structure control based on feedback and action rather than just on supervision and security; it has a self-organizing system organization structure so as to receive a minimum of communications—you need communication but you don't need too much; it exercises strategic management; it places no premium on tidiness in organization; it tolerates small mistakes; it is never surprised; it can innovate internally as well as by acquisition; it is not dependent on scale for profits.[33]

Toffler describes Information Age corporations as less top-heavy, having flatter hierarchies, smaller components linked together in temporary associations, each with its own outside connections.[34] In the organization of the future, according to James Affleck,

the old-style divisions of assigned responsibility are constantly being crossed, often without formal or official recognition, by individuals whose inquiring minds, ambition, or dedication simply will not permit them to be limited by lines on a chart.... Organizations will slowly become more fluid and less dimensional at all levels, with growing participation by subordinates in key decisions affecting them and even the enterprise as a whole.[35]

The corporation of the future will focus more fully on people in ways shown in Table 14. In a rapidly changing world, lifelong education will become the norm. An employee will learn a new job every year and begin a new career every five years.[36] Concern will shift to the intellectual and personal aspects of the job. Individualism in the work place will be

Table 13
Contrasting the Corporation in the Present and the Future

Industrial Age	Information Age
Organization structured and ordered	Organization flexible at all levels
Control based on supervision	Control based on feedback
Tall hierarchies—up to 11 levels in large companies	Flat hierarchies in companies of all sizes
Definite assigned duties as shown on organization chart	Division of responsibilities as shown on organization chart crossed frequently
Decentralization incomplete	Decentralization complete
Short-term planning	Long-term planning
Numerous raw materials	Basic raw material is information
Relies on exhaustible resources	Relies on renewable resources
Value increased by labor	Value increased by knowledge
Emphasis on achievement	Emphasis on self-actualization
Foundation for work is profit	Foundation for work is systematic acquisition of information
High profit margin is wealth	Access to information is wealth
Information acquired as needed	Information central to operations
Communication based on "need to know"	Communication is basic function
Communication efforts scattered	Communication core combines capabilities of telephone, radio, television, computer, and facsimile
Meetings a major consumer of time and money	Teleconferencing reduces costs of meetings

needed and fostered. Much of this will be in reaction to the automation that is transforming work habits in the office and factory. Word and data processors will continue to streamline the work of managers and their support staff; robots will automate most manufacturing processes.

Decentralization will occur to a degree not seen before, with emphasis on nearly autonomous groups and even individuals. Groups will function in new styles of management. Entrepreneurships will increase, and corporations will have to learn how to encourage the entrepreneurial spirit among their own employees.

Table 14
Contrasting Management and Employees in Present and Future Corporations

Industrial Age	Information Age
Management in charge	Management by "nonmanagement"
Manager a decision maker	Manager an information processor
Production workers predominate	"Knowledge workers" predominate
Workers pitted against fabricated nature	Workers pitted against other people
Workers located at plant	Workers may work at home—in an "electronic cottage"
Workers give rote responses	Workers capable of discretion and resourcefulness
Emphasis on total organization	Emphasis on small groups and individuals
Requires people who obey orders	Requires people who accept responsibility, are individualistic, and are capable of using all their skills
Employees have a single career	Employees undergo training for new career every 5 years
Education for definite period of 12 or 16 years	Lifelong education

New demands will be made on workers in the future. Employees will need to be resourceful and capable of discretion and will not be able to rely on rote responses, according to Toffler.[37] It is the difference between a classical musician who plays each note according to a predetermined pattern and the jazz musician who improvises. The employee of the future corporation will have to improvise. Toffler calls such people complex and individualistic and says they are proud of the ways they differ from other people.[38]

Employees will also require of management a new attitude. Affleck explains how and why:

We are going to have to employ people as people, taking into account all the interests, habits, attitudes, and learned skills which when properly exercised lead the human being to new heights of individual and collective achievement.... Perhaps the biggest circumstance facing management today and in the future is the rise in educational levels of the people who compose the organization.[39]

It is an entirely new system of managing people. The future of management, says Affleck, is "nonmanagement."

It will be the development and utilization of people organized to employ all of their individual creative talents to the maximum, within an environment of continuous and dynamic change.... Management's main job will be to exercise sensitivity and an educated intuition to draw the maximum from a highly skilled and intellectually sophisticated force of managers and workers.[40]

The new manager will be viewed as an "information processor."[41] The required attributes of the future manager, according to Toffler, are operating as well in open-door free-flow styles as in more rigid hierarchical modes, in organizations structured like Egyptian pyramids as well as those that resemble Calder mobiles, with few managerial strands connecting nearly independent modules.[42] The Information Age will bring a new corporation with new-style employees and managers.

The rigid hierarchical structure will loosen up because it impedes information flow. In the information economy, greater speed and more flexibility in information flow are needed.[43] Future management will want to assure that all elements of the organization have the information needed to do their jobs.[44] The computer makes that possible, says Naisbitt: "With the computer, we don't need that pyramid anymore. Those institutions that survive are going to reconstitute themselves in smaller and smaller entrepreneurial units, horizontal organizations with thousands of profit centers. And we can do that because we now have the computer to keep track of those diverse centers."[45]

Toffler describes information in the future corporation as needed to serve production methods. Information will become central to production, and managers will be "information managers." The result will be competition to control information, more demands for open accounting, more pressure for truth in advertising and lending. The future organization will be as concerned about "information impacts" to the same extent that present organizations worry about environmental and social impacts. The corporation will be viewed as an information producer in addition to an economic producer.[46]

By the next century, the communication system of a corporation will be centralized in a location from which all electronic media will connect offices and plants worldwide. Communication will be fast, flexible, and cheap.

This communication network will enable some employees, those who perform tasks that require few direct face-to-face transactions—entering data, typing, retrieving, totaling columns of figures, preparing invoices— to work at home in what is being called the "electronic cottage."[47] "You will be able to get all the information you need through your computer and telephone," says Nelson Otto, a futurist at Anticipatory Sciences, Inc., Minneapolis. "You can live on a mountaintop, by a lake, in the forest, or on the ocean beach, and still work."[48]

Another futuristic communication technique already in use is an electronic method whereby groups in different locations meet via television monitors. Teleconferencing allows images and voice to be transmitted along with images of printed documents. The company saves the travel and time costs of holding such meetings in person. Drucker explains,

The first impact [of the office of the future] will be a sharp drop in business travel. Few businessmen traveled before 1950 or so, and none, except salesmen, traveled a great deal. But as soon as the jet appeared, two decades ago, hopping a plane for a two-day meeting in Paris, Rio, or Tokyo became commonplace.[49]

COMPETITIVE EDGE?

Based on what we know about American and Japanese companies in 1984, let's now try to determine which corporation most closely matches the qualities of the Information Age organization that we have discussed. We will consider the companies in terms of their structure, management style, employee relations, and communication system.

In organizational structure, great differences exist between American and Japanese corporations. The American corporation is hierarchical, with an organization chart outlining the relationship among workers, whose duties are clearly delineated in job descriptions. There is a clear distinction between managers and employees.

Japanese corporations have a much less rigid structure and operation. Organizational charts are only formalities and very general in content. No clear delineation of individual responsibilities is set forth in job descriptions. To make that delineation, they feel, would mean that when a worker is absent from the job his duties would stop. No distinction exists between manager and employees.

The Japanese have relatively flat organizational hierarchies with two or three levels of supervision, compared with Western companies, which may have seven to ten layers of supervision.[50] These structures, shown in Figure 12, create differences in communication and coordination of Japanese and American corporations, the Japanese is more decentralized. Decisions flow upward in Japanese companies, opposite to the flow in American business.

Management style in the two companies is also considerably different. In Japan, management focuses on human relations, attempting to avoid conflict and create a stable business life. The style resists change. American managers' aggressive style follows a management-by-objectives ap-

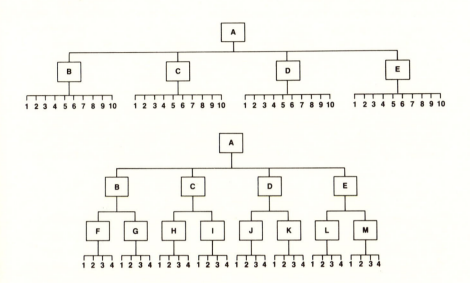

Figure 12. Changes in Structure and Span-of-Control to Facilitate Communication and Coordination.

proach that fosters change and invites conflict. Here horizontal relationships predominate, unlike in Japanese firms, where important relationships are vertical. Japanese management is known to favor a long-term approach to planning and to operate through group activity. Americans up to now have preferred a short-term view and have depended on employee individuality for the best results.

Employees of Japanese corporations have an experience very unlike that of the American employee. The employee's attitude toward his company is different, as is the company's view of the employee. This is best illustrated by who takes the blame when something goes wrong. In America, the worker does; in Japan, the manager is considered at fault.

Japanese employees are treated in a way, says Ezra Vogel, that "provides a sense of belonging and a sense of pride to workers, who believe their future is best served by the success of their company."[51] By caring for the whole person, Japanese management has created a secure employee who is committed to his job, his group, and his company.

American management is more interested in an employee's performance in his immediate job and does not have much concern for his career or outside life. The result is insecurity for the American worker and job security for the Japanese worker. The predictable outcome is a turnover rate of 25 percent in America and only 6 percent in Japan.[52]

In the textbook on American management methods, communication is a chapter, if that. In a similar textbook on Japanese management methods, communication is important throughout the book. Communication in the Japanese corporation is not delegated to one individual as it is in American companies. The personnel department in Japan is responsible for communication, but in a system that emphasizes human relations, the responsibility is easily relayed to each employee.

Williams expressed it well: "That's the core of the difference between the Japanese industrial system and ours. They communicate, we don't."[53] The payoff is enormous. It is reported, for example, that the communication technique known as the quality circle saved Japanese companies $4.6 million in 1982.[54]

Communication is important in the Japanese corporation also because information is key to the *ringi* system of decision making. For that, information is gathered systematically from around the world.[55] As stated, the Japanese do that more thoroughly than others.[56] If a business uses this information and its competitors don't, it will naturally have an advantage. The same applies to countries. Japan is using the information it gathers to good advantage.

Mitchell has explained that the Japanese learned in the Meiji Restoration how to learn; they've learned the value of information, and they don't have the cultural problems of adaptation that the rest of us do. "The Japanese get strategic control through constant acquisition and processing of information beyond knowledge up to the point of understanding. Knowledge is where most people stop. This acquisition of knowledge which is developed into understanding gives them very good strategic control."[57]

American companies have not achieved the same type of worldwide information-gathering program as have the Japanese. This is ironic considering that information is America's principal product, including "education, publishing, the media, communications, management and administration, research and development, finance and insurance, and much of the work of government."[58]

Another difference between the two companies is that in Japan upward communication—from employees to supervisors—predominates, but in America downward communication is dominant. Most communicating in American companies is by managers directing and informing employees. Affleck describes the American approach:

Information is made available on a "need to know" basis under the assumption that management knows, in fact, what employees really need to know to do their jobs effectively.... What has become lost in the process is a perception by the individual of the totality of the organization—where it is and where it is heading—and of his or her own potential for contributing to its progress.[59]

In Japan, communication is as common as the fabric of the organizational uniform; in the United States, communication is an accessory of the manager's mantle of authority.

As Table 15 shows, the answer to who has achieved a competitive edge in the Information Age is quite clear. So clear is the Japanese lead in almost every area that we could go back to the tables that contrast the Industrial Age and the Information Age and consider the criteria for the Industrial Age to represent America and those of the Information Age to represent Japan. Toffler in fact seems to be describing present-day Japanese workers when he speaks of the employee of the Information Age corporation. "What Third Wave employers increasingly need, therefore, are men and women who accept responsibility, who understand how their work dovetails with that of others, who can handle ever larger tasks, who adapt swiftly to changed circumstances, and who are sensitively tuned in to the people around them."[60]

The one item on Table 15 that is significant to both countries, however, is "Individualistic employees" under "Employee relations." If there is anything that American workers have and Japanese workers don't have it is individualism. Much of the literature indicates that employees of the future will be acting alone much of the time. Resourcefulness on the part of the individual will determine his success as well as that of his company.

Is Japan to be permanently handicapped by the lack of that one quality? Emphatically not! That changes are already occurring was demonstrated by one speaker at the Second Japan–United States Business Conference in Tokyo in early April 1983. He behaved in a manner not typically Japanese—puffing on a cigar and looking around the audience as he listened to what other speakers had to say—and, in reproachful tones, expressed thoughts that Japanese usually leave unsaid: To succeed in Japan, he said, Americans should:

1. Not assume an attitude of big brother or preacher.
2. Avoid the unwarranted superiority complex so many Americans display when in Japan.

Table 15
Contrasting the Information Age Corporation with Those of Present-day Japan and America

	Japan	America
Structure		
Fluid organizational framework	x	
Flat hierarchy	x	
Loose division of responsibility	x	
Decentralization	x	
Electronic cottage		x
Management Style		
Management by "nonmanagement"	x	
People versus people	x	
Control based on feedback	x	
Long-term planning	x	
Emphasis on groups	x	
Employee relations		
Knowledge workers	x	
Resourceful workers		x
Retraining		x
Lifelong education	x	
Individualistic employee		x
Communication system		
Information a basic raw material	x	
Systematic acquisition of information	x	
Information central to operation	x	
Communication a basic function	x	
Manager an information processor	x	

3. Don't assume you have won an argument simply because your Japanese colleague keeps quiet out of politeness.

4. Remember that what matters is not how long you have been here but how much you have gone out of your way to understand the Japanese.

5. Make good friends with at least two Japanese of high quality.

6. Do not allow yourself to be misled by a Japanese who says, "This is Japan and things must be done in a Japanese way." This may be camouflaging his lack of business acumen.

7. Be a good listener, discerner, and judge.

8. Don't overindulge in pressure techniques in business dealings. Don't view Japanese colleagues as tools to achieve your goals; regard them as human beings.

This young president of a Japanese company proved to me once again during this, my first visit to Japan in 22 years, that the country I knew then is by no means the country it is now and that no adaptation to changing conditions will be impossible to the Japanese.

However, this discussion does not necessarily mean that Japan will be more successful than other countries in the future. What the study does show is that the Information Age is here and has been for three decades; that the corporation in the Information Age will be quite different from corporations today; and that the Information Age corporation resembles present-day Japanese corporations more than it does those from all other countries.

TRANSFER OF TECHNIQUES

"I think America is awake now, but it is not out of bed yet," a Japanese businessman once said to C. Jackson Grayson, chairman of the American Productivity Center, Houston. If the nation is still in bed, at least it is pondering the future and realizing some alarming facts. To forestall the worst possibilities, America is searching for practical solutions. Among them is adopting Japanese management methods.

But can Japanese management be transferred to America? If it can, to what extent? The answers by experts to these questions are "Yes" and "More than we think." Rohlen, for example, says:

Taken separately, the methods can be a sort of gimmick. But taken as part of a coherent, cohesive management system, they can be quite significant.

The real benefits of studying Japanese management, however, will come when we begin to adopt their way of seeing the relationships within organizations as having much greater potential than we ever realized. For example, we've typically treated individuals—especially blue collar workers—like machines: we assumed they were insensitive and expendable.

It's a long, slow process to focus attention on the notions of human potential, connectedness, and mutuality. But in the process, many of the individual practices of the Japanese that have received so much attention become even more viable.[61]

Some understanding of how this is possible and the benefits it would bring can be gained by examining American companies which have been acquired by Japanese owners. Techniques that they then introduce succeed in boosting profitability and employee morale and involvement in a short time. At Matsushita Electric Industrial Company's television manufacturing plant in Franklin Park, Illinois, Japanese managers took over the former Motorola, Inc., facility and improved things dramatically and quickly. In the *Electronics* article, "Yanks Borrow Japanese Keys to Quality," Larry Waller reports: "Within six months moves were made toward improvement with revamped production using automatic equipment and a new chassis design. In three years the changes were complete and automatic insertions increased from 15 percent to 65 percent to 75 percent."[62] Steven Wheelwright in the *Harvard Business Review* article "Japan—Where Operations Really Are Strategic," states further, "Within three years after the purchase by Matsushita, the plant, which makes Quasar television sets, increased its productivity by 30 percent and reduced its defects to fewer than 4 per 100 sets."[63] Previously, there were 150 defects per 100 sets!

Another example of Japanese techniques working where applied with foreign workers is the Chrysler plant in Australia, sold to Mitsubishi in 1980. Before the sale, the plant employed 6,800 workers, who turned out a mere 228 cars a day. In two years, the new management succeeded in turning out 214 cars a day with fewer than 3,500 people.[64]

An important part of Japanese management is the attitude of management toward employees. These are treated in a way that gives them a sense of family and a feeling that what benefits the company benefits them.[65] Surely American management can change their present attitudes to something closer to that, although such a change will take a long time.

Even well-structured methods such as quality circles lose something in the transfer to foreign countries. Emphasis in America, for example, is more on human relations and less on statistical applications to quality control. If we were to try to copy Japan's nearly universal employee use of statistical analysis, the change would take time. "The United States can do it," says Deming in an article in Control Data Corporation's magazine, *Contact*, "but I'm afraid it's going to take five to ten years to teach statistics to working people."[66] In the same article, Tom Kamp, president of Peripheral Products Company, is quoted: "One of the strengths of Japan is that even the assembly worker has been trained in statistics."

NEW ECONOMIC SYSTEM

Japan is a confusing mixture of East and West. Kano Tsutomu, in the introduction to *The Silent Power*, "Why the Search for Identity?" says: "Modern Japan has been neither fully Western nor fully Asian, and yet it has aspired to more than full membership in both."[67]

Most puzzling, perhaps, is the economic order which has developed in Japan. It is neither capitalism nor communism, as this statement from *Japan, the Businessman's Guide*, shows:

The Japanese economic system resembles neither Soviet communism nor Western capitalism. It has the dynamism of capitalism but attempts to eliminate both the uncertainties of risk taking and the wastefulness of excessive competition.

It also succeeds, where communism has vainly tried, in persuading the individual to harness his efforts to the furtherance of society's interests in such a way that he ultimately benefits far more than if he followed his own inclinations.

Japan, as befits the leading country of the "third world," seems to have discovered what Harold Macmillan once called the "middle way" between capitalism and communism.[68]

Robert Guillain explains further in *The Japanese Challenge*:

When we compare Japan's planned economy with that of the socialist countries, do we find the unpleasant consequences that are so often to be observed in them: uniformity and the death of the spirit of enterprise and of competition? Nothing of the sort. On the contrary, Japanese planning is successfully united with an unusually active competition, which is chiefly owing to the existence of the powerful industrial groups that have either reappeared or come into being since the war.[69]

This new economic system includes a different view of the worker, according to Gibney.

To understand the Japanese worker, we have to scrap the Western view of work as we know it. This includes both the Marxist idea of a society divided into giant horizontal levels, in which a recognizable class called the proletariat is struggling against the domination of another class called the bourgeoisie, and the free enterprise version, in which work is seen as a struggle by the individual, sanctified or not by the Protestant work ethic, to better himself and, if possible, to become a capitalist in turn. In Japan the job is the society. The society is the job. Every man who enters a company equally shares in it. It is not so much a question of whether Mr. Sakamoto is a director, a junior department head, or the fellow who drives the company bus. What counts is that he works for Mitsubishi. If he works for Mitsubishi, he is a Mitsubishi man. Most of his friends come from Mitsubishi. He drinks with them, golfs or bowls with them, and shares his troubles with them. He competes with them, surely, but like siblings competing within a family which no one would think of leaving. With the exception of his relatives, and possibly a few school friends, most of his associations—and often those of his family's—go on within the framework of the company.[70]

Referring to this quality about Japanese business–government relations, Philip O'Reilly of Houdaille Industries suggested in the NBC program, "Japan vs. USA, the Hi-Tech Shoot-Out" that America may have to change its methods to compete: "Well I think we have to understand that the world is changing and that free enterprise, as we have known it in the past, may have to be altered."[71] Charles Sporck of National Semiconductor agreed later in the same program:

I'm a free market type. I'm an entrepreneur. However, I guess in the last five to ten years I've looked around and said, hey, the world is rapidly becoming non-free in terms of capitalism, in terms of free market, and Japan's a pretty good example of that. The only true free economy is the United States, and I no longer believe that the United States can afford it.[72]

More countries copy Japan's government-industry cooperative system than follow America's system of government-industry confrontation, the program pointed out. "We are increasingly a free enterprise island, and if we sometimes feel we are under economic siege, perhaps we are."[73]

THE FUTURE

Worldwide markets in the future will belong to those who can process information fully and quickly. The total of human knowledge that doubled every ten years up to 1950 and every five years to 1970,[74] is increasing even faster now, as discussed. The emphasis on communication, strong in Japan and gaining in America, will be the chief characteristic of the corporation in the Information Age.

"The task now for corporate communicators is to help people seize the future," said William P. Dunk, a communication consultant from New York.[75] And that means giving them the sorts of responsibility for and abilities in communication that once were reserved for the corporate communicators.

In the age of increased value of and need for information, it is natural that the electronic media, like the information system shown in Figure 13, will grow in importance against the traditional print media. An important innovation will be connecting word processors, computers, and video capabilities to enable management to communicate with large groups of employees and to receive rapid feedback.[76] Use of the teleconference will grow considerably for everything from sales and training sessions to conversations between two executives at distant locations.

However, technology can't replace human contact. With the push for higher productivity, managers will increase the number of small-group meetings, making themselves more visible to employees. There will be a greater emphasis in America on all forms of upward communication. A survey of 1500 members of IABC determined employee morale and motivation to be the most important issue confronting management today and in the near future (see Table 16). An increase in upward communication should help provide that.

Another effect of the electronics revolution will be a deemphasis in America on the management chart. John Naisbitt, chairman of Naisbitt Group, a firm that analyzes American societal trends, predicts that the computer will eliminate the need for the pyramid. Institutions that survive will structure themselves in smaller units, each a profit center. That

Figure 13. On the Xerox 8010 Star information system, the business person can create, modify, store and retrieve text, graphics and records.

Table 16
Issues of Prime Importance to Business as Identified by Corporate Communicators

Concern	Percent
Employee morale/motivation	60.6
Productivity	42.7
Inflation/recession	39.2
Government regulation	38.2
Energy situation	36.6
Cost containment	36.2
Technological advances	33.7
Economic competition	32.0
Consumerism	25.5
Equal opportunity/affirmative action	24.1
Occupational safety/health	23.5
Professionalism	22.5
Labor relations	22.0
Changing sociopolitical attitudes of the population	21.7
Environmentalism	19.7
Changing demographic composition of the population	18.6
Mental health/alcoholism/drugs	16.6
Ethics and accountability	15.9
Corporate mergers	14.6
International relations	14.5

Source: "Better Titles, More Diversified Duties Lead to Greater Advancement Potential,"
    p. 8.

will be possible because the computer allows us to keep track of those many centers.[77]

The computer also enables companies to keep track of each employee individually, and thereby treat each one differently, according to Naisbitt, eliminating the need to deal with depersonalized large groups. The paradox is that the computer will also enable companies to control employees more closely. Work can be monitored and compared to norms, tying employees closely to performance standards.[78]

Fundamental changes to the work force in America will include lower growth of labor pools due to past low birth rates. Equal opportunity pressures will continue, however, and they will be met easily as manpower shortages will provide new opportunities for inexperienced women, minorities, handicapped persons, and aliens. Retirement for older workers will be postponed.[79] In the emphasis on productivity and worker involvement, there will be a new interest in job enrichment programs like flexitime and employee participation in decision making.

These additional changes were included in the Summer 1982 issue of *Dresser News*, newspaper of Dresser Industries, Inc., of Dallas:

- Surplus among 25- to 44-year-olds: This "baby boom" generation will grow by one-third during the 1980s and will represent 50 to 55 percent of the work force by 1990. In 1975 there was an average of ten candidates for each middle management job. By the mid 1980s there will be nineteen candidates for each such job.
- Women: More than half of all new labor force entrants in the 1980s are expected to be women. By 1990 women will make up 50 percent of the work force, up from 44 percent in 1980.
- Minorities: Minorities will constitute 25 percent of the work force by 1990, up from 17 percent today. Hispanics are expected to surpass blacks as the principal minority group by 1990.
- Organized Labor: Since the mid-1960s, most U.S. labor unions have lost membership. The fundamental shift in our economic base from menial work to mental work has been a major factor. You can expect unions to step up their organizing efforts among the white collar employees in government and manufacturing and service industries to attempt to offset these losses.
- Employee Values: High salaries, job security, and pension benefits are being rated less important by employees. More important to them are meaningful work, opportunity for personal development, and advancement. Loyalty to employer will continue to decline.[80]

That same issue quoted David Snyder, a consulting futurist from Washington, D.C., as saying: "Information is America's principal product. It includes education, publishing, the media, communications, management and administration, research and development, finance and insurance, and much of the work of government." Among the implications of the "information economy" he cited for managers were:

- More money will be spent on productivity improvement for the office worker. Today about $2,500 is spent on equipment for each white collar worker's job versus about $26,000 for each blue collar worker's job.
- Increased attempts will be made by big labor unions to organize the white collar work force.

"Rising levels of education and 40 years of nearly unbroken prosperity have produced significant changes in values held by the American worker," Mr. Snyder added.

"Employee expressions of job satisfaction are declining. Workers are placing more emphasis on meaningful job situations, less on high salaries."

Mr. Snyder's message to Dresser's group staff managers was clear. Much of the demographic, economic, social, and even technological information is available to help managers interpret current trends and how they will impact on our future. But it must be studied and evaluated carefully.

"The future," he said, "evolves in an orderly manner out of the realities of the past, filtered and shaped by the decisions of the present."[81]

In general, said Herman Kahn, director of the Hudson Institute, "The next decade will be known as the 'sobering eighties,' and the best we can hope for is a time of 'lowered rising expectations' in which the standard of living for most people will continue to improve, but not as much as in the last twenty years or so. This will change the definitions of success."[82]

Many of the changes listed above, of course, will apply to Japan as well as America. Vogel predicts, however, that "Japan is going to continue to be the fastest growing of the major industrial powers of the 1980s."[83] If so, it will be amid changes to this country which values tradition. One change, according to Nathan Glazer, will be "the decline of distinctively Japanese values and practices and their replacement by more characteristically 'modern' values," an adjustment that should slow economic growth.[84]

Other changes will be made to the management structure of the Japanese corporation. The *ringi* system will have to give way to the computer. The long process of *nemawashii* will be speeded up by necessity. Some companies are already introducing rewards based on merit instead of age and length of service and are hiring employees in mid-career and compensating them more equitably than in the past.

Japan's efforts, as planned by MITI in its *Visions for the Eighties*, commit $300 million over the next decade to:

- Development of a supercomputer that would be more than 60 times faster than the best now available.
- Basic work on a "fifth-generation" computer that could follow oral commands as well as solve problems nobody told it to tackle—a capacity known as "artificial intelligence."
- Development of new, sophisticated semiconductor devices.[85]

The Japanese goal is to win 18 percent of the American computer market and 30 percent market share of global sales by 1990, which, according to Don Fabun, will be gigantic in America alone:

According to a two-year, 700-page, $500,000 study sponsored by 25 major corporations and conducted by SRI International, "Terminals in the home will be the most important consumer electronics development of the 1980s."

By 1990, they say, individual buyers—as distinguished from business or education—will be 57 percent of the market, which will be selling an estimated 10 *million* systems a year. Market value, including software (the programs that make the hardware work) will be $4.5 billion in 1985 and $7.9 billion in 1990. The entire American computer market is expected to exceed $60 billion: three times greater than the total U.S. factory sales of the automotive industry in its peak year![86]

While Japan pursues its goals, social conditions will be changing, too. Retired persons are expected to increase by the end of the century from the present 9 percent to 22 percent. That will pressure the government to do something to care for them, including pressuring business to extend the retirement age to 65. Eiko Fukuda, in "Japan's Welfare Load Too Heavy to Carry," said this about the aging:

At the moment, for example, the 2,000 government and private homes for the aged here can meet the needs of only 1 percent of those eligible. Only one out of every five old people can get into a hospital geriatric ward.

Traditionally, the elderly in Japan counted on their families for support with couples and their children living under the same roof with the grandparents. Under this arrangement, the daughter-in-law served her husband's aged mother and father. But this custom is breaking down as wives, seeking jobs and equality, increasingly refuse to act as nurses for their elderly in-laws. Crowded housing conditions are also a factor in eroding old-fashioned kinship ties....

The situation is complicated by the fact that the government is trying to persuade companies to extend the retirement age to 65 in order to ease the drain on public resources caused by pension payments.

But the companies, which normally retire workers at 55, are under pressure from their employees to retain the earlier retirement age so that there is room for promotions.[87]

Despite such problems and continuing economic difficulties that forced the resignation of Prime Minister Zenko Suzuki, Japan's influence throughout the world is expected to continue.

Kawasaki predicted about Japan's future that, as its industrial development continues, the West will have to decide whether to lower trade barriers against Japanese products to guarantee a share of the market. Japanese, on the other hand, will have to abide by commercial ethics and rules of fair trading. They will also have to accept more responsibility for developing countries in Asia and Africa.

But for many years, Kawasaki says, Japan will play an important role in trade and industry. Economic consideration will dominate foreign policy. Japan is not likely to assume political leadership of Asia, much less the whole world. For reasons of race and ideology, Japan does not feel up to the task. Instead, Japan will continue to concentrate on industrial power and improvement of the living standards of its citizens.[88] That Japan will continue to succeed in the future as it has in the past seems a certainty. Whether others can achieve similar successes is not so certain.

W. C. Redding in *Communication Within the Organization* characterized ideal managerial climate as including the following: (1) supportiveness; (2) participative decision making; (3) trust, confidence, and credibility; (4) openness and candor; and (5) emphasis on high performance goals.[89] All of these, with the possible exception of number four, describe the Japanese corporation today! If there were a sixth item on the list, it would surely have to be a strong system of communication, particularly upward communication. If America learns one lesson from the success of Japan in world industrial markets, it should be the importance to any organization of those at the top providing opportunities to those at the bottom to communicate with them, and then paying keen attention to what they have to say.

NOTES

1. Vogel, *Japan as Number 1*, p. 43.
2. Hain, "Japanese Success Model in the U.S."
3. Naisbitt, *Megatrends*, p. 12.
4. Ibid.
5. Ibid., p. 18.
6. Kennedy, "Riding the Waves of Change," p. 4.
7. Waterlow, "The 'Community' of the Future," in *Through the '80s*, ed. Feather, p. 155.
8. Fabun, "Feel Buried by Too Much Information?" p. 23.
9. Kennedy, "Riding the Waves of Change," p. 4.
10. Abbott, "Work in the Year 2001," in *1999: The World of Tomorrow*, ed. Cornish, p. 101.
11. Drucker, "Evolution of the Knowledge Worker," in *The Future of Work*, ed. Best, p. 58.
12. Fabun, "Feel Buried by Too Much Information?" p. 23.
13. Naisbitt, *Megatrends*, p. 36.
14. Toffler, *The Third Wave*, p. 136.
15. Naisbitt, *Megatrends*, p. 17.
16. Drucker, "Evolution of the Knowledge Worker," p. 60.
17. Toffler, *The Third Wave*, pp. 353–54.
18. Naisbitt, *Megatrends*, p. 19.
19. Ibid., p. 59.
20. Kennedy, "Riding the Waves of Change," p. 4.
21. Bodman, " 'Telematique'—The Telecommunications Explosion and Its Impact," in *Focus on a Changing World*, pp. 16–17.
22. "Sees Lifestyle Revolution," p. 1.
23. Friedrich, "The Computer Moves In," p. 14.
24. Naisbitt, *Megatrends*, p. 33.
25. Kennedy, "Riding the Waves of Change," p. 4.
26. Friedrich, "The Computer Moves In," p. 16.
27. Kouri, "The Global Economy—New Economic and Political Relationships," in *Focus on a Changing World*, p. 13.

28. Drucker, "Evolution of the Knowledge Worker," p. 58.

29. Kouri, "The Global Economy," p. 13.

30. Toffler, *The Third Wave*, pp. 14–15.

31. Conger, "Social Inventions," in *1999: The World of Tomorrow*, ed. Cornish, p. 146.

32. Ibid., p. 243.

33. Mitchell, "Surprise Avoidance," in *Focus on a Changing World*, p. 44.

34. Toffler, *The Third Wave*, p. 263.

35. Affleck, "The Constructive Orchestration of Chaos," in *Management for the Future*, ed. Benton, pp. 3, 8.

36. Kennedy, "Riding the Waves of Change," p. 4.

37. Naisbitt, *Megatrends*, p. 353.

38. Toffler, *The Third Wave*, p. 385.

39. Affleck, "The Constructive Orchestration of Chaos," p. 2.

40. Ibid., p. 1.

41. Black and Wilson, "The Environment of Management in the Future," in *Management for the Future*, ed. Benton, p. 22.

42. Toffler, *The Third Wave*, p. 264.

43. Naisbitt, *Megatrends*, p. 190.

44. Affleck, "The Constructive Orchestration of Chaos," p. 5.

45. Naisbitt, "Technology Can't Replace Human Contact," p. 3.

46. Toffler, *The Third Wave*, pp. 236–37.

47. Ibid., p. 197.

48. Kennedy, "Riding the Waves of Change," p. 4.

49. Drucker, *The Changing World of the Executive*, p. 36.

50. Yankelovich, "Changes in Expectations and the Work Ethic Worldwide," in *Focus on a Changing World*, pp. 23–24.

51. Vogel, *Japan as Number 1*, p. 157.

52. Harding, "Needed, a String to Pull," p. 4.

53. Williams, "Communications for Profit, the New CEO Role," p. 10.

54. "World View," p. 2.

55. Kennedy, "Riding the Waves of Change," p. 28.

56. Vogel, *Japan as Number 1*, p. 43.

57. Mitchell, "Surprise Avoidance," p. 43.

58. "Dresser Managers Urged to Plan for the Future," p. 2.

59. Affleck, "The Constructive Orchestration of Chaos," p. 5.

60. Toffler, *The Third Wave*, p. 385.

61. "Japanese Management: Can It Work Here?" p. 16.

62. Waller, "Yanks Borrow Japanese Keys to Quality," p. 98.

63. Wheelwright, "Japan—Where Operations Really Are Strategic," p. 67.

64. Burck, "What Happens When Workers Manage Themselves," p. 67.

65. Vogel, *Japan as Number 1*, p. 157.

66. Dineen, "The Force Behind Quality Consciousness in Japan Speaks to Control Data," p. 9.

67. Tsutomu, "Why the Search for Identity?" in *The Silent Power*, ed. Japan Center for International Exchange, p. 9.

68. Financial Times, *Japan*, pp. 18–19.

69. Guillain, *The Japanese Challenge*, pp. 74–75.

70. Gibney, *Japan*, p. 182.

71. "Japan vs. USA: The Hi-Tech Shoot-out," p. 4.

72. Ibid., pp. 62–63.

73. Ibid., p. 59.

74. Fabun, "Feel Buried by Too Much Information?" p. 23.

75. Howard, "More Than a Bulletin Board," p. 34.

76. Foltz, "Learning to Speak with One Voice," p. 31.

77. Naisbitt, "Technology Can't Replace Human Contact," p. 3.

78. Main, "Work Won't Be the Same Again," p. 59.

79. "Trends of the 1980's," p. 1.

80. "Dresser Managers Urged to Plan for the Future," p. 2.

81. Ibid.

82. Kahn, "On Success," p. 2.

83. Vogel, "What Can We Learn from the Japanese?" talk to Japan-America Business Conference.

84. Glazer, "Social and Cultural Factors in Japanese Economic Growth," in *Asia's New Giant*, ed. Patrick and Rosovsky, p. 890.

85. Lohr, "Japan Emerging as Capital of Computerization," p. A-11.

86. Fabun, "Feeling the Electronic World Jitters," p. 23.

87. Fukuda, "Japan's Welfare Load Too Heavy to Carry," pp. C-4, C-8.

88. Kawasaki, *Japan Unmasked*, pp. 230–31.

89. Redding, *Communication Within the Organization*, as cited in Koehler, Anatol, and Applbaum, *Organizational Communication*, p. 126.

APPENDIX
General Motors Communication Policy

GENERAL MOTORS CORPORATION

Date: March 10, 1977
Subject: *INTERNAL COMMUNICATIONS*

General Managers of Divisions
To: Plant Managers
General Operating Officers
Group Executives
Staff Executives
Heads of Staff Sections

General Motors has developed a corporate-wide internal communications program designed to achieve greater understanding and support from all employees in attaining Corporation goals. The purpose of this letter is to affirm the importance of this activity and to encourage your support in achieving continuing improvements.

In today's critical business and social environment, effective two-way communications between management and employees is needed if we are to have the full support of the entire General Motors team—both on and off the job—in several key areas:
- Better communications will encourage our employees to make a greater contribution to our organizational goals simply because they will have a clearer understanding of these goals and what they mean to their own well being.
- More effective communications will stimulate increased ideas from employees to help us run the business more efficiently.

- Better communications also will help secure wider support for the Corporation's stand on important national and local issues because employees will have the necessary background and facts. As a result, they will be better prepared to defend our positions in contacts with friends, neighbors and government officials.

The Internal Communications Section of the Public Relations Staff, working through local Internal Communications Coordinators, will provide printed and audio/visual materials and other services for use by staff, divisional and plant units. There is also a wide variety of other types of information of a local or divisional nature that can and should be conveyed to employees.

While an open climate of information sharing is desirable to satisfy both the needs of the business and of our employees, there is a need to safeguard the security of certain types of confidential corporate information, the disclosure of which might unfairly influence the sale of securities of General Motors or its suppliers. Whenever there is a question concerning the release of information to employees, the matter should be reviewed with the appropriate plant, division or staff executive. The GM Public Relations Staff also is available to assist in the clearance of informational material.

In the final analysis, the major responsibility for carrying out effective employee communications in GM must be assumed by the top management of every staff, division and plant. And every member of supervision shares this responsibility.
Effective internal communications are essential to good management and each of you is urged to give your full support and cooperation to this important activity.

Roger B. Smith
Executive Vice President

cc: Divisional Personnel Directors
    Plant Personnel Managers
    Divisional Public Relations Directors
    Internal Communications Coordinators
    Editors

GENERAL MOTORS CORPORATION

Date: June 9, 1977
Subject: *GUIDELINES FOR MANAGEMENT/EMPLOYEE COMMUNI-*
           CATIONS
   To: General Managers of Divisions
           Plant Managers
           General Operating Officers
           Group Executives
           Staff Executives
           Heads of Staff Sections

In a letter dated March 10, 1977, Executive Vice President Roger B. Smith discussed the importance of effective two-way communications between management and employees in attaining Corporation goals—both on and off the job.

The Internal Communications Section of the Public Relations Staff is responsible for coordinating corporate-wide efforts in this field, including the development of corporate information and materials, training activities and other services to help General Motor's staffs, divisions and plants maintain effective programs of information sharing with all employees. This memorandum discusses minimum standards and outlines guidelines concerning priority subjects for employee-management communications.

MINIMUM STANDARDS

To improve the general level of employee communications throughout the Corporation, minimum standards for each GM location have been developed, based on programs already in operation at some locations. These minimum standards are:
- Establish a formal, organized program of regular communication with all employees involving key information about the business and its effect on employees.
- Establish one regular, frequent channel of printed communication for all employees—at least once a week. It is also desirable to publish a larger publication—monthly, bi-monthly, or quarterly—to allow more in-depth coverage of subjects, both local and corporate, which are of prime interest to all employees.
- Encourage regular meetings between management and employees. At least once a year, management should provide all employees with a review of the state of the business (from both corporate and local viewpoints), as well as discussion of problems and opportunities and what is expected from employees.
- Make effective use of your supervisory structure to provide for two-way communication. Make sure all supervisors understand the importance of communicating key information to subordinate supervisors and to employees in their work group.

- Conduct periodic surveys to evaluate the effectiveness of internal communications and to provide direction for needed change.

GENERAL GUIDELINES

- The local Internal Communications Coordinator is the key to a successful program. The Internal Communicator should have the responsibility for organizing and managing a planned, systematic program involving various channels of employee communications. Included would be printed materials, bulletin boards, employee meetings and audiovisual materials produced both locally and at the corporate level. To insure a successful program, Internal Communicators should be capable managers who have proper professional training or experience and the full support and cooperation of top management.
- Managers and supervisors should be encouraged to share with employees all information that is useful for increasing their understanding of, and contributions to, the operation of the business.
- It is good practice to communicate the bad news as well as the good news to avoid negative effects of rumors and misinformation and to maintain credibility with employees. It also is good practice to respond promptly to rumors or negative information about your organization or GM that would be of concern to employees.
- Whenever possible, important information that is released to the news media should be given to employees at the same time.
- Make prompt and effective use of corporate materials supplied on a continuing basis by the Public Relations Staff through the local Internal Communications Coordinator. All of these materials are approved for release to all employees and to the public unless specifically restricted. Approved materials also will be distributed from time to time by other Corporation staffs and divisional offices.
- Expand Corporation information whenever possible to reflect local interests as a means of increasing its impact on your own employees. Example: In new product stories, discuss the role played by the local organization and people in development, production or sales.

PRIORITY CORPORATE INFORMATION

To help coordinate corporate-wide information sharing, a list of priority subjects for employee communications will be developed each year and made available to Internal Communications Coordinators. Corporate informational materials during the year will highlight these subject areas. The 1977 priorities are:

- Selling GM Products
- Auto Emission Standards
- Auto Safety
- Fuel Economy/Energy Use
- Mass Transit/Role of the automobile
- Product Quality
- Economic Awareness
- Benefits of Being a GM Employee

PRIORITY LOCAL INFORMATION

The corporate priorities provide a base for development of local priorities. In addition to emphasis on these subjects in both corporate and local efforts, special attention should be given to the exchange of local information with employees on other subjects, such as the following:

- Plans, goals and problems concerning GM and the local organization.
- Performance levels—production output, absenteeism, quality, reject rates, periodic reports on progress in meeting established goals; also ranking of departments or plants within an organization in such areas as quality, scrap or absenteeism.
- Expansion or modification of physical facilities, improvement of equipment; what these changes will mean to employees.
- Action or events which require special employee understanding—such as layoffs, reduction in production levels or changes in overtime needs.
- Plant safety—basic rules, reports on accidents and how employees can help.
- Personnel matters—benefit programs, changes in compensation levels, work schedules, job opportunities, training and development opportunities, employment levels.
- Role of the local unit in community relations—how its management and employees can contribute.
- Significant, interesting news about people.

HANDLING OF CONFIDENTIAL OR SENSITIVE CORPORATE INFORMATION

While an open climate of information sharing is desirable to satisfy both the needs of the business and of our employees, there is a need to safeguard the security of certain types of confidential corporate information, the disclosure of which might be detrimental to GM, its shareholders or its employees or which might unfairly influence the sale of securities of General Motors or its suppliers. For a more detailed discussion, see the booklet entitled "GM Guidelines for Employee Conduct" published in May 1977.

Special care also should be used in communicating materials directed to employees or the public which state or imply an inability of a plant or division to meet a union's economic demands or that the unit need a labor cost relief in order to remain competitive. Use of such materials could result in having to provide a union with financial data to support such claims, an action which might be detrimental to the best interests of General Motors.

Whenever there is a question concerning the release of information to employees, it should be reviewed with the appropriate plant, division or staff executive. The GM Public Relations Staff also is available to assist in the clearance of informational material.

A. G. DeLorenzo
Vice President
Public Relations Staff

Attachment

cc: Personnel Directors
Internal Communications Coordinators
Editors

Bibliography

BOOKS

Abegglen, James C. *Business Strategies for Japan*. Tokyo: Sophia University Press, 1970.

————. *The Japanese Factory*. Glencoe, Ill.: The Free Press, 1958.

————. *Management and Worker: The Japanese Solution*. Tokyo: Kodansha International, 1973.

Adams, T.F.M., and N. Kobayashi. *The World of Japanese Business*. Palo Alto, Calif.: Kodansha International, 1969.

Allen, Louis. *Japan: The Years of Triumph*. New York: American Heritage Press, 1971.

American Chamber of Commerce in Japan. *Manual of Employment Practices in Japan*. Tokyo: ACCJ, July 1975.

American Management Associations. International Management Division. *Doing Business in and with Japan*. New York: AMA, 1969.

Anderson, Richard C. *Communication: The Vital Artery*. Watsonville, Calif.: Correlan, 1973.

Aoki, Michiko Y., and Margaret B. Dardess. *As the Japanese See It*. Honolulu: University Press of Hawaii, 1981.

Austin, Lewis, ed. *Japan: The Paradox of Progress*. New Haven: Yale University Press, 1976.

Ballon, Robert J., ed. *Doing Business in Japan*. Tokyo: Sophia University Press, 1967.

————. *The Japanese Employee*. Tokyo: Sophia University Press, 1969.

Baranson, Jack. *The Japanese Challenge to U.S. Industry*. Lexington, Mass.: Lexington Books, 1981.

Barnard, Chester I. *The Functions of the Executive.* Cambridge: Harvard University Press, 1958.

Barnds, William J., ed. *Japan and the United States.* New York: New York University Press, 1979.

Barnlund, Dean C. *Public and Private Self in Japan and in the United States.* Tokyo: Simul Press, 1975.

Bassett, Glenn A. *The New Face of Communication.* New York: American Management Associations, 1968.

Benedict, Ruth. *The Chrysanthemum and the Sword.* Boston: Houghton Mifflin, 1946.

Bennett, John W., and Iwao Ishino. *Paternalism in the Japanese Economy.* Minneapolis: University of Minnesota Press, 1963.

Benton, Lewis, ed. *Management for the Future.* New York: McGraw-Hill, 1978.

Berlo, David K. *The Process of Communication.* New York: Holt, Rinehart and Winston, 1960.

Best, Ernest E. *Christian Faith and Cultural Crisis: The Japanese Case.* Leiden: E. J. Brill, 1966.

Best, Fred, ed. *The Future of Work.* Englewood Cliffs, N.J.: Prentice-Hall, 1973.

Burks, Ardath W. *Japan: Profile of a Postindustrial Power.* Boulder, Colo.: Westview Press, 1981.

Busch, Noel F. *The Horizon Concise History of Japan.* New York: American Heritage, 1972.

Caves, Richard E., and Masu Uekusa. *Industrial Organization in Japan.* Washington, D.C.: Brookings Institution, 1976.

Chamberlain, Neil W. *Enterprise and Environment.* New York: McGraw-Hill, 1968.

Cherry, Colin. *On Human Communication.* Cambridge: MIT Press, 1966.

Clark, Rodney. *The Japanese Company.* New Haven: Yale University Press, 1979.

Cleaver, Charles Grinnell. *Japanese and Americans: Cultural Parallels and Paradoxes.* Minneapolis: University of Minnesota Press, 1976.

Cole, Robert E. *Japanese Blue Collar: The Changing Tradition.* Berkeley: University of California Press, 1971.

―――. *Work Mobility and Participation: A Comparative Study of American and Japanese Industry.* Berkeley: University of California Press, 1979.

Condon, John C., and Mitsuko Saito, eds. *Intercultural Encounters with Japan.* Tokyo: Simul Press, 1980.

Cornish, Edward, ed. *1999: The World of Tomorrow.* Washington, D.C.: World Future Society, 1978.

Council on Foreign Relations. *Japan Between East and West.* New York: Harper and Brothers, 1957.

Dale, Ernest. *Management Theory and Practice.* New York: McGraw-Hill, 1973.

Davis, Keith. *Human Behavior at Work.* New York: McGraw-Hill, 1981.

―――. *Human Relations in Business.* New York: McGraw-Hill, 1957.

Delassus, Jean-Francois. *The Japanese.* New York: Hart, 1972.

De Mente, Boye. *Faces of Japan.* N.p.: Simpson-Doyle, 1966.

―――. *How to Do Business in Japan: A Guide for International Businessmen.* Los Angeles: Center for Industrial Business, 1972.

―――. *Japanese Manners and Ethics in Business.* Phoenix: Phoenix Books, 1981.

Deutsch, Arnold. *The Human Resources Revolution: Communicate or Litigate*. New York: McGraw-Hill, 1979.

Dickerman, Allen. *Training Japanese Managers*. New York: Praeger, 1974.

Dilts, Marion May. *The Pageant of Japanese History*. New York: Longmans, Green, 1938.

Doi, Takeo. *The Anatomy of Dependence*. Tokyo: Kodansha International, 1971.

Drucker, Peter F. *The Changing World of the Executive*. New York: Truman Talley Books, 1982.

———. *Technology, Management and Society*. New York: Harper & Row, 1970.

Dubin, Robert. *The World of Work*. Englewood Cliffs, N.J.: Prentice-Hall, 1958.

Duncan, William. *Doing Business with Japan*. Epping, Essex: Gower Press, 1976.

Dunham, Bob. *The Art of Being Japanese*. Rutland, Vt.: Charles E. Tuttle, 1968.

Embree, John F. *The Japanese Nation*. Westport, Conn.: Greenwood Press, 1973.

England, George W., Anant R. Negandhi, and Bernhard Wilpert, eds. *Organizational Functioning in a Cross-Cultural Perspective*. Kent, Ohio: Kent State University Press, 1979.

Feather, Frank, ed. *Through the '80s*. Washington, D.C.: World Future Society, 1980.

Feinberg, Lillian O., and Mary C. Thompson. *Applied Business Communication*. Palo Alto, Calif.: Mayfield, 1982.

Field, Percy A. "The Receiving End of Communication—Listening." In *Managerial Control Through Communication*, ed. George T. Vardaman and Carroll C. Halterman. New York: Wiley, 1968.

Financial Times. *Japan: A Businessman's Guide*. New York: American Heritage Press, 1970.

Fodor's Japan and Korea, 1982. New York: David McKay, 1981.

Forbis, William H. *Japan Today*. New York: Harper & Row, 1975.

Furstenberg, Friedrich. *Why the Japanese Have Been So Successful in Business*. New York: Hippocrene Books, 1974.

Gellerman, Saul W. *The Management of Human Relations*. New York: Holt, Rinehart and Winston, 1966.

Gibney, Frank. *Japan: The Fragile Superpower*. New York: Norton, 1979.

Gibson, Michael. *The Rise of Japan*. New York: Putnam's, 1972.

Glazer, Herbert. *The International Businessman in Japan*. Tokyo: Sophia University Press, 1968.

Goldhaber, Gerald M. *Organizational Communication*. Dubuque, Iowa: William C. Brown, 1974.

Graves, Desmond, ed. *Management Research: A Cross-Cultural Perspective*. Amsterdam: Elsevier Scientific, 1973.

Greer, Thomas H. *A Brief History of Western Man*. 3rd ed. New York: Harcourt Brace Jovanovich, 1977.

Gryna, Frank M., Jr. *Quality Circles*. New York: American Management Associations, 1981.

Guillain, Robert. *The Japanese Challenge*. Philadelphia: Lippincott, 1970.

Halloran, Richard. *Japan: Images and Realities*. New York: Knopf, 1969.

Hanneman, Gerhard J., and William J. McEwen. *Communication and Behavior*, Reading, Mass.: Addison-Wesley, 1975.

Hersey, Paul, and Kenneth H. Blanchard. "The Management of Change." In

Readings in Organizational Behavior and Performance, ed. John M. Ivancevich, Andrew D. Szilagyi, Jr., and Marc J. Wallace, Jr. Santa Monica,
Calif.: Goodyear, 1977.

Hewins, Ralph. *The Japanese Miracle Men.* London: Secker and Warburg, 1967.

Heyal, Carl. *How to Communicate Better with Workers.* Concordville, Penn.: Clem-
print, 1967.

Hoslett, Schuyler Dean. "Overcoming the Barriers of Communication." In *Management and Its People.* New York: American Management Association,
1965.

Hsu, Francis L. K. *Iemoto: The Heart of Japan.* New York: Wiley, 1975.

Imai, Masaaki. *Never Take Yes for an Answer.* Tokyo: Simul Press, 1980.

————. *16 Ways to Avoid Saying No.* Tokyo: Nihon Keizai Shimbun, 1981.

Ishida, Eiichiro, and Teruko Kachi. *Japanese Culture.* Tokyo: University of Tokyo
Press, 1974.

Ivancevich, John, Andrew Szilagyi, Jr., and Marc J. Wallace, Jr., eds. *Readings
in Organizational Behavior and Performance.* Santa Monica, Calif.: Goodyear,
1977.

Jansen, Marius B. *Japan and Its World.* Princeton: Princeton University Press,
1980.

Japan. Economic Planning Agency. *Economic Survey of Japan.* Tokyo: Japan Times,
1981.

Japan All-Around. Tokyo: Miura, 1970.

The Japan Business Guide. Tokyo: Diamond, 1964.

Japan Center for International Exchange, ed. *The Silent Power.* Tokyo: Simul
Press, 1976.

Japan External Trade Organization. *How to Succeed in Japan.* Tokyo: Mainichi
Newspapers, 1974.

Kahn, Herman. *The Emerging Japanese Superstate: Challenge and Response.* Englewood Cliffs, N.J.: Prentice-Hall, 1970.

————. *The Future of the Corporation.* New York: Mason and Lipscomb, 1974.

Kahn, Herman, William Brown, and Leon Martel. *The Next 200 Years.* New York:
Morrow, 1976.

Kahn, Herman, and Thomas Pepper. *The Japanese Challenge.* New York: Crowell,
1979.

Kahn, Herman, and Anthony J. Wiener. *The Year 2000.* New York: Macmillan,
1967.

Kaplan, Morton A., and Kinhide Mushakoji. *Japan, America and the Future World
Order.* New York: Free Press, 1976.

Kato, Hidetoshi, ed. *Japanese Popular Culture.* Westport, Conn.: Greenwood Press,
1959.

Katz, Daniel, and Robert L. Kahn. *The Social Psychology of Organizations.* New
York: Wiley, 1966.

Kawasaki, Ichiro. *Japan Unmasked.* Rutland, Vt.: Charles E. Tuttle, 1969.

Killian, Ray. *Managing by Design . . . for Executive Effectiveness.* New York: American Management Association, 1968.

Kluckhohn, Clyde. *Mirror for Man.* New York: Wittlesey House, 1949.

Koehler, Jerry W., Karl W. E. Anatol, and Ronald Applbaum. *Organizational
Communication.* New York: Holt, Rinehart and Winston, 1981.

Langer, Paul F. *Japan, Yesterday and Today.* New York: Holt, Rinehart and Winston, 1966.

Lebra, Takie Sugiyama. *Japanese Patterns of Behavior.* Honolulu: University Press of Hawaii, 1976.

Lebra, Takie Sugiyama, and William P. Lebra, eds. *Japanese Culture and Behavior.* Honolulu: University Press of Hawaii, 1974.

Lerner, Max. *America as a Civilization.* Vol. 1. New York: Simon & Schuster, 1957.

Maki, John M., ed. *We The Japanese.* New York: Praeger, 1972.

Marsh, Robert M., and Hiroshi Mannari. *Modernization and the Japanese Factory.* Princeton: Princeton University Press, 1976.

Martino, R. L. *Information Systems: The Dynamics of MIS.* Wayne, Penn.: Management Development Institute, Division of Information Industries, 1968.

Masatsugu, Mitsuyuki. *The Modern Samurai Society.* New York: American Management Associations, 1982.

Mayerson, Evelyn W. *Shoptalk: Foundations of Managerial Communication.* Philadelphia: Saunders, 1979.

McGregor, Douglas. *The Human Side of Enterprise.* New York: McGraw-Hill, 1960.

McNamara, Anne, ed. *Communications Downward and Upward.* New York: National Retail Merchants Association, 1967.

Merrihue, Willard V. *Managing by Communication.* New York: McGraw-Hill, 1960.

Molloy, John T. *Dress for Success.* New York: Warner Books, 1975.

————. *The Woman's Dress for Success Book.* Chicago: Follett, 1977.

Moloney, James Clark. *Understanding the Japanese Mind.* Rutland, Vt.: Charles E. Tuttle, 1954.

Monroe, Wilbur F., and Eisuke Sakakibara. *The Japanese Industrial Society.* Austin: University of Texas Press, 1977.

Morley, James W., ed. *Prologue to the Future: The United States and Japan in the Postindustrial Age.* Lexington, Mass.: Heath, 1974.

Moskowitz, Milton, Michael Katz, and Robert Levering, eds. *Everybody's Business: An Almanac.* San Francisco: Harper & Row, 1980.

Naisbitt, John. *Megatrends.* New York: Warner Books, 1982.

Nakamura, Mikito F. "Business English and Business Communication in Japan." In *International Business Communication: Theory, Practice, Teaching throughout the World.* Ann Arbor: University of Michigan Press, 1981.

Nakane, Chie. *Japanese Society.* Berkeley: University of California Press, 1970.

Norbury, Paul, and Geoffrey Bownas, eds. *Business in Japan.* Boulder, Colo.: Westview Press, 1980.

Northrop, F.S.C. *The Meeting of East and West.* New York: Macmillan, 1946.

Okochi, Kazuo, Bernard Karsh, and Solomon B. Levine, eds. *Workers and Employers in Japan.* Princeton: Princeton University Press, 1974.

Organization for Economic Co-operation and Development. *The Development of Industrial Relations Systems.* Paris: OECD, 1975.

Ouchi, William. *Theory Z.* Reading, Mass.: Addison-Wesley, 1981.

Pascale, Richard Tanner, and Anthony G. Athos. *The Art of Japanese Management.* New York: Simon & Schuster, 1981.

Passin, Herbert, ed. *The United States and Japan.* Englewood Cliffs, N.J.: Prentice-Hall, 1966.

Patrick, Hugh, and Henry Rosovsky, eds. *Asia's New Giant*. Washington, D.C.: Brookings Institution, 1976.

Pempel, T. J. *Policy and Politics in Japan*. Philadelphia: Temple University Press, 1982.

Pezeu-Massabuau, Jacques. *The Japanese Islands*. Rutland, Vt.: Charles E. Tuttle, 1978.

Pickins, Judy E., ed. *Without Bias*. New York: Wiley, 1982.

Pigors, Paul. *Effective Communication in Industry*. New York: National Association of Manufacturers, 1949.

Planty, Earl, and William Machaver. "Upward Communication." In *Business and Industrial Communication*, ed. W. Charles Redding and George A. Sanborn. New York: Harper & Row, 1964.

Plath, David W. *The After Hours*. Berkeley: University of California Press, 1964.

Price, Willard. *The Japanese Miracle and Peril*. New York: John Day, 1971.

Read, William H. "Upward Communication in Industrial Hierarchies." In *Readings in Organizational and Industrial Psychology*. New York: Harper & Row, 1971.

Redding, W. Charles, and George A. Sanborn. *Business and Industrial Communication*. New York: Harper & Row, 1964.

Redfield, Charles E. *Communication in Management*. Chicago: University of Chicago Press, 1958.

Reischauer, Edwin O. *Japan: Past and Present*. New York: Knopf, 1958.

———. *Japan: The Story of a Nation*. 3rd ed. New York: Knopf, 1981.

———. *The Japanese*. Cambridge, Mass.: Harvard University Press, 1977.

Reuss, Carol, and Donn Silvis, eds. *Inside Organizational Communication*. New York: Longman, 1981.

Richardson, Bradley M., and Taizo Ueda, eds. *Business and Society in Japan*. New York: Praeger, 1981.

Robbins, James G., and Barbara S. Jones. *Effective Communication for Today's Managers*. New York: Chain Store Age Books, 1974.

Roberts, John G. *Mitsui: Three Centuries of Japanese Business*. New York: Weatherhill, 1973.

Rogers, Everett M., and Rehka Agarwala-Rogers. *Communication in Organizations*. New York: Free Press, 1976.

Rohlen, Thomas P. *For Harmony and Strength: Japanese White-Collar Organizations in Anthropological Perspective*. Berkeley: University of California Press, 1974.

Roy, Robert H. *The Cultures of Management*. Baltimore: Johns Hopkins University Press, 1977.

Schneider, Arnold E., William C. Donaghy, and Pamela Jean Newman. *Organizational Communication*. New York: McGraw-Hill, 1975.

Scholz, William. *Communication in the Business Organization*. Englewood Cliffs, N.J.: Prentice-Hall, 1962.

Seward, Jack. *The Japanese*. New York: Morrow, 1972.

Sheldon, Walt. *Enjoy Japan*. Rutland, Vt.: Charles E. Tuttle, 1961.

Simon, H. A., D. W. Smithburg, and V. A. Thompson. *Public Administration*. New York: Knopf, 1950.

Sinha, Radha. *Japan's Options for the 1980s*. New York: St. Martin's Press, 1982.

Swindle, Robert E. *The Business Communicator*. Englewood Cliffs, N.J.: Prentice-Hall, 1980.

Thayer, Lee. *Communication and Communication Systems*. Homewood, Ill.: Richard D. Irwin, 1968.

Timm, Paul R. *Managerial Communication*. Englewood Cliffs, N.J.: Prentice-Hall, 1980.

Toffler, Alvin. *The Third Wave*. Toronto: Bantam Books, 1981.

Tortoriello, Thomas R., Stephen J. Blatt, and Sue DeWine. *Communication in the Organization*. New York: McGraw-Hill, 1978.

Trater, James. *Letters from Sachiko*. New York: Atheneum, 1982.

Treece, Marla. *Communication for Business and the Professions*. Boston: Allyn and Bacon, 1978.

Tsurumi, Yoshi. *The Japanese Are Coming*. Cambridge, Mass.: Ballinger, 1976.

———. *Japanese Business*. New York: Praeger, 1978.

U.S. Department of Commerce. Bureau of the Census. *Statistical Abstract of the United States, 1981*. Washington, D.C.: Government Printing Office, 1981.

van Helvoort, Ernest. *The Japanese Working Man: What Choice? What Reward?* Vancouver: University of British Columbia Press, 1979.

Vardaman, George T., and Carroll G. Halterman, eds. *Managerial Control Through Communication*. New York: Wiley, 1968.

Vogel, Ezra F. *Japan as Number 1*. Cambridge, Mass.: Harvard University Press, 1979.

———. *Modern Japanese Organization and Decision-Making*. Berkeley: University of California Press, 1975.

Warshaw, Steven, and C. David Bromwell. *Japan Emerges*. Berkeley: Diablo Press, 1974.

Webber, Ross A. *Culture and Management*. Homewood, Ill.: Richard D. Irwin, 1969.

Whitehill, Arthur M., Jr., and Shin-Ichi Takezawa. *Cultural Values in Management-Worker Relations*. Chapel Hill: University of North Carolina Press, 1961.

The World Almanac and Book of Facts, 1982. New York: Newspaper Enterprise Association, Inc., 1982.

Woronoff, Jon. *Japan: The Coming Economic Crisis*. Tokyo: Lotus Press, 1979.

———. *Japan: The Coming Social Crisis*. Tokyo: Lotus Press, 1981.

Wren, Daniel A. *The Evolution of Management Thought*. New York: Ronald Press, 1972.

Yamaguchi, Shozo, ed. *We Japanese*. Yokohama, Japan: Yamagata Press, 1950.

Yoshino, M. Y. *Japan's Managerial System*. Cambridge, Mass.: MIT Press, 1968.

———. *Japan's Multinational Enterprises*. Cambridge, Mass.: Harvard University Press, 1976.

Zelko, Harold P., and Harold J. O'Brien. *Management–Employee Communication in Action*. Cleveland, Ohio: Howard Allen, 1957.

ARTICLES

"Annual Reports Help Sell Organizations." *iabc news* 11 (December 1981): 1.

Asperry, John. "Would Readers Pay for Your Publication?" *Journal of Organizational Communication*. iabc reprint (n.d.):38–39.

Awaya, Mariko. "Japan's 'Unwritten' Law." *Japan Times*, April 3, 1983, p. 12.

Bauder, Donald C. " 'Open Plan' Advocated for Offices." *San Diego Union*, July 13, 1981, p. B1.

———. "U.S. Productivity West's Lowest." *San Diego Union*, November 7, 1982, pp. H-11, H-18.

"Bell Labs: The Threatened Star of United States Research." *Business Week*, no. 2746 (July 5, 1982): 46–52.

"Better Titles, More Diversified Duties Lead to Greater Advancement Potential." *Profile/81, Special Report* (iabc) (1981): 6–9.

"Breakfast Meetings Work at Bailey Controls." *Communication World* 1(August 1982): 6.

"A Brief History of Suggestion Systems." *Personnel Journal*. Reprint received from National Association of Suggestion Systems, n.d.

Brown, Arnold. *The Futurist* (August 1981), as cited in *Journal of Communication Management* 11 no. 4 (1981): 5.

Brown, William. "Japanese Management: The Cultural Background." *Monumenta Nipponica* 21 (1966): 47–60.

Bruce-Briggs, B. "The Dangerous Folly Called Theory Z." *Fortune* 105 (May 17, 1982): 41–53.

Brush, Douglas P. "Internal Communications and the New Technology." *Public Relations Journal* 37 (February 1981): 10–13.

"Bulletin Boards Provide Quick Information." *iabc news* 11 (May 1982): 6.

Burck, Charles. "Can Detroit Catch Up?" *Fortune* 105 (February 8, 1982): 34–39.

———. "What Happens When Workers Manage Themselves." *Fortune* 105 (July 27, 1981): 61–69.

"Business Hotline." *Boardroom Reports* 12, no. 12 (June 15, 1983): 6.

Caplan, Jerome A. "Dial 6." *ABCA Bulletin* 39 (December 1976): 12–13.

Cole, Robert E. "Made in Japan—Quality Control Circles." *Across the Board* 16 (November 1979): 72–79.

"Corporations Expand Shareholder Communication." *iabc news* 11 (October 1981): 3.

Davis, Keith. "Care and Cultivation of the Corporate Grapevine." *Dun's Review* 102 (July 1973): 46.

———. "Management Communication and the Grapevine." *Harvard Business Review* 31 (September–October 1953): 43–49.

Deming, W. Edwards. "What Top Management Must Do." *Business Week* no. 2697 (July 20, 1981): 20–21.

"Don't Let Technology Defeat Productivity." *Communication World* 1 (July 1982): 1, 3.

Drucker, Peter F. "Behind Japan's Success." *Harvard Business Review* 59 (January–February 1981): 83–90.

———. "What We Can Learn from Japanese Management." *Harvard Business Review* 49 (March–April 1971): 110–22.

Dunsing, Richard. "You and I Have Simply Got to Stop Meeting This Way—Part 1: What's Wrong with Meetings?" *Supervisory Management* 21 (September 1976): 5–6.

"Electronic Mail Speeds Communication." *iabc news* 11 (March 1982): 11.

"Elsewhere." *Communication World* (formerly *iabc news*), iabc 1 (June 1982): 18, 20, 22.

"Elsewhere." *Communication World*, iabc 1 (September 1982): 18.

"Elsewhere." *iabc news* 10 (January 1981): 16.

"Elsewhere." *iabc news* 11 (August 1981): 6.

"Elsewhere." *iabc news* 11 (September 1981): 12.

"Elsewhere." *iabc news* 11 (November 1981): 14, 16.

"Elsewhere." *iabc news* 11 (January 1982): 6.

"Elsewhere." *iabc news* 11 (March 1982): 10.

"Elsewhere." *iabc news* 11 (April 1982): 16, 22.

"Elsewhere." *iabc news* 11 (May 1982): 18.

Emanuel, Myron. "Productivity Improvement—Japanese Style." *Communication and Management* (January–February 1981): 1–4. Reprint furnished by author.

"Employee Annual Reports Grow Up." *iabc news* 11 (December 1981): 6.

"Employees Annual Reports Rarely Shine." *iabc news* 11 (December 1981): 1.

Fabun, Don. "Feel Buried by Too Much Information?" *iabc news* 11 (October 1981): 23.

———. "Feeling the Electronic World Jitters." *iabc news* 11 (May 1982): 23.

"Family Life in Japan Deteriorated in '82: Government." *Japan Times*, April 9, 1983, p. 2.

Farinelli, Jean L. "Fine Tuning Employee Communications." *Public Relations Journal* 33 (January 1977): 22–23.

Foltz, Roy G. "Learning to Speak with One Voice." *Public Relations Journal* 38 (July 1982): 29–31.

"Frenetic, Automated Future Awaits Communicators." *iabc news* 11 (November 1981): 1, 6.

Friedrich, Otto. "The Computer Moves In." *Time* 121 (January 3, 1983): 14–24.

Fukuda, Eiko. "Japan's Welfare Load Too Heavy to Carry." *San Diego Union*, July 11, 1982, pp. C-4, C-8.

Gildea, Joyce Asher, and Myron Emanuel. "Internal Communications: The Impact on Productivity." *Public Relations Journal* 36 (February 1980): 8–12.

Goodman, Ronald, and Richard Ruch. "The Role of Research in Internal Communication." *Public Relations Journal* 38 (July 1982): 16–19.

Gray, Dr. Christopher S. "Japan, Corporate Strategies for the 1980s." *Business Week*, no. 2748 (July 19, 1982): 20–46.

Grayson, C. Jackson, Jr. "Closing the Gap." *Executive* 7 (January 1980). Reprint furnished by the American Productivity Center.

Hall, Richard W. "When a Champ Is a Loser." *Nation's Business* 59 (November 1971): 47–48.

Haneda, Saburo, and Hirosuke Shima. "Japanese Communication Behavior as Reflected in Letter Writing." *Journal of Business Communication* 19 (Winter 1982): 19–32.

Hanley, J. "Our Experience with Quality Circles." *Quality Progress* (February 1980): 22–24.

Harding, Ed. "Needed a String to Pull." *Journal of Communication Management* 11, no. 4 (1981): 3–5.

Hayes, Robert H. "Why Japanese Factories Work." *Harvard Business Review* 59 (July–August 1981): 56–66.

Hennington, Jo Ann. "Memorandums—An Effective Communication Tool for Management." *ABCA Bulletin* 41 (September 1978): 10–14.

Hirota, Minoru. "History Told in Communications Development." *Business JAPAN* 27 (March 1982): 31–34.

Holtz, Shel. "ARCO Installs Internal Teleconferencing System." *iabc news* 11 (April 1982): 19.

"Honda's U.S. Plant not Likely to Follow Japanese Pattern." *San Diego Union*, August 1, 1982, p. 1.

"Hotlines Make Communication a Call Away." *Communication World*, June 1982, p. 6.

Housel, Thomas J., and Warren E. Davis. "The Reduction of Upward Communication Distortion." *Journal of Business Communication* 14 (Summer 1977): 49–65.

Howard, Elizabeth. "More Than a Bulletin Board." *Public Relations Journal* 38 (July 1982): 34–35.

"How Are We Doing?" *Journal of Communication Management*, no. 4 (1982): 3–11.

Hunter, Bill. "Organizational Video Use Booms as Costs Shrink." *iabc news* 11 (September 1981): 19.

"Internal Publications Keep Managers Informed." *Communication World* 1 (September 1982): 3.

"The Japan Productivity Center." *Japan Report* 26 (December 1980): 1–2.

"Japanese Attribute Much of Success to Quality Circles." *Data Management* 19 (October 1981): 34.

"Japscam for Computer Spies." *Fortune* 106 (July 26, 1982): 7.

Kahn, Herman. "On Success." *Learning Scene* 1 (September 1982): 2.

Koestler, Arthur. "Her Course Is Set." *Life* 57 (September 11, 1964): 63–68.

Lohr, Steve. "Japan Emerging as Capital of Computerization." *San Diego Union*, September 6, 1981, pp. A-11, A-19.

Main, Jeremy. "Work Won't Be the Same Again." *Fortune* 105 (June 28, 1982): 58–65.

"Mazda RX-7." *Business Week*, no. 2748 (July 19, 1982): 28–29.

"Media Use Survey Shows AV Popularity Nudging Print." *Communication World* (July 1982): 13.

"Meetings Are Versatile Communication Tools." *Communication World* 1 (September 1982): 7.

"Meetings Offer CEOs Communication Impact." *iabc news* 11 (September 1981): 1, 7.

"Mitsubishi: A Japanese Giant's Plans for Growth in the U.S." *Business Week*, no. 2736 (July 20, 1981): 128–31.

Morgan, Neil. Column. *San Diego Union*, June 4, 1982, p. B-1.

Naisbitt, John. "Technology Can't Replace Human Contact." *iabc news* 11 (March 1982): 3.

"New Survey Supports Technology." *Communication World* 1 (August 1982): 1, 11.

Nichols, Ralph. "Listening Is Good Business." *Management of Personnel Quarterly* 1 (Winter 1962): 2.

"Organizational Publications Tackle Economic Issues." *iabc news* 11 (June 1982): 10.

"Outsiders Inside Japanese Companies." *Fortune* 106 (July 12, 1982): 114–28.

Pascale, Richard. "Communication and Decision Making Across Cultures: Japanese and American Comparison." *Administrative Science Quarterly* 23 (April 1978): 90–109.

————, and Mary Ann Maguire. "Communication, Decision Making and Implementation Among Managers in Japanese and American Managed Companies in the United States." *Sociology and Social Research* 63 (January 1978): 1–23.

Pauly, David, Joseph Contreras, and William Marbach. "How to Do It Better." *Newsweek* 96 (September 8, 1980): 59.

"Productivity Called By-Product of Respect." *iabc news* 11 (September 1981): 9.

"Quality Circle Programs Bypass Information." *iabc news* 11 (June 1982): 7.

"Quality Circles: Putting Better Ideas Into Production." *Sales Digest* (November 1980): 1–2.

"Quality Control Circles Pay off Big." *Industry Week* 175 (October 29, 1979): 17–19.

Ramsey, Douglas, and Frank Gibney, Jr. "Japan's High-Tech Challenge." *Newsweek* 98 (August 9, 1982): 48–54.

Rearwin, David. "Japan and the U.S.: Mutual Survival in the International Arena." *Business Review Project* 1 (Spring 1982): 4–7, 15–18.

Ringle, William M. "The American Who Remade 'Made in Japan.' " *Nation's Business* 64 (February 1981): 67–70.

"Satellite Helps Emhart Reach Shareholders." *iabc news* 11 (December 1981): 15.

Schwartz, Charles. "Want to Plan Livelier Meetings? Use Audiovisuals." *iabc news* 11 (September 1981): 18.

"Script for the New Trends Session." iabc, unpublished paper.

"*The Shop Rag* Improves Communication." *iabc news* 11 (December 1981): 7.

"Six Yesses Mean You Could Use Teleconferencing for Meetings." *Communication World* (April 1983): 313.

"Stemming the Paperwork Tide." *New Jersey Bell*, as cited in *Communication World* 1 (August 1982): 16.

"Survey Suggests Teleconference Guidelines." *Communication World* 1 (August 1982): 10.

Tanako, Atsuko, as presented in Jean Johnston, "Business Communication in Japan." *Journal of Business Communication* 17 (Spring 1980): 65–70.

"Teleconferences Can Cut Communication Costs." *iabc news* 11 (March 1982): 9.

Tsurumi, Yoshi. "Productivity: The Japanese Approach." *Pacific Basin Quarterly* 6 (Summer 1981): 7–11.

Waller, Larry. "Yanks Borrow Japanese Keys to Quality." *Electronics* 53 (December 4, 1980): 95–100.

"War Atrocities, Revisited." *Newsweek* 98 (August 9, 1982): 29.

Weiss, W. H. "Breaking the Fear Barrier." *Nation's Business* 59 (July 1971): 64–65.

"What Goes with a Formal Communication Policy." *Personnel Management* 13 (January 1981): 13.

"What Happens When Workers Manage Themselves?" *Fortune* 105 (June 27, 1981): 64.

Wheelwright, Steven C. "Japan—Where Operations Really Are Strategic." *Harvard Business Review* 59 (July–August 1981): 67–74.

Whitburn, Merrill D. "An Experimental Telephone Information System." *Journal of Business Communication* 12 (Spring 1975): 33–34.

"Why Some Won't Circle," in Robert E. Cole, "Made in Japan—Quality Control Circles." *Across the Board* 16 (November 1979): 72–78.

Widfeldt, James R. "Jumping on the Quality Control Bandwagon." *Data Management* 19 (October 1981): 32–35.

Wiesman, Walter. "Effective Communication." *Vital Speeches* 36 (September 15, 1970): 723–25.

Wood, Marion M. "The Give-and-Take of Communication." *Supervisory Management* 21 (June 1976): 24–28.

"World View," column in *Communication World.* iabc, February 1983, p. 2.

Zemke, Ron. "Quality Circles: Using Pooled Effort to Promote Excellence." *Training* 17 (January 1980): 30–31.

COMPANY PUBLICATIONS

"Advanced Office Systems." *Hercules Mixer*, no. 2 (1981): 3–10. Hercules Inc., Wilmington, Delaware.

Agee, William M. "Bendix in Japan." *Bendix 82* (February 1982): 16–17. The Bendix Corporation, Southfield, Michigan.

"Annual Report: A 'Must' to Read." *Ford World* (April 1983): 8. Ford Motor Company, Detroit, Michigan.

"Cash in on Your Ideas." *Ford World* (July 1982): 10. Ford Motor Company, Detroit, Michigan.

"Common Ground, Mutual Goals." *Ford World* (September 1981): 8. Ford Motor Company, Detroit, Michigan.

"Communication." *Burlington Employee Handbook* (September 1980): 10–11. Burlington Industries, Inc., Greensboro, North Carolina.

"Communication Meetings Reach 1500 Employees." *Nalco News* (April 1982): 1, 2. Nalco Chemical Company, Hinsdale, Illinois.

"Communications." *Managing at Xerox* (May 1981). Xerox Corporation, Stamford, Connecticut.

"The Crisis." *1980 Annual Report*, p. 10. Cincinnati Milacron Inc., Cincinnati, Ohio.

"Crosby's Seven Manufacturing Plants Represented at Action Teams Training." *Amhoist Overview* (May 1982): 9. American Hoist and Derrick Company, St. Paul, Minnesota.

Cunningham, Mary E. "A Return to Balance." *mgr*, no. 3 (1981): 19–23. AT&T Long Lines, Bedminster, New Jersey.

"Deming Pitches Quality, Productivity." *Ford World* (April 1982): 3. Ford Motor Company, Detroit, Michigan.

Dineen, Mary. "The Force Behind Quality Consciousness in Japan Speaks to Control Data." *Contact* (July–August 1981): 8. Control Data Corporation, Minneapolis, Minnesota.

"Document Dumping Leads to Leaner Files." *Formula* (July 1982): 1. Rohm & Haas Company, Philadelphia, Pennsylvania.

Donnelly, Michael L. "Productivity at the Top." *mgr*, no. 3 (1981): 2–5. AT&T Long Lines, Bedminster, New Jersey.

"Dresser Managers Urged to Plan for the Future." *Dresser News* (Summer 1982): 1, 2. Dresser Industries, Inc., Dallas, Texas.

"Employee Responses Strong to RJR World Readership Study." *RJR World* (October 1981): 10. RJ Reynolds Industry, Winston-Salem, North Carolina.

"Employees Star in New Fire-Police Safety Film." *News Meter Digest* (January 16, 1981): 1. San Diego Gas & Electric Company, San Diego, California.

"Face-to-Face Meetings Keep Channels Open." *Gifford-Hill Times* (February 1982): 1, 2. Gifford-Hill & Company, Inc., Dallas, Texas.

"Feedback: Study Reveals Employees Attitudes Toward Bendix." *Bendix 82* (May 1982): 13. Bendix Corporation, Southfield, Michigan.

"Foreman's Development Program Launched This Month." *Whiting Refinery News* (May 1981): 4, 6. Amoco Oil Company's Whiting Refinery, Whiting, Indiana.

"From the Editor." *Consolidated Aluminum Quarterly* (second quarter 1981): 1. Consolidated Aluminum Company, St. Louis, Missouri.

"From Telex to Telecommunications." *Headquarters News* (April 1982): 2, 3. AMAX Inc., Greenwich, Connecticut.

Funderburk, Brenda. "Suggestion Systems: Ours vs. Theirs." *Sonoco News* (September 1981): 5. Sonoco Products Company, Hartsville, South Carolina.

General Motors Corporation Communications Policy.

"Good Communication Is Important to These Five." *Formula* (October 1981): 8. Rohm & Haas Company, Philadelphia, Pennsylvania.

"Grabill's GREAT Program Gets People Involved." *Sheller-Globe Insight* (Winter 1982): 3. Sheller-Globe Corporation, Toledo, Ohio.

"Growth Appraisal and Review: A Management Methodology." Unpublished report, June 9, 1969. Aerospace Division, General Electric Company, King of Prussia, Pennsylvania.

"How Do We Rate: Here's What You Said." *General-ly Speaking* (February 23, 1983): 2. General Tire & Rubber Company, Akron, Ohio.

"How to Conduct Productive Meetings." *Gillette Company News* (December 1981): 10. Gillette Company, Boston, Massachusetts.

"The HP Organization." *Measure* (January–February 1982): 14–15. Hewlett-Packard Company, Palo Alto, California.

"Ideas at Work." *Weyerhaeuser Today* (June 1982): 4–5. Weyerhaeuser Company, Federal Way, Washington.

"J&L Leads New Trend in Cooperative Programs." *Upfront* (July–August 1981): 5–6. LTV Corporation, Dallas, Texas.

"Japan Diary." *Ford World* (August 1981): 10–13. Ford Motor Company, Detroit, Michigan.

"Japanese Formula for Success Proves Healthy for Bonnell's Carthage Plant." *Ethyl Intercom* (September–October 1981): 4. Ethyl Corporation, Richmond, Virginia.

"Japanese Management: Can It Work Here?" *mgr*, no. 3 (1981): 14–18. AT&T Long Lines, Bedminster, New Jersey.

Kennedy, Griff. "Riding the Waves of Change." *Contact* 8 (September–October 1982): 4. Control Data Corporation, Minneapolis, Minnesota.

Kirby, Dave. "HP Employee Publication Guidelines." May 1975. Hewlett-Packard Company, Palo Alto, California.

"Letters Column on the Way." *Xerox World* (June 1981): 1. Xerox Corporation, Stamford, Connecticut.

"Live from Palo Alto." *Measure* (May–June 1981): 6–9. Hewlett-Packard Company, Palo Alto, California.

"Made in Japan." *Mgr.*, no. 3 (1981): 6–10. AT&T Long Lines, Bedminster, New Jersey.

"Mandarin Oranges and Origami." *Alcoa News* (June 1982): 9–11. Aluminum Company of America, Pittsburgh, Pennsylvania.

Mooney, Karen. "Getting It All Together . . . via Video." *Hercules Mixer*, no. 2 (1980): 2–8. Hercules Incorporated, Wilmington, Delaware.

"New Circles Chosen." *Hoover News* (February 19, 1982): 4. Hoover Company, Canton, Ohio.

"Newsletter Expanded and Localized." *Corporate News* (July 1981): 1. Carpenter Technology Corporation, Reading, Pennsylvania.

"1981 Top Suggestion Award Winners." *Sonoco News* (April 1982): 5. Sonoco Products Company, Hartsville, South Carolina.

"No Substitute for People's Efforts in Productivity Equation." *Amhoist Overview* (February 1982): 9. American Hoist and Derrick Company, St. Paul. Minnesota.

"Orientation Film Wins Top Honor in Competition." *News Meter Digest* (December 3, 1982): 2. San Diego Gas & Electric Company, San Diego, California.

"The Owners of Inland Steel." *Inland Now*, no. 4 (1981): 6–8. Inland Steel Company, Chicago, Illinois.

"Participation Is a Way of Life." *Ford Times* (September 1981): 11. Ford Motor Company, Detroit, Michigan.

"President's Communication Luncheon." *Sonoco News* (March 1982): 4. Sonoco Products Company, Hartsville, South Carolina.

"Productivity: The Problem That's Made in America." *Grace Digest* (Spring–Summer 1982): 22–26. W. R. Grace & Company, New York.

"Productivity . . . What It Is, Why It Matters." *Consolidated Aluminum Quarterly* (third quarter 1982): 10. Consolidated Aluminum Company, St. Louis, Missouri.

"Quality Circle Employees Become Problem Solvers," *Dresser News* (Winter 1982): 4. Dresser Industries, Inc., Dallas, Texas.

"Quality Circles Activities Boom." *Schering-Plough World* (June 1982): 1, 6. Schering-Plough Corporation, Kenilworth, New Jersey.

"Quality Circles . . . Sharing Ideas Voluntarily." *Firestone Nonskid* (April 22, 1982): 1. Firestone Tire & Rubber Company, Akron, Ohio.

"Quality Circles Group Given $5000 Award." *Northrop News* (March 26, 1982): 8. Northrop Corporation, Los Angeles, California.

"Quality Circles Work at Plastics Inc." *AnchorScope* (Winter 1981–82): 10–11. Anchor Hocking Corporation, Lancaster, Ohio.

"Salaried Survey." Special Supplement to *Ford World* (July 1982): 1–4. Ford Motor Company, Detroit, Michigan.

"SDG&E Summer Power Reserves Good, Employees Told." *News Meter Digest* (July 17, 1981): 4. San Diego Gas & Electric Company, San Diego, California.

"Sees Lifestyle Revolution." *Emhart News* (September 1982): 1, 2. Emhart Corporation, Farmington, Connecticut.

"Sharing Ideas and Information via TV." *Xerox World* (May 1981): 4. Xerox Corporation, Stamford, Connecticut.

"Some Answers on Company Finance, Rate Publicity, Interconnection." *News Meter Digest* (December 12, 1980): 2. San Diego Gas & Electric Company, San Diego, California.

"Statement of Policy on Relationships with Employees." *Policies and Public Thoughts* n.d., pp. 2–3. Atlantic Richfield Corporation, Los Angeles, California.

Stephens, Bill. "Visions: The Rising Sun of Productivity." *mgr*, no. 2 (1981): 3–11. Atlantic Richfield Company, Los Angeles, California.

"Suggestion Campaign Winners Chosen." *Galaxy* (December 1981): 9. Gillette Company, Boston, Massachusetts.

"Suggestion Committee Responsible to You." *Sonoco News* (August 1981): 10. Sonoco Products Company, Hartsville, South Carolina.

"Suggestion Program Celebrates 30th." *Bendix 81* (February 1981): 18–19. Bendix Corporation, Southfield, Michigan.

"Suggestions Earn Extra $ in Contest." *General-ly Speaking* (September 16, 1981): 1. General Tire & Rubber Company, Akron, Ohio.

"Survey Indicates Employees Want More 'First-hand' Data Versus 'Grapevine' Information." *Ethyl Intercom* (March–April 1981): 4. Ethyl Corporation, Richmond, Virginia.

"Teamwork Is Basis of New Management Style." *Burlington Look* (March 1981): 4. Burlington Industries Inc., Greensboro, North Carolina.

"Teamwork Takes Off." *Measure* (September–October 1981): 8. Hewlett-Packard Company, Palo Alto, California.

"Telecast Annual Report." *Emhart News* (August 1981): 6. Emhart Corporation, Farmington, Connecticut.

"Telegraph System Can Reach 1000 Locations." *Firestone Nonskid* (October 8, 1981): 3A. Firestone Tire & Rubber Company, Akron, Ohio.

"They Cost Less than in the U.S." *Ford World* (September 1981): 9. Ford Motor Company, Detroit, Michigan.

"This Is What Happens to Your Suggestions." *Sonoco News* (November 1981): 5. Sonoco Products Company, Hartsville, South Carolina.

"3 Employees Send 'Messages' in Film." *Ford World* (May 1982): 17. Ford Motor Company, Detroit, Michigan.

"Top Management Discusses Issues at Employee Meetings." *News Meter Digest* (November 14, 1980): 4. San Diego Gas & Electric Company, San Diego, California.

"Trends of the 1980's." *Public Issue Trends: A Review for Stauffer Management* (July 30, 1980): 1. Stauffer Chemical Company, Westport, Connecticut.

"Try Teleconferencing!" *Ford World* (July 1982): 13. Ford Motor Company, Detroit, Michigan.

"Until Death Do Us Part?" *Gifford-Hill Times* (March 1982): 3. Gifford-Hill & Company, Inc., Dallas, Texas.

"Very Special Delivery." *Communicate* (January–February 1982): 17. RCA Corporation, New York.

"Videotapes Now Available for Home Use." *Headquarters News* (August 1981): 6. AMAX Inc., Greenwich, Connecticut.

"Want Company Information? Dial 2001, or Read FYI Flyers." *News Meter Digest* (August 13, 1982): 4. San Diego Gas & Electric Company, San Diego, California.

"What's the Answer?" *Columbine* (August 1980): 19. CBS Inc., New York.

Whitehouse, Alton W. "The Corporation: A Good 'Person' to Have Around." *Sohio* (Summer 1982): 9. Standard Oil Company (Ohio), Cleveland, Ohio.

"Workers Give TEC Ideas." *Grace News* (July–August 1981): 3. W. R. Grace & Company, New York.

"Workforce Changes in '80s." *Dresser News* (Summer 1982): 2. Dresser Industries Inc., Dallas, Texas.

"Work Quality Circles Concept Approved." *Schering-Plough World* (July 1981): 1, 8. Schering-Plough Corporation, Kenilworth, New Jersey.

"Worldwide Survey Profiles Emhart News Readership." *Emhart News* (October 1981): 4. Emhart Corporation, Farmington, Connecticut.

"Write to Know." *Gulf Oilmanac* (May 1982): 18–19. Gulf Oil Corporation, Pittsburgh, Pennsylvania.

OTHER SOURCES

Blair, John, and Jerome V. Hurwitz. "Quality Circles for American Firms? Some Unanswered Questions and Their Implications for Managers." Transcript talk presented at Japan-America Business Conference, Lincoln, Nebraska, October 6, 1981.

Brown, Robert Edward, Manager, Business Communications, Corporate Communications Division, W. R. Grace & Company, New York. Comments on questionnaire received July 11, 1981.

Callahan, Roger. "Quality Circles: A Program for Productivity Improvement Through Human Resources Development." Transcript of talk presented at Japan-America Business Conference, Lincoln, Nebraska, October 6, 1981.

"The Comment Program." Xerox Corporation, Stamford, Connecticut.

Easterly, Donald A., General Manager, Corporate Communications, Armco, Inc., Middletown, Ohio. Comments on questionnaire, received June 20, 1981.

Ferrell, James, General Manager, Manufacturing Division, Hewlett-Packard Company, Palo Alto, California. Letter to former student, dated March 10, 1978.

Focus on a Changing World. Proceedings of symposium sponsored by Emhart Corporation in Monte Carlo, Monaco, June 27–29, 1982.

Hain, Tony. "Japanese Success Model in the U.S." Transcript of talk presented at the Japan-America Business Conference, Lincoln, Nebraska, October 6, 1981.

Hamilton, Gordon C., Public Relations Manager, Texaco, Inc., White Plains, New York. Letter to author dated June 19, 1981.

Hanada, Mitsuyo. Comments in panel discussion at Japan-America Business Conference, Lincoln, Nebraska, October 5, 1981.

Hyland, Kathleen, Director, Public Relations and Advertising, Kaiser Steel Corporation, Oakland, California. Letter to former student, dated March 6, 1978.

"If Japan Can, Why Can't We?" Transcript of NBC documentary, 9:30 P.M., June 24, 1980.

"Japan, Inc.: Lessons for North America." PBS, 4 P.M., June 12, 1982.

"Japan vs. USA: The Hi-Tech Shoot-Out." NBC documentary, 10 P.M., August 14, 1982.

Japan Prime Minister's Office, "White Paper of the Youth." (*Seishōnen Hakusho*) 1978.

Katz, Richard, Chairman, California Assembly Committee on Small Business. Letter to Leslie Yerger, San Diego State University, dated June 25, 1982.

Kelley, Lane. "Japanese Management and Cultural Determinism." Transcript of talk presented at Japan-America Business Conference, Lincoln, Nebraska, October 6, 1981.

Kim, Ken I., and Harold I. Lunde. "Quality Circles: Why They Work in Japan and How We Can Make Them Work in the U.S." Transcript of talk presented at Japan-America Business Conference, Lincoln, Nebraska, October 6, 1981.

Lauber, Patricia F., Manager, Editorial Services, Allied Chemical Company, Morristown, New Jersey. Letter to author dated June 23, 1981.

Mayes, James H., Director of Publications, Standard Oil Company, Cleveland. Letter to author dated June 25, 1981.

Nathan, Emmett, Manager, Employee Communication, Western Electric, New York. Letter to author dated June 19, 1981.

O'Connell, James B., Director, Internal Communications, IBM, Armonk, New York. Letter to former student, dated March 16, 1978.

Orman, David A., Manager, Employee Communications, Atlantic Richfield Company, Los Angeles, California. Letter to author received June 17, 1981.

Robbins, Jerry T., Manager, Internal Communication Section, General Motors Corporation, Detroit. Letter to author dated July 1, 1981.

Sederberg, George, Cincinnati Milacron Company. Comments in panel discussion on "Quality Control Circles: A Comparison of U.S. and Japanese Practices," Japan-America Business Conference, Lincoln, Nebraska, October 6, 1981.

"6:1 Savings to Cost Ratio?" Brochure of Quality Circle Institute, Red Bluff, California, n.d.

Sours, Martin H. "Influence of Japanese Culture on Japanese Management

Systems." Transcript of talk presented to Japan-America Business Conference, Lincoln, Nebraska, October 6, 1981.

Vogel, Ezra. "What Can We Learn from the Japanese?" Talk to Japan-America Business Conference, Lincoln, Nebraska, October 7, 1981.

Williams, Louis C., Jr., Senior Vice-President, Hill and Knowlton, Inc. Transcript of speech: "Communications for Profit, the New CEO Role."

Wilson, W. E., Special Assistant, Corporate Marketing, Hyster Company, Portland, Oregon. Comments made on questionnaire, received June 19, 1981.

Index

ments, 68; silence, 68; smile, 67; suggestion system, 92-93; teleconference, 93; telegraph, 85; typewritten, 64, 88; Volunteer Reporting System, 92; word processor, 64-65
The Company Paper, 137
CompuServe, 162
Computers, 242, 247, 256
Confucianism, 14, 21, 39
Connecticut Mutual Life Insurance Company, 197
The Consolidated Aluminum Quarterly, 189, 206
Control Data Corporation, 215, 254: *Contact*, 215, 254
Copeman, George, 27
Cox, Kenneth, 133
Craig, Albert, 39, 69-70
Cultural opposites in Japan and America, 5-8
Culture, 4-5; anthropologist's definition, 5; organizational, 4-5; societal, 4-5

Dale, Ernest, 166
Dana Corporation, 149
Davis, Keith, 116, 167, 170, 172
Delta Drilling Company, 188
De Mente, Boye, 41, 43, 45, 54, 65, 69, 70-72, 74
Deming, Dr. W. Edwards, 77-78, 205, 214-15, 254; Deming prize, 215; statistical methods, 77-78
Dewar, Donald, 207
Dickson, William, 102
Digital Equipment Corporation, 201
Dilts, Marion, 15
The Dispatch, 138
Dixie Cup Company, *Dixie News*, 136
Dofasco, Inc., *Management Newsletter*, 139
Doi, L. Takeo, 39, 226-27
Dresser Industries, *Dresser News*, 217, 259
Dress for Success (Molloy), 117
Drucker, Peter, 40, 44, 70, 165-66, 168, 242, 248

Dunk, William P., 256
DuPont Corporation, 147, 157

Earle, Peter, 139
Early Bird, 242
Easterly, Donald A.,, 120-21
Eastman Kodak Company, 183
ECOM (Electronic Computer-Originated Mail System), 161
Economic Planning Agency, 59
Economic Survey of Japan (1979-80), 32, 55
Editor's Newsletter, 134
Effective Communication in Industry (Pigors), 104
"Electronic cottage," 247-48
Electronics, 253
El Paso Electric Company, *Epeople*, 137
Emanuel, Myron, 56, 59, 78, 86, 90, 174
The Emerging Japanese Superstate (Hall and Beardsley), 20
Emhart Corporation, 133, 136, 149: *Emhart News*, 136
Emperor Jimmu, 12
English language, 115
Enjoy Japan (Sheldon), 19
Epeople, 137
Ethyl Corporation, 175-76, 212-13
Europe, 15, 32-33
European Economic Community, 28
Exxon Corporation, 157, 200

Fabun, Don, 260
Fayol, Henri, 102
Federal Communications Commission, 241
Federation of Economic Organizations, 29
Ferrell, James, 131
Field, Percy A., 168
Firestone Tire and Rubber Company, 161, 217; *Firestone nonskid*, 218
First National Bank, 149
Forbis, William, 13-14, 16, 18, 64, 68
Ford Motor Company, 60, 149, 156,

ABOUT THE AUTHOR

WILLIAM V. RUCH teaches graduate courses in organizational communication, business law, and organizational behavior in the European division of the University of Maryland. He has presented talks at the Japan-U.S. Business Conferences and published articles in several professional journals.